INFANT MUSICALITY

Infant Musicality

New Research for Educators and Parents

JOHANNELLA TAFURI

Conservatorio de Musica "G.B. Martini" di Bologna, Italy

Edited by Graham Welch

Translated by Elizabeth Hawkins

ASHGATE

Published by
Ashgate Publishing Limited
Wey Court East
Union Road
Farnham
Surrey GU9 7PT
England

Ashgate Publishing Company
Suite 420
101 Cherry Street
Burlington, VT 05401-4405
USA

www.ashgate.com

British Library Cataloguing in Publication Data
Tafuri, J. (Johannella)
  Infant musicality : new research for educators and parents. – (SEMPRE studies in the psychology of music)
  1. Musical ability in children
  I. Title II. Welch, Graham III. Society for Education,
  Music and Psychology Research
  153.9'478'0832

Library of Congress Cataloging-in-Publication Data
Tafuri, J. (Johannella)
  [Nascere musicali. English]
  Infant musicality : new research for educators and parents / by Johannella Tafuri,
translated by Elizabeth Hawkins and edited by Graham Welch.
      p. cm. – (SEMPRE studies in the psychology of music)
  Includes bibliographical references (p.   ).
  ISBN 978-0-7546-6506-9 (alk. paper) – ISBN 978-0-7546-6512-0 (pbk. : alk. paper)
  1. Musical ability in infants. I. Hawkins, Elizabeth. trl II. Title.

  ML3838.T3413 2008
  153.9'4780832–dc22

                                                                            2008007002

ISBN 978-0-7546-6506-9 (HBK)
ISBN 978-0-7546-6512-0 (PBK)

Printed and bound in Great Britain by
TJ International Ltd, Padstow, Cornwall

To my mother
who carried me in her womb
and rocked me
while singing

Contents

List of Figures and Tables

Figures

Tables

Foreword

It was the summer of 1998. Johannella and I had been invited to South Africa to participate with international colleagues in a research seminar on music education. One afternoon, we had time out from our discussions to explore the wonderful countryside that surrounded the conference centre and to visit a game reserve. Johannella and I sat next to each other on the coach and we discussed her proposed longitudinal study of infant singing development. Her plan was to begin with volunteer Italian mothers-to-be during the final stages of their pregnancy and to continue the research across succeeding years. It was (and is) a bold and visionary study; something that had not been attempted before, but essential if we were to take forward our understanding of how early singing behaviours actually develop over time from the earliest beginnings.

Previous research into singing behaviours had largely focused on studies of particular age groups at specific moments in time, with "development" having to be inferred from the juxtaposition of different sets of research data. Although it is possible to put such findings together to generate some kind of overall picture of development, this is not equivalent to a sustained investigation of a group of children over time that also takes account of the context in which their singing develops. Previously, only a few researchers had attempted longitudinal and/or comparative studies of different age groups and singing (such as Wilson, 1973; Moog, 1976; Davidson, 1994; Dowling, 1999; Welch, 2002) and none had focused on this very young age group. What Johannella proposed was of a different scale – a much larger group of participants for whom there would be regular monitoring over many years of singing in the home, recorded by the mother, and supplemented by data from weekly communal sessions in the local conservatoire. Data were to be gathered by audio (some video) and written diaries completed by the mothers.

The outcomes of Johannella's research have been as exciting and wonderful as was the original vision. For the first time, we have evidence of how individual children develop their singing behaviours from the earliest months of life onwards. And the data is both informative and surprising.

Earlier research indicated that singing development pre-school is characterized by an increasing interaction with the sounds of the experienced maternal culture. This interaction is reflected in a mosaic of different singing behaviours that are evidenced between the ages of one and five years. It is the young child's nature to have an acquisitive, playful, creative and spontaneous engagement with their "local" musical world. According to this previous research, the variety of vocalization includes two-year-olds' repetition of brief phrases with identifiable rhythmic and melodic contour patterns (Dowling, 1999) and three-year-olds' vocal interplay between spontaneous improvisation and selected elements from the dominant song culture, termed "pot-pourri" songs (Moog, 1976) and "outline songs" (Hargreaves, 1996).

Overall, there is evidence of increasing sophistication and complexity in relation to young children's learning of songs from the dominant culture.

The previous research had also suggested that singing development tends to be relatively linear in nature, following a path of increasing complexity. For example, a USA study of the spontaneous singing of two-year-olds' first songs reported evidence that "phrases are the initial musical units" (Davidson, 1994, p. 117). Such phrases are characterized by limited pitch range, a certain disjunction of key/tonality and a descending contour.

In contrast, Johannella's new Italian data of two- to three-year-old children provides evidence of much greater developmental diversity. Some children followed the expected linear hierarchy pattern, with song phrases being more accurately reproduced than complete songs. Yet other young children, exposed to similar amounts of parental support and singing experience, were much more advanced. This latter group were already able to reproduce complete songs in tune and with an artistic expression of all their basic musical characteristics (see lighter bars in the figure).

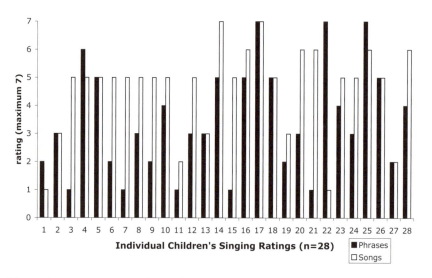

Figure 0.1   Accuracy ratings of Italian children (n = 28) aged 2.6 to 3.3 years in imitating song phrases and complete songs modelled by their mothers. Ratings are based on a seven-point scale of perceived accuracy (Tafuri and Welch, in Welch, 2006).

Overall, this research has generated a unique data set that is both informative and powerful in its implications for music education policy. The research design not only provides evidence of detailed variations in musical growth, it also implies that we should seek to ensure the widest possible sustained engagement in singing between carers, especially mothers, and their children throughout the pre-school years.

We know from other research that musical activity embraces multiple neural networks (*cf* Parsons, 2003) and that sustained engagement in the arts has lifelong positive benefits of higher levels of cognitive functioning (Arts Education Partnership, 2002). In this book, Johannella details for the first time how it might be possible to link such previous findings and their underlying principles. What her research proposes is that we can bring about a major beneficial shift in many children's development if we are able to provide sustained opportunities to support mother-carer-child interactions in singing from the first months of life. This is hugely important research and owes much to her personal commitment, drive and imagination, as well as the ongoing dedication and enthusiasm of her colleagues and participants, both younger and older.

All those who have an interest in fostering and maximizing the musical, social, emotional and intellectual growth in our children – whether parents, carers, teachers or policymakers – should read, recommend and act on this book.

Professor Graham Welch,
Institute of Education, University of London
May 2008

References

Arts Education Partnership, *Critical Links: Learning in the Arts and Student Academic and Social Development* (Washington, DC: The Arts Education Partnership, 2002).

Davidson, Lyle, 'Songsinging by young and old: A developmental approach to music', in Rita Aiello with John A. Sloboda (eds), *Musical Perceptions* (New York, Oxford: Oxford University Press, 1994): 99–130.

Dowling, W. Jay, 'The development of music perception and cognition', in Diana Deutsch (ed.), *The Psychology of Music* (2nd edn, London: Academic Press, 1999): 603–625.

Hargreaves, David J., 'The development of artistic and musical competence', in Irène Deliège and John Sloboda (eds), *Musical Beginnings* (Oxford: Oxford University Press, 1996): 145–170.

Moog, Helmut, *The musical experience of the pre-school child* (trans. C. Clarke) (London: Schott, 1976).

Parsons, L.M., 'Exploring the functional anatomy of music performance, perception, and comprehension', in Isabelle Peretz and Robert Zatorre (eds), *The Cognitive Neuroscience of Music* (New York: Oxford University Press, 2003): 247–268.

Wilson, D.S., 'A study of the child voice from six to twelve', *Bulletin of the Council for Research in Music Education,* 34 (1973): 54–60.

Welch, Graham F., 'Early Childhood Musical Development', in Liora Bresler and C. Thompson (eds), *The Arts in Children's Lives: Context, Culture and Curriculum* (Dordrecht, NL: Kluwer, 2002): 113–128.

Welch, Graham F., 'Singing and Vocal Development', in Gary McPherson (ed.), *The Child as Musician: a handbook of musical development* (New York: Oxford University Press, 2006): 311–329.

Acknowledgements

The study that forms the core of this book was made possible through the collaboration of many people to whom I wish to express my deepest gratitude. Most of all, I would like to thank the friends and colleagues who have encouraged and supported the research project with helpful advice right from the beginning, in particular, Roberto Caterina, Graham Welch, Michel Imberty, Mario Baroni and Gianni Zanarini.

My thanks also to the Regional Health Service and to the local health services of Bologna and Imola, including their Directors of Childbirth Courses for their support in promoting the project among the expectant mothers, particularly Patrizia Stefanelli and Maria Anita Cutini in Bologna and Doctor Suzzi in Imola.

For their hospitality and support for our meetings, special thanks are given to Rossana Dalmonte who welcomed us to the Liszt Institute in Bologna. Thanks also to the educators and collaborators (in particular Patrizia Cacciari and Mara Balestri) who gave us hospitality at the 'Castle of 100 games' run by the Bologna City Council, and Franco Giovannelli, Director of the Vassura-Baroncini School of Music where we were made to feel very welcome.

I thank those who collaborated in different aspects of the research and book, specifically: those involved in leading the meetings, in particular Claudia Gazzotti; in researching some of the themes, particularly Franca Mazzoli and Maravillas Diaz; in data analysis, in particular Silvia Rossi, Michele Privitera, Susanna Felisatti, Caterina Gornati, Fabio Regazzi, Beatriz García Rodriguez and Cecilia Pizzorno who also managed the control group; and Roberto Caterina for his help in the statistical analyses.

I wish to thank the paediatricians Giancarlo Biasini and Stefano Gorini for their interest and encouragement and for helping me to discover the importance of paediatrics, such as in relation to the role of music in children's lives.

Thanks also to my family and all those friends who have followed the phases of the *inCanto* Project with keen interest and listened patiently to my accounts. A particular thank you goes to my sister Maria Teresa for having collaborated with dedication and competence in the final revision of the book.

However, the biggest thank you must go to all the children and their parents and relatives (grandparents, sisters, brothers, aunts...) who took part in the project, to the 119 mothers who took part in the first phase and also to all those who were able to participate for short periods. I am especially grateful to those children and parents who managed to reach the final stages of the project or at least to stay in contact from time to time:

Alessandra Conti and parents Lucia and Lino
Alessia Rossini and parents Maria Giuseppina (Mary) and Damiano

Adriano Rossi and parents Natalia and Alessandro
Andrea Pasquali and parents Anna Rita and Matteo
Andrea Ricciardelli and parents Gloria and Antonio
Arianna Giorgi and parents Manila and Gianni
Bianca Degli Esposti and parents Cristiana and Gian Franco
Bianca Gironda and parents Flavia and Francesco
Chiara Celeghin and parents Anna Rosa and Loris
Chiara Collina and parents Gabriella and Silvano
Clara Bartolini and parents Maria and Sandro
Claudia De Vita and parents Milena and Lino
Eleonora Fabbri and parents Simona and Fabrizio
Enrico Rossi and parents Lisa and Marcello
Francesca Pasini and parents Elisa and Enrico
Francesco Cavedoni and parents Silvia and Fabio
Fulvio Rossi and parents Valentina and Ivan
Gabriele Cioli and parents Monica and Federico
Gea Grassi and parents Denise and Italo
Giorgia Ropa and parents Federica and Gabriele
Giulia Bilanzuoli and parents Antonella and Marco
Greta Narducci and parents Micaela and Massimiliano
Greta Spada and parents Laura and Alberto
Irene Galli and parents Laura and Daniele
Irene Sermenghi and parents Katia and Marco
Kady Giunia Ka and parents Cristina and Nago
Leonardo Melchiorri and parents Silvia and Riccardo
Linda Lanzoni and parents Cinzia and Gianfredo
Lorenzo Calocero and parents Stefania and Massimiliano
Luna Balestra and parents Silvia and Alberto
Manuel Vergnani and parents Beatrice and Marco
Manuele Martignani and parents Marina and William
Marco Angelini and parents Silvana and Donato
Margherita Mengoli and parents Emma and Paolo
Margherita Ripoli and parents Anna and Pasquale
Martina Renda and parents Annalisa and Salvatore
Martina Landi and parents Cristina and Massimo
Matteo Galimberti and parents Simona and Gianluca
Matteo Missana and parents Paola and Mauro
Michele Fontana and parents Rita and Franco
Noemi Collina and parents Armida and Gianni
Riccardo Garruto and parents Giovanna and Clemente
Riccardo Morelli and parents Roberta and Giuseppe
Riccardo Poli and parents Barbara and Andrea
Sara Ghiddi and parents Giuliana and Alessandro
Sara Petrovic and parents Giovanna and Darco

Tobia Sermenghi and parents Alessandra and Vainer
Viola Murer and parents Claudia and Sergio
Virginia Bernardi and parents Rita and Enrico.

Introduction
The Reasons for a Research Study

One day, six-year-old Michele returned home in tears: "Mama, the teacher told me I sing out of tune." His mother was surprised; to her, the child usually sang in tune. Maybe at times he was little bit off key in some passages, especially if he did not know the song well or if he was playing; sometimes, he had fun distorting the songs with his little sister. He never thought that he sang out of tune; in fact, he was quite proud of his musical abilities. This was why the teacher's comment frustrated and humiliated him. What could have happened? Perhaps he sang badly at that moment because he was distracted, and the teacher, who did not yet know him well, had immediately passed judgement and put him in a category that some teachers appear to use often quite confidently.

Episodes like this appear to be very frequent and we hear it over and over again from teachers and parents. Is it possible that so many children sing out of tune? Or is it something that is not generally understood, particularly by educators? Should their role not include "teaching children how to sing in tune"?

This last question is how it should be, in fact. Nevertheless, we very often hear, on precisely such occasions, a prejudice that does not die easily: you are born with a good ear! The ability to sing in tune is a "gift" of nature from which some are excluded. Is this really the case? Or is it simply a convenient excuse to justify this widespread failure in education? What if we should try to discover when and how this skill is formed? What if we should attempt to understand the mechanisms, to find out how much can depend on hypothetical gifts of nature and how much comes from the development of physiological and psychological processes, in addition to the influences that come from the environment and education? These nagging questions gradually led to the idea that there was a need for scientific research to investigate, in a rigorous and systematic way, the development of the ability to sing in tune.

What really convinced me of the importance of this objective was the anthropological, cultural and social value of singing in all cultures. It is a profoundly human activity, practised in the most diverse circumstances as a collective (as well as personal) instrument of shared communication. On the numerous occasions when people sing together, events like festivities and religious functions, as well as political gatherings, if a person feels that his or her voice does not blend with the others but is out of tune with the rest because he or she is not producing exactly the same melody that the others are singing, it causes embarrassment, both for the person in question and for the people nearby, and the individual feels somewhat excluded. Singing can be, and in fact is, a significant instrument for uniting or dividing.

Before initiating the actual fieldwork of the research project, it was necessary to do something that in practice was the first step of the project itself, and that was to embark on a thorough study of the theoretical fundamentals of the problem and the research already undertaken.

This groundwork led me progressively to a wider research project, from both the temporal and musical perspectives.

First of all, I saw that there was the need to study younger and younger children: age 3 ..., age 2 ... until, on the basis of important research results, I came to the point at which the auditory system begins to function, and that occurs during the final months of prenatal life.

Secondly, I saw the limitations that would ensue from following only the vocal production of children, isolating this from the ensemble of instances of musical production from which it derives, develops and becomes apparent.

It was in this way that a rather demanding project began to take shape. To begin with prenatal life, follow up the children for several years, at least until they were about to commence elementary school and to take into account various aspects of musical development: this all meant preparing a research protocol that was rather complex, yet highly appealing.

I spoke about this with my friend and colleague, Donatella Villa, a teacher at the Vassura-Baroncini Municipal School of Music in Imola and she was soon as enthusiastic as I was. Yes, we would definitely have to get to work on this. We felt that it was worth the effort. Friends and colleagues who are psychologists and musicologists gave their approval and encouragement.

In this way the *inCanto* project was born. It was to be a longitudinal research project (meaning that it would take place over a fixed number of years) to study musical development, in particular the ability to sing in tune, in children of age zero to six. Whilst making an initial overview of the panorama of studies available in this field, I became aware of their variety and also noted a definite change in perspective. Notable advances had been made since the 1940s when Revesz claimed that the first year of a child's life is unimportant for musical development and that musicality (musical sense, talent) is innate and impervious to education (as recounted by Teplov, 1966, p. 53).

The first (and until now the only) ample and systematic study on the musical development of children during the early years of life was that undertaken by Moog in 1960–61 for his doctoral thesis (published in the English version of 1976), a work that still marks a milestone in this field for the number of subjects (about 500 children), for the period examined (ages zero to six) and for the musical experiences taken into account (singing, motor responses to musical stimuli, language-music-rhythm).

On the basis of the results obtained, Moog traced an interesting profile of musical development – from which we shall note some aspects in the pages that follow – but his research left some questions open. One of these related to the influence of family and environmental conditions on the development of the identified skills.

From that time on there was a progressive increase in studies undertaken on the perceptive-cognitive and productive skills of infants from the neonatal stage to the first years of life. Whilst retaining Moog's study as a basis, we could not ignore the fact that almost forty years had passed. This was another factor that convinced me to embark on new research that would put greater focus on methodological aspects and would respond to the questions left open by Moog himself, as well as by subsequent studies.

The Reasons for this Book

This book is not meant to be a research report in the strictest sense. That would mean employing a literary genre with precise rules as used by the scientific community. Particular results of this research had been published already in recent years in specialized journals as segments of the whole project were studied and interesting findings emerged. However, this book is intended to be an instrument for the general transmission of the major research outcomes. These are examined panoramically in a synthesis that highlights the most important data. We shall not describe here all the results obtained during those six years of work. We shall limit ourselves to highlighting those obtained during the first three years. The main reason for this is because, during the course of research, we realised that these are precisely the decisive years in which the ability to sing in tune is indicated and is decisively established. The activities of the further three years (three to six) can confirm or contribute to its development in the event that this has not already occurred, but they do not appear to have the same decisive importance as those of the previous phase, a period to which there is normally not enough attention paid.

Accordingly, in this book, we wish to describe a process of development related to the musical ability of children, taking into consideration the space of time from the later months of prenatal life until age three. The innovation of this work that we are presenting here lies in the fact that it is the first research project to deal with the systematic study of the development of several musical abilities through observation of the skills gradually learned by the same group of children, stimulated by an appropriate programme of activities and accompanied by the support of family members.

As the programme of musical activities offered to the children in this research study had a specific role, this book also presents some pedagogical-didactic guidelines that had proved to be effective when applied during the study. The plentiful results that were obtained allow for educational processes to be planned that take into consideration the initial predisposition of all children, and that follow the stages of development of musical skills from the first months of life. In this way, it is suggested that all can achieve the full development of their musical ability.

The first part of the book deals with the research. It opens with a panoramic view of the most significant studies carried out on the musical development of children. Besides the intrinsic value of the data, it is hoped that our presentation will also help to better capture the significance of the results of our research which is the subject of this book.

The next chapter presents the core of the *inCanto* Project encompassing the stages of planning and execution.

The results are presented in the succeeding chapters from two points of view: that of the researchers (Chapter 3), which is the point of view of those who adhere to the data with precision and methodological rigour, and that of the parents (Chapter 4) who relate how they lived through that long experience with the children, actively collaborating in their education and in the execution of the research.

The sources used to create Chapter 3 are of different kinds: on the one hand, they are from the diaries prepared by the researchers and completed by the parents and, on the other hand, we have the recordings of the children produced at home by the parents and at times during our encounters.

The sources for Chapter 4 are the accounts that the parents gave freely in answer to a letter of invitation that gave pointers to make sure that nothing would be overlooked. After six years working together, the parents' point of view could not be left out. It was they who were with the children every step of the way and who proved to be the real educators by creating in their homes the best conditions for learning. They spoke out spontaneously, freed from the rigid interrogation of the diaries and they were able to cast more light on the processes followed by the children in the intensive experience that they had lived through at home.

The second part of the book focuses on the educational aspects: the theoretical-methodological stipulations that constitute the basis of an educational programme (Chapter 5) are followed by a series of specific recommendations of musical activities (Chapter 6) which stimulated and accompanied the children of the *inCanto* Project in their growth.

Who Does this Book Address?

Instinctively (probably because of my professional background), I would say that this book is intended for educators of music, primarily those teachers and other adults working in early years' settings, such as nurseries, playschools and kindergarten. They will find here a series of educational proposals that are justified by theoretical-methodological fundamentals. These derive from the research and from the results obtained from those same programmes.

In a more general way, it is intended also for all music teachers, whatever age their pupils may be. Awareness of what happens during the first years of life should make teachers more attentive to the skills that can actually be achieved in the early years and hence to the kind of progress that can be encouraged at later stages.

However, if we ask ourselves who the first educators may be, without any doubt we must reply that it is the parents. Therefore, this book is addressed to them, not only the "musical" parents who might find it useful in assuring them of their own intuition on the subject and who wish to find further encouragement in their educational activities, but to all the parents who may wish to sing for and with their children, and to listen to music with them together. It is intended for parents who may already have a certain background in music and parents who have little, each can take the opportunity of their baby's arrival to set out on a musical path together. It is for all those parents who wish to respect their children's right to develop their musical abilities.

In addition to parents and educators, I would like to address this book to a set of people who dedicate their lives to the care of children: paediatricians, the real pillars of the childhood years who do not limit their attention to physical care. I am sure that many of them already have combined (I am thinking of the paediatricians in the Paediatricians' Cultural Association who gave life to the project "Born for Music") or might like to combine an interest in music with medical science, and they will be happy to discover the important role that the musical experience can have in the lives of children and family life in general.

Addressing such diverse readers has presented a challenge of style. How could I make myself understood by colleagues in the world of music and also by early years' teachers, parents and paediatricians who are often not familiar with musical techniques and (with the exception of the paediatricians) to the methodological demands of scientific research? How could I reconcile data, tables and statistical calculations with educational requirements?

It would be necessary to use language that is agile and at the same time scientifically correct. It would have to balance the requirements of theoretical premises with practical proposals and examples. It should not have too many numbers and tables that would make it tedious, but at the same time there should be sufficient for scientific requirements.

I have accepted the challenge. Let the readers respond.

PART I
Musical Development

Chapter 1
The Literature on Musical Development from 0 to 3 Years of Age

There has always been a certain fascination with the topic of when musical development begins. Not only musicians are curious about this, but also parents and educators, the former because they are anxious (and perhaps ambitious) concerning the future of their offspring, and the latter because they wonder how they can advance the potential of something that may seem to be mysterious and beyond their control.

When science, or to be more specific, musical psychology, began to take an interest in musical ability at the end of the nineteenth and start of the twentieth century and first attempted to "measure" it with the further intention of trying to "predict" musical development, they concentrated on school-age children. A major reason for this choice was because of the difficulty of giving "pen and paper" tests to children any younger. In subsequent studies, with the help of a different kind of testing, they targeted younger and younger children. After the discovery that a foetus begins to hear at about the 24th week of pregnancy, attention was directed to studying the effects of prenatal hearing on the development of musicality and the early reactions of newborn infants.

Nowadays, literature on the various aspects of musical development abound. If we wanted to compile a full and detailed catalogue of research done so far, one chapter would certainly not suffice. (The interested reader is directed towards Hargreaves (1986), Lucchetti (1992), Deliège and Sloboda (1996) and McPherson (2006) for more research-based background literature.) We shall, therefore, limit ourselves to a synthetic presentation of studies that are considered to be the most relevant, especially in relation to those aspects most closely studied in the research dealt with in this book. Ample citations of research and studies will be given in order to enable further reading by interested readers who wish to examine the topic further.

1.1 Prenatal Memory and Early Experiences of Newborn Infants

Over half a century ago, the otorhinolaryngologist Alfred Tomatis suggested that, based on his experiments, the auditory system starts to function during prenatal life and, therefore, children can hear before they are born. He was accused of charlatanism and threatened with expulsion from the medical association (Tomatis, 1977). Nevertheless, his research and that by others subsequently has led to this claim being accepted and there are numerous scientific studies on the hearing ability of the foetus, as well as on motor reactions to auditory stimuli in general or to musical stimuli in particular (such as Porzionato, 1980; Dumaurier, 1982; Shetler, 1989; Woodward, 1992; Lecanuet, 1996; Parncutt, 2006).

In the light of these numerous contributions, it is possible to summarize some essential points:

- the auditory system starts to function at around the 24th week in some foetuses and after the 30th week in all of them (see, in particular, Lecanuet, 1995; Parncutt, 2006);
- the foetus reacts to sounds in the interior environment (intrauterine sounds of various kinds, from the mother's heartbeat to the ripples made by their own movements) and from the exterior environment (voices, sounds, music), with variations in heartbeat (acceleration/ deceleration) and with movements, varying from brusque to gentle, of the eyelids, the head, the limbs, the trunk;
- the quality and quantity of the reactions depend on the sound quality of the stimulus, of the behavioural state of the foetus (deep sleep, active sleep, quietly awake, actively awake) and, in the case of musical stimuli, also probably on the effects of music on the mother;
- during the foetal stage it is possible already to bring about habitual reactions to certain stimuli (for example, babies who have spent the prenatal period near an airport do not wake up or give a start if an aeroplane takes off nearby), a phenomenon that shows the discriminatory ability of the foetus and the possible effects on learning that can be detected subsequently at the postnatal stage.

Recent years have also been marked by an increase in research on newborn behaviour (cf. Aucher, 1987; Woodward, 1992; Papoušek H., 1996; Papoušek M., 1996; Fassbender, 1996; Trehub, 2001; 2003) and the results can be summarized as follows:

- the newborn are sensitive to sounds and musical stimuli; they demonstrate this with various gestures (for example, they bat their eyelids, open their eyes wide and stare, turn their head towards the source of the sound and stop crying);
- they demonstrate an ability to distinguish sounds by reacting in different ways to the changes in any of the qualities of the stimulus (such as intensity, speed, timbre, melody) and they soon demonstrate that they have preferences;
- some reactions by newborns seem to reveal a kind of memory and learning with respect to prenatal auditory experiences (for example, they prefer their mother's voice, they are soothed by recordings of the mother's heartbeat and by music that they have heard during the prenatal phase, they show familiarity with loud noises that they seem to have heard before).

On this last point concerning the presence of possible forms of prenatal memory, we would like to cite two studies in particular. Wilkin (1996) invited a group of expectant mothers, beginning from the 32nd week of pregnancy, to listen to four pieces of music. Six weeks after delivery the reactions of the newborns were observed when they listened to the same tunes. Comparisons were made with the reactions of an equal number of newborns who had not been exposed to this music. The first group displayed more attention, receptiveness and motor responses than those in the control group.

A study by Woodward (1992) attempted to demonstrate prenatal memory by measuring its effect on the rhythm of non-nutritive sucking behaviour. A group of expectant mothers, from the 34th week, listened twice a day to a piece of music, one of a choice of two presented by the researcher. Between the third and fifth day after birth, the same piece of music was played to the infants in addition to a new tune, after giving them a pacifier that could register the rate of non-nutritive sucking. Analysis of the graph lines showed that sucking was interrupted for longer when listening to a known piece of music rather than to a new one. This difference in behaviour, considered as a form of attention, was interpreted, although cautiously, as a possible demonstration of conditioning resulting from prenatal listening.

Furthermore, if we look at the studies of one of the most famous and extensive researchers of auditory perception during the early months of life, Sandra Trehub, we find a series of insightful results: babies are born with a predisposition for music; the basic principles of perceptive organization are already functioning in early infancy (Trehub, Trainor and Unyk, 1993). As other researchers have also demonstrated, they are sensitive to the elements of music, in particular to changes in pitch, tempo, beat, duration and tone (Trehub, 2003). Babies categorize musical sequences on the basis of global and relational properties, while the melody plays a critical role in perception (Trehub, Thorpe and Morrongiello, 1987; Trehub, Bull and Thorpe, 1984).

Stern also found that infants between eight and 11 months were able to distinguish the transformation of a melody if the melodic contour is altered or if some sounds are changed (Stern, Spieker and Mackain, 1982). Similarly, other researchers have found that the ability to group sounds appears already at the age of two months (Fassbender, 1993). From the age of four to six months, infants are able to group and segment units, both in speech and music (Fassbender, 1995) and they show sensitivity to musical phrase structures based on pitch and rhythmic patterns (Krumhansl and Jusczyk, 1990; Jusczyk and Krumhansl, 1993).

1.2 Vocal Communication: Leading to Speech

When do infants begin to communicate?

During the early months of life, newborns do not yet speak but, for their own affective and mental health, they need to receive information from and about the world and to communicate their needs and desires. From birth onwards, infants manifest their discomforts (and later also their satisfactions) by reactions that use sounds. After crying and screaming (the three basic functions of which are to signal pain, satisfaction and hunger), they soon discover the existence of different kinds of sounds (such as wailing, whimpering, whining and gurgling) and produce these in a richer and more varied way, such as by using sounds with vowels and consonants, as they gradually progress towards mastering phonation (due also to the development of the larynx) and in relating to the world beyond themselves. Very early on, the newborn are sensitive to the reactions that their sounds provoke. Already towards the end of the first month, the newborn expects to receive satisfaction of the need that gave rise to the cry. At times, the infant starts with a long low whimper that increases in volume until it becomes a cry, according to the carer's speed in reacting (Wolff 1969).

Newborns also communicate with their eyes, with an increase in motor activity, and very soon also with facial expressions and smiles. Nevertheless, sound communication continues to be most important and varied. Elicited by their mothers, young infants also imitate vocal intonation in an increasingly active way. Through this interaction with the mother, they learn to recognize and share emotions and knowledge of the world.

In this interaction, according to one researcher on the birth of language, Bénédicte de Boysson-Bardies, a special part is played by the exchange of vocalization that takes place around three months of age, and only for a short period, called *turn-taking*, where "mother and child respond to each other by taking turns vocalizing. [...] The infant begins to vocalize when the adult stops talking to him, a situation that occurs again several times, giving the impression of a conversation" (Boysson-Bardies, 1999, p.76).

The way that adults speak to small children is instinctively higher-pitched. It has an exaggerated modulation of intonation contour, moderate intensity and gentle sonority, syllabic and word repetition, with decelerated pronunciation. Infants show special interest towards this form of communication (termed 'motherese', 'infant-directed speech' or 'parentese') with positive effects on interactive communication.

Key prosodic characteristics of speech (frequency, intensity, rhythm), which many researchers classify as "musical" qualities, "melodies of maternal language", are therefore important for newborns who perceive them very early. They prefer their mother's speech with a high-pitched voice and sing-song intonation (Fernald, 1989, 1992; Papoušek M., 1995). As Fernald added, "...the prosodic patterns of maternal speech serve psychobiological functions central to the development of communication in the first year of life" (1992, p. 270). In the first mother-infant dialogues, or *protoconversations*, both try to synchronize on the same rhythmic beat. This behaviour was studied by Malloch (1999/2000) who analysed the temporal characteristics and the pitch in the responses of some newborns (from six weeks old) during dialogue activities with the mother. In his studies of mother-infant communication, Malloch identified the high level of attunement as a manifestation of a communicative interaction which was described as both co-operative and co-dependent.

According to Trehub and Nakata (2001–2002) the melodic contours used by mothers in this interaction are unique to each one, and they seem to have beneficial effects on the newborn, serving both as an aid to distinguishing their mother from other people, and as a reinforcement of emotional ties.

In addition to relational or "social" vocalizations, other authors identify vocalizations that Dumaurier calls "private" in her survey (1982). They consist of vocal sounds produced by newborns when they are alone, awake and very active. They are a form of exploration of their own phonation. It is almost an exercise, an inner sensory (proprioceptive) satisfaction, brought about by the "massage" caused by the sound waves the infant produces, vocalizations that stop if an adult appears.

Newborns show their ability to produce sounds early on, also by imitation, before they manage to produce real syllables (confused at times with similar sounds or pseudosyllables). This happens at around six to seven months. Contrary to what was claimed in earlier publications, recent studies say that real babbling begins towards the sixth month (Thurman, 1997; Trevarthen, 1999–2000) or the seventh month (Boysson-Bardies, 1999), when the vocal tract is able to produce syllables that respect the linguistic constraints of natural languages. Before this, from four months, infants start to produce quasi-consonantal sounds with vowels, similar to syllables in the spoken language and, therefore, commonly called babbling.

1.3 Leading to Song

We have seen how interactive communication between mother and infant benefits linguistic capacity as well as the sharing of emotions and social behaviour. After closely observing their baby daughter (Papoušek and Papoušek, 1981), Mechtild Papoušek (1995) studied the vocal production of infants from two to 15 months during interactions with their mothers. On the basis of the results of this and of other research, she reported several stages in the vocal production of infants: during the first month of life they produce simple sounds, and from the second month they produce more articulated and modulated sounds; during the next stage (from about four to six months) they play at exploring their own voice by producing a series of sounds that at first tend to be repetitive, then more varied, and then lead on to their first words at about one year old.

Early in this process there are traces of the appearance of two separate skills: one that leads to language and thought and the other that leads to song and the creative and imitative activity of vocal music. Both are closely linked to the affective (emotional) functions of the voice and communication.

At this point we ask ourselves: could music have the same potential in the musical field as it has in verbal language? If it is true that in order to learn a language well it is necessary for the linguistic model to be presented within a framework of interactive communication (Boysson-Bardies, 1999, p. 94), then is this also true for music? What happens if mother sings? If she tries to open an interactive dialogue by singing, does the newborn begin to "respond"? And, if so, what form do these responses take?

As we have said, newborns very soon distinguish melodic contours and speech rhythms, and this is all the more reason why they should be able to do the same with music, as its pitch and duration are organized in a more precise way.

At this point, perhaps we should clarify some of the terminology used. Whilst researchers of verbal communication use musical terms in a broad sense – for example, they speak of the melody of the mother's speech to describe how her voice rises and falls as she speaks, in the study we are addressing here, the terms pitch, melody, rhythm, metre, etc. will be used in the strict sense to indicate the specific features of the musical system of the Western world.

Returning to the question just posed, we immediately reply that the ability of infants to distinguish verbal language from song and other kinds of sound appears quite early on, between the first and fourth months (Eimas *et al.*, 1971). We should not forget that the auditory system is functional for three or four months before birth.

We can, therefore, surmise that a mother's singing (or a father's) could have, for the purposes of musical stimulation, the same effect as their speaking, and that the infant's need to communicate could be equally satisfied with this form of "language" as long as the mother and father sing, for example, to interact with them, to attract their attention, to sooth them and to share different emotions.

Here we touch on a fundamental point concerning relationships and that is the human need for communication that cannot be satiated by verbal language. It is for this reason that every society has created other forms of symbolic communication. Even if music has generally taken on a less powerful structure than spoken language, the tonal system used by a large part of our music – a system that the psychologist Robert Francès considered to be "the musical mother language of the West" (1972), is structured with its own grammar and syntax (Baroni, Dalmonte and Jacoboni, 1999; Francès, 1972) that allow composers to convey meanings and emotions and for listeners to understand them (Meyer, 1956; Imberty, 1986).

If we look at the research conducted in this field, we notice that few researchers have asked what happens in the first year of life if the mother sings. One of the first to take a closer look and try to identify first signs of "singing" in newborns was Moog (1976). When studying the vocal sounds produced in the early months of life after birth, he identified the progressive presence of a certain assortment of sounds of varied pitch. He reported that the sounds produced towards the sixth to seventh month are similar to singing and they happen mostly when adults sing to the infants or let them listen to music. Moog calls this "musical babbling".

Other researchers have shown how newborns prefer the song that their mother sings to them rather than songs in general, as the former are more expressive and emotionally intense, as well as being produced by their first human sound source. Researchers have demonstrated how babies show greater attention (by fixing their stare and reducing movements) if their mother sings rather than speaks. It seems, therefore, that the relationship that the mother (and also the father) establishes with the newborn through song is more intense and elicits a more emotional response than speech (Trehub and Nakata, 2001–2002).

The importance of this relationship is generally grasped through a mother's intuition. Even if they do not feel that they sing well or have a great voice, mothers are still observed singing to their babies to calm them, entertain them, make them laugh and play, being (other-than-consciously) aware of the emotional role that their voice plays in the child's experience (Street, 2003).

A newborn's earliest vocalizations increase in variety and duration if the parents continue to encourage it. This is affirmed by Moog (1976), who continued to analyse the musical production of infants after the first few months, and by other researchers. In a study carried out in the United States at Harvard University, for example, nine children were followed up from the ages of one to seven. The researchers went to the house of each one every week for the first three years of life and after that every two months to observe and record moments of free singing, as well as the singing of songs that the infants had memorized. The results obtained from these children were checked against those obtained by researchers who had studied another 70 children grouped according to age (Davidson, 1985, 1994). Another American researcher, Jay Dowling, studied the songs produced by two children from their first year until age six (1984, in Dowling, 1988). A later contribution to the topic, also from the United States, came from Edwin Gordon who formulated his own theory (1990) on the way that children learn music from the time they are born.

Putting together the results of these studies, there emerges a very interesting picture that demonstrates quite a deal of convergence regarding the earliest manifestations of music in children. In the period between the ages of one and two, vocal sounds can begin to resemble little songs as the pitches of the vowels are sustained and therefore are clearly discernable – even if the sounds do not yet correspond to conventional musical scaling. In addition, there is also a certain degree of rhythmic regularity. After the first year, these sounds progressively take the form of phrases and then (closer to the second year) of songs of some duration. At times, these songs are without words and at other times they have repeated syllables that will develop into real words over a period of some months. Sometimes it is possible to recognize in babies' singing some fragments of songs that they know. At other times it is not, and these are the so-called 'spontaneous songs'.

In this process, words play a fundamental role in supporting the rhythmic-melodic structure. Moog's (1976) data suggests that infants first manage to imitate the words, then the rhythm and then the pitch (a sequence also identified in other research, see Welch 1994). When studying the assimilation of tonal structure in particular, Davidson (1985, 1994) presented some interesting findings. After classifying the songs produced by infants in the Harvard study into three categories, depending on the manner in which they were performed "as either spoken, sung with diffuse pitches, or sung with articulated pitches" (1994, p. 115), he made a specific study of the way that infants proceed to assimilate intervals. He came to the conclusion that melodic processes are first assimilated by skips (intervals of a third then a fifth or a fourth) and that, as they gradually master an interval, they go back to assimilate the degrees connecting the extremities of that interval.

After the age of two years, songs appear that are based on repetition of one melodic phrase, then with phrases that increase progressively in variety, number and consistency (Dowling 1988, 1994). In conclusion, we can say with Moog that, by the age of two, all children who have developed normally can sing.

1.4 Imitative Song

It is undoubtedly a great joy for parents when they recognize in the more or less uncertain singing of a two-year-old infant the song that they often sing to the child. Our child can sing! It is like the joy of hearing their first words. They may rush to record it (if they have the means) so that this special moment will not be lost. Although there is great excitement at the arrival of speech, it is considered normal, whereas when babies sing for the first time, their parents may think that this is exceptional and that their children must be gifted musicians.

In fact, as reported by Moog (1976), all two-year-old children can sing, and between the ages of two and three they do so more clearly and more often, enabling this to be more easily documented. According to the researchers cited earlier, the sounds infants produce increase in quantity and quality, in the sense that the structures of our musical system begin to appear more clearly in the children's vocalizations, even if they are not yet stable. The fact that infants have this ability has allowed researchers to study more closely the assimilation of our musical system and the development of the ability to sing "in tune", that is, to correctly match the pitches of the melody learned. This is the study of imitative song.

During observations made over the course of months and years of the melodic reproduction of familiar songs (learned through imitation), it was noted that children first reproduce correctly the melodic profile (that is the rise and fall of sounds). This is followed by the intervals (beginning with the third) between the most important notes of the melody, and then finally the sounds within the intervals. In this way, the infant vocalizations gradually come closer to the original model (Davidson, 1985).

The research on children over the age of three is more plentiful, not only because it is easier to collect the required documentation, but also because many scholars retain that it is only from that age onward that we can see the ability to sing in tune. (Interesting studies and reviews can be found in Welch, 1979; Lucchetti, 1987; Björkvold, 1990; Davidson, 1994). From analysis of the level of intonation in sequences sung by children of three and over, Moog deduced that 44% of three-year-old children produce songs that "resemble" the original (although we note that the expression is imprecise in the sense that the author does not specify the features of this resemblance). At four years of age, 38% of the children correctly imitate songs, apart from small errors.

As children approach the age of five, there is an increase in the tonal stability of their songs (Dowling, 1994), as well as in the interval distances performed correctly, and the precision of each pitch interval (Davidson, 1985). There are also more precocious and more delayed instances. For example, four American children who had received prenatal stimulation at the ages of 21, 27, 30 and 46 months demonstrated noticeable ability in singing many songs correctly and in playing percussion instruments (Shetler, 1989). On the other hand, children aged three to four in some Italian kindergarten schools were found to have uncertain intonation, and oscillated between speech and song (Lucchetti, 1987). Of 78 children in the first year of elementary school who sang some well known songs, only 15% had developed the ability to sing moderately in tune (Jorquera *et al.*, 2000). Likewise, in a longitudinal study carried out with children aged five by the English scholar Graham Welch, together with other collaborators (Welch and White, 1994; Welch *et al.*, 1996, 1997, 1998), children's ability to reproduce the texts of songs was impressively accurate, and significantly better than their pitch intonation (even allowing for an overall improvement in pitching across the three years). By taking the results of these and other studies, Welch (1998, 2006) traced a model of development of the ability to sing in tune divided into four phases:

- Phase 1: The words of the song appear to be the initial centre of interest rather than the melody, singing is often described as "chant-like", employing a restricted pitch range and melodic phrases. In infant vocal pitch exploration, descending patterns predominate.
- Phase 2: There is a growing awareness that vocal pitch can be a conscious process and that changes in vocal pitch are controllable. Sung melodic outline begins to follow the general (macro) contours of the target melody or key constituent phrases. Tonality is essentially phrase-based. Self-invented and "schematic" songs "borrow" elements from the child's musical culture. Vocal pitch range used in "song" singing expands.
- Phase 3: Melodic shape and intervals are mostly accurate, but some changes in tonality may occur, perhaps linked to inappropriate singing register usage. Overall, however, the number of different reference pitches is much reduced.
- Phase 4: No significant melodic or pitch errors in relation to relatively simple songs from the singer's musical culture (2006, p. 317).

As we can see, Welch does not propose ages of referral, both because this model is the result of numerous studies in which the results were collected from children of different ages, and also because this schema would suggest a process somewhat independent of the children's ages, each of whom has the right to grow according to their own rhythm of development.

1.5 Original Song

Needless to say, many parents and educators have noticed children playing alone in a corner and singing. Perhaps they are singing with others and conversing in song ("don't pull", "it wasn't me"). They could be using the melodic formula of *Ring a ring o' roses*. However, it is possible that few people will have given any importance to the fact that, at that moment, the children were inventing phrases in song or snippets of songs or entire songs. In the area of research, several authors have focused attention on the study of spontaneous song, meaning (by that expression) the songs produced by children at free moments, individually and collectively, when in playschool, in kindergarten or at home. Researchers report a great variety of examples of spontaneous production, from vocalizations without words to phrases invented to commentate on individual or collective games, from reproduction or re-processing of familiar songs to the invention of actual songs. We shall not deal here with imitative song as that has already been addressed in the previous section, but we shall look at all the other kinds of song production that Lucchetti called "original" in her classification (1987), that is, invented by the children.

In order to better understand what is happening at those moments when there is spontaneous song, we can turn to some studies that have been conducted in this area. We have chosen a pioneering study carried out in the 1930s at a centre created for that purpose in California (Moorhead-Pond, 1941), another conducted in several kindergarten schools in Stockholm in the 1960s (Sundin, 1963, and taken up again in 1988), in Oslo and Venice in the 1980s (Bjørkvold, 1985; Lucchetti, 1987) and more recently in London (Young, 2003).

Although the studies were carried out in very different places and at different times, it is interesting to note that all the authors attest to a great richness of song production. They point out various elements that are important in the study of spontaneous song, including the context in which children invent, the functions taken on by their song, the methods used, the presence of specific intervals or melodic modules and the consequent evidence of a continuing process and originality.

Despite the systems of observation and classification used in the various studies being different, as is the terminology used, some very interesting convergences emerge. All the authors agreed that in spontaneous singing there are at least two kinds of song production: the socializing kind that children invent in collective situations (to play, to tease, to call each other), and the more personal kind that children invent when they are alone, or when they want to be by themselves and do not sing for others but only when there is no one there. This does not necessarily mean that children have to be alone in a room, but that no one is there asking them for some kind of communication, and so they can be absorbed in themselves.

The songs of the first kind are more conversational and consist of melodic phrases with words ("my mummy's car is nicer than your mummy's car", "no-o, my mummy's is nicer"; "I want the red sponge", "and I'll give you the green one"). They develop around very few different sounds and finish with cadenced inflections at the end of the phrase (similar to a musical recitative). They have a fairly regular rhythmic structure that is linked to the syllables of the words (the notes tend to have the same duration with some intensification according to the text and long sounds at the end). Of note are the variety of functions that this kind of song can have: such as to tease, protest, call, ask and command (Bjørkvold, 1985).

The songs of the second kind are the individual ones. They are much more varied and can be divided into a further internal classification (Lucchetti, 1987; Young, 2003): *vocal expressions* without words that are connected to movement, the use of objects or state of mind; *monologues*, when the children are absorbed in themselves and repeat vowels or syllables with few sounds, often while they are doing something else (a little girl on a swing, a little boy with building bricks, etc.); and *songs*, such as when children sing as they tell a story or recount an experience or describe what they are seeing.

While the monologues often present a rhythmic cell that is repeated in a fairly regular way, the songs are characterized primarily by free rhythm or at least flexible rhythm, by free use of intervals – without excluding the presence at times of melodic modules typical of children's songs – and by the use of fantasy words, or even nonsense words. By observing the level of pitch accuracy, it can be seen that children show less control over intonation with respect to what they can achieve in imitative songs, probably because imitation is based on specific memorized examples, whereas invention is improvised and, therefore, guided by an impromptu idea. Besides, the ability to sing in tune while inventing new melodies requires considerable experience, bearing in mind that learning a lot of songs plays a role in the stabilization of the musical scale model typical of one's own culture. If the intonation is still poor, this means that the production of precise pitch intervals is not yet well controlled by a stable scale model (Dowling, 1984).

Original song then tends to diminish and disappear as they grow older, likely because children acquire a greater aesthetic sensitivity and learn to appreciate the song models presented through the media or that come from the world of adults (claimed to be "nice"). They pay no attention to their own inventions and might even be ashamed of them as they think that they are no good in comparison (Lucchetti, 1987).

1.6 Rhythm, Instruments, Movement

We often see infants from the fifth or sixth month shaking rattles or banging their little drums if given the opportunity. They do it spontaneously in order to explore the object and get to know it, and they do this even more if someone sings or if they are listening to music. Babies are certainly fascinated by sound and, in a more general way, by a global situation in which the object, with its shapes and colours, the action itself of shaking or banging and the sound that comes from it is all one whole.

There is another kind of behaviour that infants begin to show as they approach the first year, an activity that is a well known psychological-cultural need: they clap their hands. There are numerous songs in the popular repertoire that call for this action. Sometimes, it is the parents themselves who take the child's hands and clap them, although really the children should have the freedom to do so when they have developed this skill and feel the desire to do it. These are the first games of motor coordination present in children's education, at home and at play school, precisely with the aim of encouraging this development.

Another commonly observed practice that we can add is a little in the same direction, and that is to bounce the baby on your knees, generally while singing a song. The bouncing can have variants (it can be faster or slower) and it often finishes with pretending to fall.

Making noise, clapping hands, bouncing: three components that entertain and amuse infants and at the same time help their motor coordination, their emotional involvement and the development of the ability to structure time (Imberty, 2002). These actions are usually encouraged by songs and music that have a very clear rhythmic-metric structure and, more precisely, a distinct regular beat, that is, a regular alternation of strong beats and weak beats, as in a march (1:2 binary metre) or in a waltz (1:3 ternary metre), and that also have regular rhythmic combinations (sounds of varying duration), that contribute to the perception of pulse.

This presence of regular pulse in a song or a piece of instrumental music to which children can join in by clapping their hands, banging percussion instruments or bouncing on an adult's knee, allows them, as we said before, to learn to organize time (which in physical reality flows by in a uniform manner). It also helps them to develop a particular basic musical skill: the so-called "keeping time", or rhythmic-motor synchronization, a skill that comes into the wider context of rhythmic sense in general.

Although it may seem that we all understand what we mean by "rhythmic sense", in fact we are not all aware of the implications of this expression. First of all, rhythm is not a quality of sound. Among the various qualities that we can attribute to one or more sounds, particularly relating them to each other, we can, for example, speak of high/low, light/dark, loud/soft, light/heavy and, coming closer to our field, long/short, but we cannot yet speak of rhythm.

If we follow the studies of the French psychologist, Paul Fraisse (1974), a master in this area, we discover that it is we ourselves who grasp the relations between the durations of sounds when listening to a sequence (with or without melody). In order to do this it is necessary for the durations to be perceptible and groupable (therefore, neither too long nor too short). In other words, on the one hand physics tells us that there are consecutive sounds of specific duration (equal or varied) whilst, on the other hand, our perceptive-cognitive skills work at grouping and enable us to say, on the basis of the experienced criteria of our culture, that there is or there is not any rhythm. Briefly, rhythm is an arrangement of relationships of duration by those who listen according to their own perceptive-cognitive development and their own culture, not forgetting that the first to listen are precisely those who produce (by inventing or reproducing) rhythmic sequences.

The importance that is attributed to the person who listens allows us right away to appreciate the determining role of age in the development of rhythmic sense. To this we add that it is a complex area in which there are varying types of abilities: those that are perceptual (at what age can we perceive and arrange durations?) and those that are productive (at what age can we produce and reproduce rhythmic structures?). The latter are produced by means of the voice when speaking and singing and through movement, from the more subdued, necessary for playing an instrument, to the more expansive that involves the whole body, whether in free movements responding to music or in dance.

This complexity means that we must consider a great diversity of research results, since researchers who have explored this area have approached it in different ways, from the perceptual to the productive, and in this second case, from the vocal to the instrumental and the motor fields.

Although the theoretical clarifications on the nature of rhythmic perception may look alarmingly complex, if we look at the research carried out from the perceptual point of view we are immediately put at ease, because children manage to perceptually arrange sounds in rhythmic patterns from the age of two months (Demany, McKenzie, Vurpillot, 1977). A researcher that we encountered earlier, Sandra Trehub, together with some collaborators, has found that infants of around seven to nine months are able to work with groupings and to distinguish different rhythmic sequences, as long as they contain few sounds. Whilst observing what happens in a slightly older age group, Arlette Zenatti (1981) observed that four-year-old children begin to distinguish between two rhythmic sequences without melody, and they improve notably by the age of five and a half.

Going over now to rhythmic production, we first of all look at this in speech and song. On this subject, Moog (1976) tells us that the first musical babbling is rhythmically amorphous, whilst at around 18–24 months, in their earliest fragments of spontaneous song, children begin to use two durations: the longer one is less frequent and tends to be twice as long as the other, and it can be found in different positions (at the start or middle of a phrase). Moog does not consider the long sound at the end of a phrase to be significant musically in the same way, as he does not attribute to this an expressive value but merely a "rest" function, generally connected with the need to take a breath: in practice, the breath before the next phrase. In imitative song, Moog observes that children first repeat some words without precise rhythm, and later they repeat some words (still without melody) to the rhythm of the song. After three years of age, there is a higher number of children capable of correctly reproducing a song with its rhythm and melody.

Rainbow (1981) also studied the ability of children to repeat words modelled by a teacher with a given rhythm, and found that this aptitude is already quite good at age three (50% of the children managed it correctly) and distinctly better at age four (70–90%). Moorehead and Pond (1941) also came up with interesting data when, as we have said, far back in 1937 they conducted pioneering research on the spontaneous song of children. In communicating their results, the authors did not consider matching them to age, but rather wanted to point out the variety of vocal sounds produced by children (such as exploring their own abilities, imitating the sounds of animals or instruments) and the rhythmic freedom and flexibility of their inventions in which at times there emerges the presence of rhythmic patterns typical of a child's repertoire.

When dealing with the relation between perception and movement, Moog (1976) emphasized the transition that takes place at around age six months from responding calmly to responding with movement when listening to music. Explicit gross motor responses, not yet synchronized, increase considerably until about 15–18 months, and then diminish in number, though not in variety which continue to increase. This development is also aided by a progressive domination of space – an observation that is of prime importance because the child begins to use movement, it also being temporal, as the preferred way of expression when there is music. When examining the degree of coordination, that is, the synchronization of children's movement when relating to music, Moog says that very few of them between the ages of three and four (10%) were able to synchronize with the music. Nevertheless, this skill becomes quite good between the ages of four and five (71–74%), especially when the children are asked to clap their hands together or to bang them on a table.

To clap hands, to play a percussion instrument (drum, rhythm sticks, etc.) or to march in time with the music, are three kinds of rhythmic motor synchronization. In other words, they are three kinds of motor response synchronized with the beat of the music. They are experiences in which music and movement join together in one temporal dimension. These three activities present different levels of difficulty connected to motor control. It is easier to synchronize using small movements than to use movements that involve greater muscular mass, research has confirmed. According to Rainbow (1981), the ability to synchronize by clapping hands or tapping rhythm sticks is low in three-year-olds (10–14%), but it improves at age four (40–60%). It seems to be more difficult to march in time with the music, as we see in the percentages that are very low at age three (4–10%) and slightly higher at four (18–20%). Finally, it is almost impossible to march and clap hands at the same time at age three (less than 4%) and still very difficult at four (less than 15%).

The improvement from age three to four is confirmed in various studies and from different viewpoints. For example, Gilbert (1981), when studying motor coordination in children playing a percussion instrument and their eye-hand coordination, as well as speed and fullness of movement, also noticed an improvement between age three and four. This suggests a determining influence of age in motor and perceptive-cognitive development.

A particularly important contribution to the understanding of the skill of rhythmic-motor synchronization came from the Argentinian researcher, Silvia Malbrán, who used a sophisticated research protocol to identify and verify the various components. She based it on theoretical studies that demonstrate the main cognitive processes involved in this activity. These include the mental representation of a succession of intervals of regular tempo, transforming the perception into a mental image, locating the information in memory for a short time and transforming it into gesture (Shaffer, 1982; Parncutt, 1994). With this, Malbrán identified the presence of four components that concur in determining the ability to synchronize:

- the ability to grasp the presence of pulsations and to accompany them with the appropriate instrument (*correspondence*);
- the ability to keep going (*sustainability*);
- the ability to approach as much as possible the precise instance of each pulsation (*adjustment*);
- the ability to maintain the same level of synchronization (*regularity*).

Malbrán's protocol provided for the children to play with a digital drum that was connected by MIDI interface to a computer, and the recording and analysis was undertaken with Cakewalk software and a statistical calculations programme. In a first study conducted with 30 children aged three (Malbrán, 2000–2001), at that age the ability to synchronize with the pulse of a piece of music is still quite limited. Children can do it, but it is very unstable and irregular. The next study (Malbrán, 2002) was longitudinal, in the sense that nine children were followed up from the age of three to five. Here a general improvement was noted, with some internal differences, and the most significant improvement in "correspondence" came at age four to five, while for "sustainability" it came at age three to four.

On the basis of numerous studies, we can conclude, with Malbrán, by saying that rhythmic skills:

- play a very important role in development;
- appear soon;
- require double involvement, perceptual and motor;
- depend on enculturation;
- require the activation of interactive relations with the environment.

Mention should be made of the use of instruments because of their importance in the development of rhythmic skills, and also because of the function that they can have in children's musical development. Studies are not many, and most of them were directed towards other skills. Rhythm sticks and drums are often mentioned in studies on rhythmic skills. Instruments are often alluded to in studies on creativity as this behaviour cannot be studied only in spontaneous song and, for this reason, it is necessary to provide children with opportunities to improvise with instruments of various kinds, from small percussion instruments to keyboards (see Swanwick and Tillman, 1986; Barrett, 1998; Baldi, Tafuri, Caterina, 2003; Tafuri, Baldi, Caterina, 2003–2004; Young, 2002).

If we think of the use of instruments considered in themselves as objects of attention and exploration, the panorama of research is very much reduced, even if some notable studies have been conducted. Firstly, there is an important study by Mario Baroni (1978) who assigns to instruments a fundamental place in the experience of children in kindergarten and elementary school in which the focus is to explore sound and carry out activities of personal expression. In contrast, a study that deals mainly with the interaction between instruments and children was conducted in Bologna by Anna Rita Addessi and François Pachet (2005). In this study, children age three to five were given the opportunity to play a programmed electronic keyboard so that they could "respond" by producing music in the same "style" as used by the one that they heard. The children were very interested in this experience and it gave rise to a great variety of reactions. There was enthusiastic playing and extraordinary attention and aesthetic participation in listening to the keyboard. They began to do things together with other children and explore different ways of playing the keyboard (such as using their finger, elbows, head and forearm).

Several years earlier, a French expert in musical education, Jean-Pierre Mialaret (1997), had carried out research on children's exploration of instruments. The study dealt with the exploration of a chromatic glockenspiel by 61 individual children, ranging in age from two years ten months to nine years six months. His objective was to observe how children would express themselves in exploring instruments and, at the same time, demonstrate how they had absorbed the musical culture around them. There were interesting results, especially on the level of the expressiveness of their exploratory behaviour. Similar research was undertaken with playschool children age one to three in Lecco by the French psychologist of music François Delalande (2004, 2009). This study was a follow up to his previous research (1993) on the sensory-motor pleasure that is felt on "touching" an instrument – a tactile, gestural and auditory pleasure that is one of the three musical "*conduites*" (behaviours) considered to be the "universals" in music. The objective of the 2004 study was to observe how exploratory behaviour develops from age one to three and what factors reinforce it. The results were quite extraordinary. Besides confirming the fascination that children have for instruments, the results showed a diversity of behaviour that, according to age, could be used and encouraged by educators and parents.

Chapter 2
The *inCanto* Project

2.1 The Journey Begins

Following our panoramic view of the research into young children's musical behaviour and development, we now look at how the *inCanto* project was put into operation. After studying this research evidence and learning many interesting things, Donatella Villa and I were left feeling that there were numerous questions still unanswered. In particular, we realized that there was need for a study that, although following the line taken by Moog, would not only have something more updated to say on the subject (Moog's research published for the first time in 1968 had actually been carried out in 1960–61, over 45 years ago), it would also, most especially, have something to say that is based on ongoing observation of an established group of children. We had to consider the need, therefore, for a longitudinal research project, even though we were well aware of the extent of the commitment that would be required.

In comparison to the German study, we could see two conditions that could constitute a new element:

- that the children would take part in musical activities organized and conducted by us, the researchers;
- that the parents would continue these musical activities at home, surrounding the children with a family environment that had plenty of musical stimulation, and the parents would accompany them with encouragement and praise as they grew.

At this point, we were ready to formulate our hypotheses. The first, chosen deliberately as a key element of the whole project, referred to singing.

All children can learn to sing correctly, that is, to sing in tune according to the musical system of their culture, as long as certain conditions are present:

- the presence of music (vocal and instrumental) in the children's surroundings from the sixth month of prenatal life;
- the systematic allocation of time dedicated to singing and listening to music, beginning from birth, in a family atmosphere that is emotionally positive;
- encouragement and praise when they sing and request music, right from the time they begin to do this;
- help with singing in tune using appropriate strategies.

The other hypotheses referred to musical ability in general.

All children are predisposed to music in the sense that they are attracted to it from birth and show interest in and attention to musical experiences.

Elementary musical ability, singing, playing instruments and moving in time develop earlier, with respect to their peers, in children who live in a continual musical environment.

2.2 The Preparation

The ideas were there, the desire to initiate this enterprise was in place, and the time it would take did not frighten us; the hypotheses for the moment seemed to be quite clear, but ... where and how were we to find the people? Should we hand out flyers on the street? A notice in the newspaper ("Attention. Pregnant women wanted")? The internet? No, these were not the right means. The category we needed was too specific and narrow, and besides, we wanted this to be taken seriously, and a project that would take six years was no joke. We had to have recourse to official channels: childbirth courses.

After making inquiries and speaking with obstetricians and gynaecologists, in September 1998 we made an official request to the Regional Director of Health Services, and after receiving approval, we spoke to the coordinator of childbirth courses run by the Health Service of Bologna and Imola. It was generally well received and we were authorized to circulate the invitation and to put up a notice. On occasion, the obstetricians allowed us to speak about the project during their childbirth classes.

We made no stipulations regarding cultural or musical preparation, ability to sing, age, ethnic group, other children in the family, etc. There was only one condition: to be in the sixth or seventh month of pregnancy, more or less. However, there were difficulties finding a venue. After looking around for a while asking organizations and friends, we were generously received in Bologna by Rossana Dalmonte at the Liszt Institute and later by Patrizia Cacciari at the "Castle of 100 games" (a centre owned by the Municipality where children go to play) and also in Imola by Franco Giovannelli at the Vassura-Baroncini School of Music.

Finally, only the financial question remained. The research should be free for the participants, but we also knew that people who take part in research often receive compensation. Again we had to knock on several doors, Italian and foreign research organizations, universities (in view of the fact that the teaching staff in conservatories do not have the right to receive financing as is the case with their university colleagues), but without success. Taking courage, we decided to meet the expenses out of our own pockets.

At this point we had to decide how to organize the meetings: how many people to gather together in each group, taking into account that perhaps some mothers-to-be would take part with the future father? How regular should the meetings be?

What would we do, and, in particular, what would we ask them to do at home? We were very clear that we would be in need of their collaboration.

We decided to solve one problem at a time and so, taking several requests into consideration, we formed groups of eight to ten expectant mothers (some of them with their partners) who, during pregnancy, would participate in a cycle of ten weekly one-hour meetings. About one month after giving birth, we would continue the weekly meetings with the babies and parents.

On the question of "homework", we would ask the mother, possibly together with the father, to continue the musical activities at home during the pregnancy and, even more so, after the birth of the child.

As regards the collection of data to be studied, it was clear that we required a series of observations that only the parents could carry out and so we decided to ask them to compile a diary and a series of periodic recordings. Each diary contained a list of questions on the activity carried out at home and the reactions of the children. The questions were to be answered once a week (except for those concerning singing and listening, for they were to be answered daily). The questions were changed from time to time in accordance with the child's gradual development. During the infant's first year, each mother received a diary every two months, and after a year it was every three months.

We encouraged them to be as truthful and honest as possible and not to include what they wished would happen or what they thought we would like to hear. If they did not have time to sing or listen to music or play musical games, they should just say so without a sense of shame, otherwise it would compromise the results of the research. Their sincerity was the most important aspect of their activity.

We would ask the mothers-to-be and their partners to complete an individual form to provide us with information (such as town of origin, studies, interests and musical activities) that could be helpful when interpreting the results.

Finally, we would ask the parents regularly to record the child's vocal productions according to a protocol established by us (times, activities and method) suited to each stage of development. The meetings with parents and care givers would be led by the researchers (Donatella Villa and me).

2.3 The Invitation

Dear mother,

The *inCanto* Project would like to give you the possibility of offering your child a gift, a treasure that cannot be consumed: the gift of musicality. Music is fundamental in the life of each one of us: it enriches us, accompanies us, gives us moments of deep joy. Music is also a language that allows us to communicate with others in a different way from words, and the activity we propose is an alternative way to allow for communication between you and your child.

The musical activities of the *inCanto* Project to which we invite you will contribute to the following:

- the *well-being* of both you and your child;
- it will reinforce your *communication* with the child, both now and after the birth, with another language that will allow you to say those things that cannot be said in words;
- it will develop the child's musical intelligence: this development is a child's *right* that is still being ignored, that society often does not recognize; but the *inCanto* Project provides you with the opportunity not to deny this to your child.

The activities that we shall offer you *free of charge* – singing, listening, vocalizing, sonorous dialogue, instrumental and vocal games – develop the musical potential present in each one's genetic heritage, so that all can experience music as a source of enrichment and pleasure, independently of a possible future professional choice.

If we are able today to offer musical activities suited to expectant mothers and children during the prenatal stage, it is thanks to all those mothers who were the first to accept to be pioneers in carrying out these activities, observing the reactions of their children in the uterus and allowing music researchers to study these reactions. There have been many of these studies and we know of plenty in this field today.

We want to go further and we are freely offering you the opportunity to allow your child to develop his/her musical intelligence from before birth until about age six, by asking you to allow us to study this development.

Our research marks the first time, at international level, that the development of musical intelligence, and in particular the ability to sing in tune, is encouraged and observed from prenatal life until age six, and we wish to disprove the general opinion that we are born either with or without a musical ear. This, therefore, is an important event, and we want it to make a decisive contribution to the world of science, culture and education, in relation to the development of musical intelligence.

If you would like to and are able to participate, one day you will feel proud of having contributed to scientific progress by offering your child this gift. It is a story you will tell your child later. The results will help children all over the world because we shall communicate this far and wide. It will be thanks to you who have agreed to take part that music education will improve in Italy and in the rest of the world.

What are we asking of you?

First of all, to take part in the weekly meetings until the birth of your child and to continue later, together with the baby, for as long as possible. It would be great if you take part in the whole project, that is until the child begins elementary school, but you can stop earlier. You can decide along the way.

Secondly, we ask you to follow up at home by listening to music and singing, according to the suggestions that we shall give you. We ask you to take note of your observations on the child's reactions in a diary that will be given to you periodically.

If you accept our invitation to participate in the project, we shall expect you on ….

This is the invitation that many expectant mothers were told about or read from notices distributed in Bologna and Imola during the childbirth classes.

What were the reactions?

2.4 The Participants

Everything began by chance the day I called into the local medical clinic to inquire about childbirth courses. Among the various notices about things like yoga lessons, relaxation courses, etc., there was a yellow flyer. I do not quite remember what was written on that flyer nor what attracted my attention, but I remember that it said something briefly about a project and that in order to take part you had to be pregnant and that it was not necessary to be able to sing. It was the *inCanto* project. I hasten to say that I was and am very keen on music, but it would never have entered my head to sing, or even to hum. I had never felt the desire to sing, not even under the shower. I glanced through the flyer and put it in my pocket, although I was sure that sooner or later it would end up in the waste paper basket. However, I found myself telephoning, taking information and showing up at the first meeting. My husband and family, knowing how shy and reserved I am and how reluctant I am to sing, were surprised, and I am sure they wondered if I had been subject to a hormonal storm due to pregnancy. [Silvia]

It started by chance. My wife had seen a publicity flyer about the *inCanto* Project at a childbirth course and she told me about it. I did not think it made much sense. It seemed more like an opportunity for her to meet other mothers-to-be and share anxieties and expectations. To play music for a baby in its mother's womb from the sixth month ... absurd! I am a bit like Saint Thomas. If I can't touch something, it seems ridiculous, and then, what music course could it be? My wife was convinced that it was a good thing and so she signed on for the course. Besides, I think that every maternity experience, in the prenatal stage and perhaps during the early months, is something exclusively for women, and so this experience that was being offered to expectant mothers complicated this separation from the experience of the soon-to-be born child. It was something only intended for mothers and would later be addressed to the baby, and as usual the father had nothing to do with it. [Marco]

When the *inCanto* Project was presented to us in 1999, during the childbirth course, I was charmed by the idea as it looked like a terrific experience for me and my baby! I was very impressed with what the music teacher said when she presented the project. She said that it is thought that babies from the early months in the womb can hear sounds and therefore music, and that this not only makes them more receptive to music itself, but that it helps them to develop their own particular abilities. [Flavia]

One afternoon in winter, when I had been carrying Bianca for five months, we were there for the presentation of the project. It was cold outside. The warmth of the room filled with cushions scattered around, the knowing smiles of all those stomachs that spoke of a hidden treasure carefully tended within, the men-boyfriends-husbands still few in number even though they were daddies and feeling a bit out of the general harmony but curious to be admitted into a secret world ... it all contributed a little magic to something that we did not then realize would unite us and be with us for the next six years. The proposals and modalities studied by the originators of the project, Johannella and Donatella, from that moment on became a reason to find a way, a link with which to transmit and communicate love for the life that was growing within. There was a hidden ear, an invisible channel that brought the sound of our voices inside us, that calmed the anxieties of future mothers who were nervous about what would happen, that helped the future daddy (separated from the baby growing slowly in the mother's womb that was welcoming and expanding) to feel less left out of the miraculous event. [Cristiana]

I received the flyer about the *inCanto* Project at the childbirth course I was doing, and as I am very curious and eager for new experiences, I decided to give it a try. The meeting place was difficult to reach, but I was convinced that it would be worth it. Something within me (perhaps my child? It was my seventh month of pregnancy) told me that life was not only about work, about housekeeping, preparing clothes, visits to the doctor to see if the baby was all right, but I also had to "cure" my spirit and heart ... and music seemed to me to be the perfect way to communicate with my child. I don't really sing in tune, but I have always enjoyed singing and listening to music. [Claudia]

Let me return to the past. Here I am, hurrying, breathless, with my big stomach, to Donatella's place to sing, dance and vocalize. How nice it is to communicate with Francesco through this new world I have discovered, to feel him move when I sing *Jack and Jill* or when I lose all sense of time at home with my "la, la, la" or "plume, plume". I want to try this experience with music. I love to feel him move when I sing. I am thrilled to think he can hear my voice. It seems to me that he is already here among us. [Silvia]

2.5 What Do We Do? Experiences and Repertoire

I remember the first meeting for mothers-to-be, all a little disoriented by the new experience but at the same time enjoying it. I remember clearly the first song they taught us, just as I clearly remember the faces of the mothers with whom I sang. We sang *Questo è l'occhio bello* two by two, and they taught us to accompany the song with gestures. I remember perfectly all the songs we learned during pregnancy, and I still enjoy humming them because they remind me of when I was expecting my first child. [Silvia]

It was an important meeting and satisfying for both Margherita and me, and we happily took part. Listening, songs, jingles, nursery rhymes, dances, little musical instruments. These are the things that gave us so much fun. [Emma]

The planning of the meetings soon became quite demanding. On the one hand we had to guarantee a good level of music and worthwhile activities; on the other hand we had to do something that was attractive, stimulating and also entertaining. But first of all we had another choice to make; in fact, when we came to deciding on the research procedure we had essentially two possibilities:

- to observe the musical development of a fixed group of children without intervening in their experiences;
- to offer the children a specially prepared music course.

In the first case, the children would receive greater or fewer stimuli according to the interests and routine of the family, the environment and the playschool teachers; in the second case a common programme would also be part of the procedure.

We opted for this second hypothesis because we felt that it was more interesting to observe the development of specific abilities when connected with certain requirements. Also, there would be a variety of situations in this option for two reasons: because of the greater or lesser regularity of attendance at the meetings and because of the frequency and manner of carrying out the activities at home. These two variables would have to be factored into those that pertained to each of the children themselves and the context in which they lived. The decision to present the children with a musical adventure meant that, before settling on its formulation, we had to choose the areas of musical experience on which to focus, drawing on suggestions offered by the existing literature. As this was quite scarce, we concentrated on some theoretical fundamentals on the one hand, coupled with our didactic competence on the other, in order to fine-tune the specific experiences to be followed. This meant, moreover, that the educational activities themselves were becoming objects for experimentation and validation.

As for the theoretical fundamentals, we drew mostly on active educational methods and the principles that guide them:

- the centrality of the child;
- attention to the child's needs and interests;
- the natural manner and pace of the child's development;
- the individuality of an education that is "made to measure";
- the demands of the social dimension;
- the significance of concrete experience.

It was on this basis that we opted to encourage the active participation of the children and to give them ample space for any possible intervention that they might make, as well as for interaction with their parents and companions.

Referring to the field of music, we see that research carried out by anthropologists and ethnomusicologists (Blacking, 1976; Nattiez, 1987) confirms that all cultures have musical practices that revolve around two basic actions: the production of vocal sounds, which is "singing"; and the production of sounds with objects/instruments, which is "instrument playing". In addition to these, there is a third action that in some cultures is inseparably linked to singing and instrument playing, and that is dance. As for listening as an 'activity' practised in Western culture, it is not so common elsewhere. Sometimes it does not appear to exist at all because making music is essentially a collective action.

The ways in which people sing, play instruments and dance obviously vary from culture to culture, and consequently the repertoires change. Particular support in this direction came from research by Delalande (1993) on musical 'conducts', and from the theory that he then formulated that states that the aims of enjoyment and pleasure in music are satisfied by three dimensions that the author recognizes as being present in all cultures and all ages: the sensorimotor, the symbolic and the game of rules. Delalande argued that, in musical practice, we find the search for sensorimotor pleasure at the level of gestures, tactile as well as purely listening; a symbolic investment of the musical object connecting with an experience (of movement, signs of affection) or with certain aspects of culture (myths, social life); and finally, an intellectual satisfaction that results from the rules of the game. These behaviours correspond to three kinds of game that children are seen to play and that were analysed by Piaget (Delalande, 1993). These behaviours should be characterized by intentionality, a fundamental concept in understanding an evolutionary process. A one-and-a-half-year-old child who inadvertently hits a tumbler with a spoon is surprised and begins to strike it at different points (to explore the sounds) and then alternates two of the sounds discovered (organizing them). The child started out with sensorimotor behaviour (exploration) and then moves on to the game of rules (organized event).

Studies in music psychology, as we saw in Chapter 1, for their part emphasize the perceptive-cognitive mechanisms that come into play in an encounter with sonorous events: how we perceive them, process them, recognize them, and how we organize them, both during production (by imitation or invention) and while listening.

In the light of all these studies, we decided to revolve our musical proposals around singing, instrument playing and dance. Listening was accounted for by the fact that, if we sing, play or dance, it means that we listen, and was incorporated through motor interpretation or other particular ways that we shall discuss later.

From what we have said, it is clear that in this educational process, we did not place the accent on the musical structures (such as melody, rhythm, form), but on the social practices: singing, playing and dancing, through which the assimilation of structures takes place. For this reason, the first criterion that guided us in the choice of songs to be taught to the children was the way that they are used in popular tradition and this is suggested by the song itself, according to its musical form and verbal text.

In popular tradition, as we are told by the Italian ethnomusicologist, Roberto Leydi (1973), children's songs (such as word games, action songs, game songs) have more than the functions of diversion and enjoyment; they also have an educational role. Their purpose is to increase motor coordination, to stimulate control of the emotions, to teach words (like the numbers, days of the week, months) and concepts. They are used, by the very fact of being sung by children, as models of socialization through a ritual that has the appearance of fun. Within this tradition, we find many children's songs (Goitre, Seritti 1980), including recent ones (Piatti 1980). As we go on to look at a possible classification of songs that most lend themselves to the proposed objectives, we notice that they have structures present not only in the Italian repertoire, but also in those of other countries.

Therefore we have:

- number songs (numbers, days, months, etc.);
- cumulative songs (a new element is added each time and everything named so far is repeated);
- songs with a *riff*, that is, that have some word or phrase that is repeated as an "incorporated refrain";
- songs with an echo (of syllables, words);
- concatenated songs (each verse begins with the last word or words of the preceding verse);
- cumulative songs with motor substitution (at each repetition, some words are substituted by an action);
- songs with actions or positions that can be changed, thus making way for new verses;
- songs for gestures, movements and dances.

Later when deciding on the kind of repertoire to choose, we also took into consideration some structural aspects of the music. Because children assimilate the musical culture of their own environment, we went for repertoire that contained the musical syntaxes common in the various kinds of song that circulate nowadays. This choice was based on two considerations in particular, one being psychological and the other biological.

With regard to the first, we based it on a declaration by Leont'ev (1969) that states that when we are born, our organs are not ready to carry out functions that are the product of historical human development, but that these organs (like a tonal ear) are formed and developed throughout life on the basis of historical experience. It follows then that, if children do not experience musical productions organized according to a certain system, these "cultural organs" do not develop.

The biological consideration is based on the discoveries of the Dutch biologist De Vries. At the beginning of the twentieth century, he focused on the presence of "sensitive periods in development". By this he referred to periods in which nature gives an organism a special flexibility to learn specific abilities. When the sensitive period is over, animal species have no further possibility of acquiring that particular ability (for example, for mole rats to dig tunnels), while for the human species it is just slower and more laborious. The clearest example is that seen in the acquisition of the mother tongue. The sensitive period goes from the last few months of prenatal life until age two. A baby who is born deaf and acquires hearing at age three, will have great difficulty in learning to speak. The later the child learns to talk, the more effort it will take, and the level reached will be lower.

The above considerations convinced us of the importance for children from the prenatal stage to be exposed to musical materials from their own culture, and to begin to assimilate their own "maternal musical language" (widespread today through the music industry), from the time that their ear is ready physiologically. The variety of genres and styles found at home and school facilitate the assimilation of a musical language that is rich and diversified, but always belonging to a specific system.

Taken together, this directed us towards the choice of a repertoire that would include mostly tonal songs, in major and minor keys, but also to include some modal and pentatonic songs. We felt there was no need to make a choice between tonal or pentatonic because several studies have shown that the pentatonic is not easier *per se*. What is easier is whatever belongs to the children's culture and there is evidence that those that learn tonal and pentatonic songs learn faster and are more mature in singing than those who only learn pentatonic songs (Jarjisian, 1983).

From the rhythmic-metric point of view, we inserted songs with regular rhythms, in both binary and ternary metre, and in simple and compound time. Our sources were popular tradition and author collections.

Another aspect studied in formulating the educational programme was the relationship between imitation and invention. As we have seen in the first chapter, studies in musical psychology have tended to be more interested in melodic invention than in imitation, but it is to be expected that, in order to invent something, you need to possess, even at a minimal level, the elements to be arranged. If we think of invention as a mental process, we should speak of creative thought. Webster, an American authority on musical creativity (1987) chooses this expression to put an emphasis on the working of the mind. If a child does not learn the words of his or her culture, and it is clear that they are learned by imitation, the child cannot produce a personal phrase that is more or less original in the combination of concepts.

In music it is a little different because children can freely produce sounds, but the assimilation of musical structures that occurs while learning songs through imitation and listening is found to be particularly necessary so that children can invent "their" songs. These are "original" in the sense that they move away from those already memorized. The more children acquire mental models and reproductive skills, the more they can develop their own ability to invent, moving further away from the said models by making new combinations.

For instrument playing, we thought of giving the children those instruments that are called "small percussion". These are instruments used in popular music and also in orchestras. Because of their small dimensions, they are also suitable for children. They are instruments such as bells, maracas, rhythm sticks, and tambourines. The evident use that children (and their teachers) make of these instruments is shown also by the fact that manufacturers of didactic materials and objects for newborns and small children put these on the market.

In the area of dance, which we had defined broadly speaking as "music and movement", we decided to insert an array of activities with appropriate repertoires:

- songs that are completed with movements (*Elephants walk like this*);
- songs that suggest actions (*Ring a ring o' roses*);
- real dancing, for which we looked at the Italian and foreign ethnic repertoire, and at some of the classical repertoire;
- musical pieces to listen to and experience through motor interpretation (such as Mussorgsky's *Ballet of the Unhatched Chicks*, and Ponchielli's *Dance of the Hours*) and sometimes even being still as in the musical fable *Peter and the Wolf* by Prokofiev.

2.6 Ready to Start

Ten, seven, twenty, twenty-two ... Each month brought new groups of mothers-to-be knocking on our door. The invitation that had been extended during the childbirth courses was a pleasant surprise for some, for others it gave rise to a sense of longing but also of fear (of not being good enough, of not being able to keep it up...), others had practical difficulties or were simply somewhat indifferent. During certain periods, the responses at a centre (Bologna or Imola) averaged eight to ten; once there were even 20 which meant two parallel groups had to be organized; sometimes there were only five or six.

Over the space of 14 months (February 1999–April 2000) the number of expectant mothers who had joined the project had reached the total of 119. During the regular activities, you could reckon each child's growth by the mother's girth. The future mothers continued to sing and listen to music at home, noting in their diaries the activities undertaken and the reactions of the baby within.

After the birth, the activities contained in the project were carried out by the mothers with the babies in their arms.

> I was used to singing with the other girls on the course, all of them pregnant. For me, it was difficult to take it up again after Sara was born when she was a couple of months old. I was tired and these weekly meetings seemed to be too demanding. I kept thinking, "What happens if I've to feed her, and she cries, and her nappy needs changing, and if she disturbs everyone?" Obviously, it was only a case of getting into the rhythm because we were all in the same boat. We could see how all the newborns were soon attracted to the music. They were relaxed during the slower songs and smiling with contentment with the faster ones. We seldom heard the babies cry during those meetings (those incidences were always linked to hunger or some kind of discomfort). They were all very attentive or so relaxed they fell asleep. [Giuliana]

As planned, our sessions included singing, listening accompanied by movement, singing games, rhythmic nursery rhymes, dancing, and exploration and use of percussion instruments. As the months passed, the babies began to take a more active and autonomous part as they gradually achieved the skills of grasping and shaking bells or maracas and banging drums (four to six months), of walking (10–16 months), of emitting sounds (two months), repeating syllables, words and songs (from 12–13 months onwards).

As stated in Guiliana's personal account above, the babies hardly ever cried. If there was some whimpering, it was a sign of hunger, and once they were fed the problem was solved. Every two months a new diary was given and the previous one was handed in. Of course, the diaries! They were very precious and necessary instruments, but they were onerous for the parents:

> What a bore! To have to write all those diaries, mark in the crosses and then answer the same questions ... But that's okay. In any case, it was my choice. [Silvia]

In fact, the diaries became a real mine of information, as we shall see in the next chapter. Although they were a burden for the parents (some never handed them in), they really demonstrate their commitment and collaboration that were so necessary for this collaborative research undertaking. When the babies reached two months old, their parents began to record their vocal productions, generally on audiocassette, but there were also some videos. This work involved a certain amount of effort, when you consider how difficult it is to be organized to capture the right moment when the children are psychologically at their best.

The recordings reached a point of great difficulty when, at about age one, the children began to notice the recorder. They were so attracted to the object that they refused to sing, and the parents had to find hiding places and use various strategies. Later on, towards age two, the parents adopted an explicit strategy: "If you sing first, then you will hear your voice again coming from here."

How constant was participation in the project?

Some mothers did not return after giving birth, others gave up after one, two, four years for various reasons: incompatible working hours, the children were ill, they moved to another area or town, they had another baby, the family situation changed, etc. Those who managed to keep going till the end came to around forty sessions, although with different levels of regularity of attendance.

Most of the children took part with their mothers, sometimes substituted by their fathers or a grandparent, some with both parents and some always with the father or a grandparent.

Chapter 3
Procedures and Results

3.1 Prenatal Memory

> Music and singing were an integral part of the day, a lovely way to communicate with Andrea and let him recognize, appreciate and love music. We were calm when going to sleep and we woke up happy. Andrea recognized some songs and then I could feel my stomach contract. This kind of dialogue through music was very moving. When Andrea was born, we made our first recordings in hospital. When he heard again the songs we had been singing before he was born, Andrea turned his head to listen. I think that it was reassuring for him to know that here too, outside the womb, we have music. [Gloria]

The children were born and the mothers watched them anxiously and attentively, wanting to witness the first manifestations and maybe some sign that would show them that the baby had really heard their voice and singing while they were still in the womb. Some of the mothers who were more involved had taken up our suggestion to have a special "recurring" song that could be a kind of affectionate link with their child. They could choose any song that they liked (not necessarily one we had recommended) and they were to sing it several times a day, especially during the later months of pregnancy. This song, besides being pleasing to the mothers-to-be, would help us to set up an experiment to study prenatal memory (Villa and Tafuri, 2000). On the basis of previous research studies (as we have seen in Chapter 1), we had wondered whether the newborns, during the first week of life, could show signs of recognition of a song that they had heard repeatedly before birth. We had given "instructions" concerning how the experiment should be conducted according to a precise research protocol and this involved using a video-recording. The methods agreed for the video-recording in this protocol were the following:

- choose a moment immediately after feeding when the baby is awake (if necessary, help them to stay awake);
- be in a quiet room where, if possible, background noise is at a minimum and the light is soft;
- the mother should sit comfortably with the child held in a lying position on her lap, their head supported by her hand in a way that they can see her. The child's clothes should be loose enough to allow the legs and arms to move freely;
- during the video-recording, the mother should look at the baby without changing expression and without speaking;

- the recording of the newborn should begin after the prepared audiocassette is set to record (explained below), beginning with a minute's silence. The recorder should be placed to the right or left of the baby.

In preparing the audiocassette (perhaps kept in the bag that expectant mothers keep at hand to have ready for the hospital), we recommended that they do the following:

- let the "recurring song" (or piece of music) play a few times in a row so that there are three minutes of music. There should be a minute's silence before this to allow for observation of the newborn's reactions at the moment in which, during the video-recording, the music starts;
- immediately after the "recurring song", without pause, allow a "new" piece of music to play that has not been sung or heard during pregnancy.

We also asked the mothers not to sing or listen to the two songs or instrumental music just after the birth of the child, but to conduct this experiment between the third and fifth day, not only to observe any reactions, but also because in that period the amniotic liquid is still present in their ears and so their hearing, filtered by this liquid, is similar to prenatal hearing.

The couples who wanted to and could conduct this experiment within the first five days after the birth were 13 in number, 12 of whom did it with a video-recorder and one couple who observed the child with other people present and took note of what happened.

> During the course it was suggested that we choose a song from among those most used in the prenatal period. We were not to sing it or listen to it just after the birth of the baby, but to present it again between the third and fifth day after birth, followed by a song that had not been played before. We did that. We were really very moved when we observed Riccardo's reactions. He listened to the prenatal song calmly, keeping his head turned towards the source of the music, and then when the new song was played, his attention was lost. Then, after showing expressions of disappointment, he calmed down again, and there was almost the same sensation of reassuring familiarity that was brought about by the previous song. [Roberta]

In analysing the videocassettes, we concentrated our attention on the reactions of the newborns at the moment between the silence and the beginning of the prenatal song and on the passage between that song and the new one. As some babies made more than one gesture (for example, they stopped and opened their eyes wide, or they opened their eyes wide and turned their head), the total number of reactions that were recorded is greater than the number of babies. Here are the reactions that we could observe (video nos. 1–2):

- all of the newborns reacted when they heard the prenatal song;
- five of them stayed still and some of these opened their eyes wide, whilst others relaxed and half-closed their eyes;

- five opened their eyes wide and gazed attentively;
- four moved their eyes from side to side and some of these turned their head at the same time;
- three turned their head towards the source of the music.

Three minutes later, at the moment when the new song began immediately without pause:

- four did not show any reaction (one of these had already fallen asleep and one had started to cry);
- five made grimaces. One of these opened his eyes and gazed attentively and two moved their hands with tension;
- three turned their heads and one of these moved his eyes;
- two moved their eyes;
- two gazed ahead.

After about 30–40 seconds, most of the babies had returned to a state of calm, although some were more attentive.

Of course, these data have to be interpreted with care, given the difficulty of controlling all the variables at that age. However, as the observed reactions were seen with a certain clarity and abundance, we believe that it is possible to consider them as signs of familiarity with the prenatal song and of recognition of the change to a new song. These results could confirm the presence of prenatal memory that had already been identified in other research cited in Chapter 1.

Some mothers were asked to do the opposite experiment, that is, to let the child hear the unknown song first and then the prenatal song. Unfortunately, only one mother videoed this experiment. However, in that recording it was clearly visible that there was a reaction of relaxation when the prenatal song began after the new one.

These reactions allowed us to note the presence of a certain discriminative ability in the newborn, a fact that had already been amply demonstrated by Sandra Trehub (see Chapter 1).

On the whole, our analysis of the video-recordings showed that, following the gestures that we interpreted as signs that the newborns had noted something different in the music, most of them returned to a state of quiet, even when the new song was rock music. We could consider this return to tranquillity to be a consequence of prenatal listening in that the particular experience could have produced familiarity with music in the broad sense.

All the mothers, even those who had not done this experiment, still gave their opinion on prenatal memory by means of the diary. Here they were asked if they thought that the child had recognized their voice when they sang and how this was made apparent. This was obviously not an "objective" question, nor could it have been in the strict sense, given the delicate nature of the subject. It was a question aimed at gathering the "feelings" of a mother.

The vast majority of the mothers replied "yes" to this question, 92.4% to be exact, if we calculate the average of the period ranging from zero to two months. The most interesting responses, however, are those from the first four weeks. Even though these were naturally less numerous than those of the second month when assimilation from the surroundings takes over – the exact figures were: first week: 89%; second: 85%; third: 88%; fourth: 89% (average: 88%), the reports of "recognition" are still numerous and we believe can only be explained by prenatal memory.

Recognition of the spoken voice produced a slightly higher result in the total average for the two months (93.2%), but was narrowly lower in the average for the first four weeks (87%). This almost testifies to a certain prevalence of singing compared to speaking in the early months of the children's lives. In order to specify the signs of recognition that the babies could give, we proposed four possibilities:

- batting their eyelids;
- staring;
- turning their head;
- moving their hands.

The most commonly reported behaviour was "staring" (48% in the first month and 40% in the second) followed by "turning their head" towards the voice (24% in the first month and 28% in the second). Perhaps this result could be viewed with a certain scepticism: "Imagine how emotional new mothers can be! Surely they see and hear more than there actually is ... ." This scepticism is often directed towards the "naturalistic" type of research in which the parents observe their children's behaviour at home, whereas research that is strictly experimental measures behaviour in controlled situations.

Nevertheless, there are notable advantages to the home-based type of research because, especially with such very young children, it is precisely the family environment and observation by those caring for the children that allows for interesting data to emerge, even if they must be interpreted with some caution. We had, nonetheless, put some necessary mechanisms in place in order to give more accurate weight to the parents' responses. These were: constant reminders to be as objective as possible in order not to alter the value of the research; the breadth and variety of the examples that in part act as correctives; and the statistical treatment of the data that gives a certain guarantee to the significance of the results and filters out, within the limits possible, any inconsistency and uncertainty that may be in the responses.

3.2 If the Mother Sings ...

> Francesco is here with us! He looks like a baby seal, but he's lovely. When he doesn't sleep? Well, we try *Buona notte Fiorellino*. When he cries? Of course, *Il grillo John* is ideal, and how he laughs when his dad sings *Il trenino corre*. [Silvia]

> It was lovely to see how Andrea changed expression when we sang the songs we had sung with you. As soon as he was born and still in the incubator, he was a bewildered, disoriented, frightened little thing who tried to look around, but only saw shadows; but when I (the father) started to sing *L'occhio bello* (heard so often while he was still inside his mother), peace and tranquillity came over him like a warm covering. [Matteo and Anna Rita]

> I observed the first positive aspect during the first few months. When I let her hear the song that she used to hear so often before birth, she stopped crying. [Annarosa]

Yes, the moment had come to test the effects of singing and music. Although the parents were very motivated to take part in the project, there was always a doubt, which was legitimate, that lingered in the background: "Could music really have any effect?"

Expectations were high.

The wait was rewarded: with the passing of days, the recourse to music, the listening to mother's songs or the recorded songs took on an almost magical role. The babies calmed down and were quiet, sometimes opening their eyes wide. Of course, when there was hunger or colic, no music could solve that, but the positive responses were there and they were amazing. The grandparents soon learned this too: "Mum, if he cries, play this cassette!" Naturally, people will say that mothers have been singing to babies to put them to sleep since the world began. It is true that popular wisdom knows and experiences intuitively the role of maternal song, but our project was to pinpoint and document the real power of communication in music.

This is why we wanted to take a closer and more detailed look at how these effects (almost prodigious) would be witnessed by mothers and studied by us (Tafuri, Villa and Caterina, 2002). The main instrument that allowed us as researchers to enter into the secret of maternal communication was provided by the diaries in which we had included several questions on this aspect. The responses examined were taken from about 40 diaries. From the 77 mothers who returned with their babies, not all gave us their diaries. To be exact, the number of responses analysed was as follows: infants from 0 to 2 months = 53; 2–4 = 46; 4–6 = 43; 6–8 = 46; 8–10 = 40; 10–12 = 36; 12–15 = 31.

Before looking closely at the effects of listening to music, we wanted to know, with data in hand, how much these willing participants had sung and listened to music. The first question posed in the diary asked them how many times a day they had sung and how many times they had listened to music for at least 15 minutes, both during pregnancy and afterwards with the baby. There were three possible responses:

- never or just once;
- two to three times;
- four times or more.

The results showed interesting differences between the period of pregnancy and that after birth in the sense that the mothers sang more with the child subsequently and the difference is statistically significant. If we wish to take a closer look at the average percentage, we see that during pregnancy:

- a good number of mothers sang two to three times a day (50.5%);
- a few sang three to four times or more (13%);
- a fair number never sang, or did just once (36%).

Listening to music during pregnancy was a little different, in that it showed that there was greater recourse to CDs or audiocassettes:

- the group that had listened to music two to three times a day was slightly more numerous (53%);
- a notable proportion listened three to four times or more a day (28.7%);
- a much smaller number either never listened, or did so just once a day (18.3%).

It can be seen that during pregnancy there was greater recourse to listening and less to singing. After the birth it is easy to understand how a thriving bouncing baby in one's arms is more likely to induce one to sing. However, the option to use recorded music remains high.

If we look at the average percentages obtained in the first 15 months after birth, we notice the following:

- there were many who sang two or three times a day (69.2%, with an increase from 66% to 77% during the 15 months);
- a significant minority group (22.9%) four times or more daily;
- there were very few who only sang once a day, or not at all (7.8%).

If we look at the option to use cassettes or disks, we notice that:

- many used recorded music 2-3 times a day (74.1%, with variations from 65% to 80% during the 15 months);
- very few took this option 4 times or more daily (12.5%);
- and also very few did this only once a day, or not at all (13.3%).

The differences between listening to the mother singing and to recorded music were always statistically significant, except for the age range from zero to two months and from ten to 15 months (Tafuri, Villa and Caterina, 2002).

Another statistical calculation allowed us to verify that the mothers who sang most were also those who listened most. In other words, those who dedicated more time to this musical experience did so both by singing and by using disks and cassettes.

At that point we went on to study the effects of listening.

It was hot that day, really hot. It was the first meeting after the summer break. All the new arrivals were irritable after the drive, the perspiration, their disturbed nap. They were so small. Some were just a few days old, others a month or less. There was some whimpering, some screaming, some demanded feeding, and then there was magic (the magic of *inCanto*). The usual greeting song began *Benvenuti tutti quanti* (*Welcome everyone* ...) and for the first time, in addition to the presentation of the names of the mums and dads, there were also the names of the babies. What a sudden silence! An hour of absolute quiet. The dances with the babies in our arms, the songs sung looking at their faces ... This miracle also took place at home. When the baby cried and I sang some of the songs that had been sung during pregnancy or let her hear some of the music we had heard so many times during the previous months, she would stop, turn her head towards the source of the sound and calm down. And she fell asleep. And she enjoyed it. [Cristiana]

During the meetings with the newborns, the chorus of satisfied testimonials continued. They wanted to tell us how Andrea stopped crying or how Chiara was better humoured when she heard her mother singing or the music coming from the disk player. We were obviously delighted and shared their enthusiasm, but we also had to put it on paper and make a few calculations because, as we all know, when people are optimistic, negative experiences are quickly forgotten.

So, what was recorded in our precious (though perhaps not always exciting) diaries? There was an entire page with a series of questions regarding the effects of the mother's singing or of the recorded music in four situations:

- when the baby was crying (for no serious reason like hunger, colic, etc.);
- when the baby was restless;
- when the baby was quiet;
- when the baby was about to fall asleep.

For each question there was a list of possible answers. For the first two, the possibilities suggested were:

- the baby continued to cry or be restless;
- the baby stopped and calmed down;
- the baby stopped and paid attention.

For the third and fourth (calm or about to fall asleep) there was a wider variety of responses as we shall see later.

The same questions were asked with regard to listening to recorded music ("if the baby cries for no serious reason and you put on some music ..."). The results were quite remarkable: the presence of positive effects was very high, especially when the baby listened to the mother singing, and a little less if they listened to recorded music.

With the figures in hand, that is, on the basis of percentages that are statistically significant, we can say that:

- the average number of infants who stop crying if their mother sings is very high (94.5%) and it is lower when recorded music is played (78.4%);
- the average number of children who cease to be restless if their mother sings is a little less than in the case of crying, but it is still very high (89.4%) and the same difference occurs with recorded music (74.8%).

At this point it is interesting to point out the greater number of positive results in the case of crying over restlessness and the greater effect of maternal singing over listening to recorded music in both those cases (Tafuri, Villa and Caterina, 2002).

We now go to the third question which attempted to find out the effects of listening in an apparently "neutral" situation, that is, a quiet situation. During the first three weeks, five possible reactions were listed. If the newborn was quiet and the mother sang:

- the child fell asleep;
- became more alert;
- showed no reaction;
- became restless;
- cried.

From the fourth week on, we added another three:

- the child moved his/her arms;
- moved his/her legs;
- smiled.

The questions were then repeated to refer to when they listened to recorded music. Given the variety of results, and these generally showed that the music had more effect when the baby was quiet, it is interesting to consider the responses in more detail.

If we observe the results covering the first three weeks, we notice a distribution that is almost equivalent (slightly in favour of sleeping) between when they fall asleep (43.2%) and become more alert (41.5%), but this difference increases if the mother plays recorded music. In this case they have less tendency to fall asleep (36.4%) and are more likely to show alertness (44.9%).

The effect of putting them to sleep falls suddenly from the fourth week on, both when the mother sings (from 43.2% to 15.14%) and when recorded music is played (from 36.4% to 16.11%) and it progressively diminishes, with highs and lows being slightly irregular, until the twelfth month, when the incidences become much lower (7.31% for the singing, 6.6% for recorded music).

On the other hand, the effect of music making them more alert increases. This is evident in all the age ranges, even if there are highs and lows (between 19% and 30% if the mother sings, and between 20% and 35% with recorded music).

The new reactions are movement and smiling. As regards the first, the answers document a motor reaction that is almost equivalent between legs and arms (the arms slightly more often), both with the singing and the recorded music, and a marked increase of leg movement in the period from four to six months. However, it is clear that the motor responses are increasing, even if irregularly, until the twelfth month.

Smiling becomes more established at around four months (25.96% and 21.43%) and, as a reaction to the mother's singing, it maintains a good level (between 25% and 28%), but it is a little less frequent with recorded music (between 12% and 23%).

Finally, we looked at the negative effects that we had suggested: no child cried, except maybe very occasionally when one of them was restless, or maybe from time to time one of them did not react to the singing or to the recorded music.

A final situation on which we wanted to test the effects of music was that of going to sleep. We asked the question: "if the child is about to go to sleep and you sing ...":

- Does the child fall asleep sooner?
- Or become alert?
- Or become restless?
- Or cry?

As previously, the question is asked again, this time with regard to listening to recorded music (If the child is about to go to sleep and you play some music ...").

In this situation, too, there is a clear prevalence of positive effects when the mother sings over when recorded music is played. The average number of babies who fell asleep sooner was reported to be quite high in the first case (80.25%) and markedly lower in the second (53.51%). Besides this positive effect of the mother singing when the child is about to go to sleep, we also find some babies showing more alertness (11.03%), very few signs of indifference (7.3%), an occasional child became restless (1.3%) and almost none cried (just two cases on one occasion only).

It is interesting to note the reactions of those babies (a little less than half) who did not fall asleep more easily if the mother played recorded music when they were about to sleep: a fair number (23%) were attracted by it and showed more attention, another group (23%) remained uninterested, a few became restless (2.7%), but almost none cried (only three cases on one occasion only).

With all of this data, something began to take shape before our eyes. The mothers' accounts were also documented in the diaries, so these were not incidences that had taken place the day before. These things were repeated and confirmed week after week and month after month with a certain constancy.

Another last question completed the picture and it dealt with the efficacy of the song, or the piece of music, chosen as the recurring song during the prenatal period. To the question repeated during the first two months: "Have you noticed any difference if you use the recurring song?", a positive response was clearly higher (50.9%) than the negative responses (28.3%) only during the first week. From the second week onwards, the number of positive responses was always slightly lower than that of negative responses (33% for the first, 39.6% for the second) and a fair number never gave any answer (27.4%). When they had to indicate the differences observed, the mothers wrote down the effects that they had seen: the baby calmed down, was quiet, became alert, turned his head, looked fascinated, smiled.

None of the couples reported any reactions by the newborn to the singing of the father because – we apologise to the fathers – we did not put in a precise question regarding the four situations. We had thought of the fathers, but in the diaries the question was general. Their participation was documented, but there is not an explicit reference to particular situations. Each week there was a question asking if the father had sung. The possible responses were: every day, occasionally, never. The results tell us that the fathers felt quite involved, for a good number sang every day (28%), many sang now and then (58.4%, varying from 62.1% to 52.5% during the first 15 months), and a few did not sing at all (13.5%).

3.3 Playing with Songs

During the meetings with the mothers-to-be, we had taught them singing games and had also given them suggestions about how to invent new ones. "The days are long", we used to say to them, "and when they begin to sleep less, babies need to be entertained more. It is good to repeat, but there is also a need for change: repetition and variation as the psychologists say, and then fantasy ... ."

In practice, during the meetings, we gave preference to singing songs with gestures or movements of different kinds (jumps, turns ...), with pauses at strategic points, getting faster and getting slower. We asked them (with good results) to invent words for existing songs, or to invent songs (music and words) based on situations that the babies would experience at certain times: bath time, feeding time, going out for a walk, etc.

This activity was continued at the meetings after the birth of the babies. Besides being for the entertainment and amusement of the newborns (after the second or third month), it also had the purpose of giving the mothers some technical knowledge related to musical language, and to lay the basis for the gradual assimilation the children would acquire.

In order to have this activity documented for the purposes of our study, and also to prompt the parents to do it, the questions to be answered in the diary were the following:

- Have you made up words to go with known songs?
- Have you made up songs (music and words)?
- Have you used singing games?

We were pleasantly surprised to find that many mothers had made up words to go with known songs, a good half of them (52%) did so at least a couple of times a week, and almost a third did so more often. Evidently the composing activity carried out during the meetings with mothers-to-be had stimulated and amused them, and so they had found it fun to do at home with the babies.

They were not quite so courageous in making up words and music, but that activity was still present: less than half of the mothers (47%) did this twice a week, and only a small group (16%) did it more often.

Besides, it is interesting to note the constancy shown by the mothers in this activity that turned out to be statistically significant. It is seen in the fairly regular distribution of the responses throughout the first year and there are no major changes from one month to the next, almost indicating that a habit had been formed.

As regards the use of singing games, until the babies were six months old we had only made allowances for two possible answers, simply "yes" or "no". The results are very interesting because they show the progressive involvement of the mothers as the months went by. It could be seen that they enjoyed this activity. This was partly because they were stimulated by the reactions of the children. A sizeable group (62.4%) began to play singing games already at two to four months, and the number increased for four to six months (69.7%).

In preparing the questions for the post-six months period, we guessed that the mothers themselves would feel more involved in the singing games that they were to do with the children and so we increased the number of possible responses to "never, sometimes, or often". If we add the results for "sometimes" (49.7%) to "often" (31.83%) in the period from six months to one year, we see that the number that played singing games, even with varying frequency during the six months, is very high (81.53%). For the following period, from one to two years, it increased slightly (82.65%), because the number of those that did it more often increased (35.6%). It is easy to imagine that this change could have been due to greater participation by the children and their possible requests.

What reactions did the babies show to this activity? Many categories emerged from the responses which means that there is much dispersion. However, some general categories are present with greater frequency, even if with quite low values (between 12% and 28%). From these answers we saw that the children expressed enjoyment. They laughed or smiled, became alert (eyes wide open, staring), they moved their legs and/or arms, and after six months they jumped, rocked, danced. Among the reactions given, we only occasionally find vocal reactions like squealing, babbling, gurgling and whooping, or excitement or clapping. The mothers rarely marked indifference or annoyance, but sometimes grumbling or crying ... if the game was over.

3.4 First Vocal Sounds

From the time that they are born, babies need to make their vital needs known and, as we have seen in Chapter 1, the only instrument available to them is their voice. Crying and screaming are the key signals, those sounds that pierce the heart (and sometimes the eardrums) of new parents who immediately go to the baby's assistance. This sets up a connection between vocal call and satisfaction of need, a connection that the newborn absorbs in the first month and soon learns to use to full advantage.

However, very soon the uses of the voice begin to extend. The voice acquires new connotations and becomes a real instrument of communication. When did the babies on our project begin to produce these freer sounds? When did they start using their voice to attract attention or even only for the pleasure (proprioceptive-based) felt through the vibrations of their own voice? How did this vocal production evolve, transform, or improve?

These are the questions we asked ourselves and with which we aroused the interest of the parents, and so they agreed to make more and more recordings. Some of this was already happening during the meetings. If we stopped still after a song, and in absolute silence looked at the babies with an air of invitation, there was often one who would make one or more sounds. We had to be very patient, however, and wait in silence.

Apart from the direct experiences that aroused our enthusiasm, we had to deal with this behaviour in a rigorous manner, and so we studied the sounds emitted by the babies under two different aspects and using two separate sources.

Our first study (Tafuri, Villa and Caterina, 2002) concentrated on the quantity and quality of sounds produced by the infants in their first 15 months whilst, or immediately after, their mother sang or they had been listening to recorded music. The study was based on the responses given in the diaries.

A second study (Tafuri and Villa, 2002) dealt with the vocal interactions between mother and child by analysing from a strictly musical point of view the quality of the vocal productions that responded to the mother's singing. This study, which will be presented in the following section, was based on analysis of the recordings made in the family homes.

Returning to the first aspect, a question in the diaries asked if the baby produced any sounds during the singing or immediately afterwards. The answers from which to choose were that the baby produced just one sound, several different sounds, or the same sound repeated more than once. These three questions arose from several requirements: the difference between various sounds or the same sound repeated more than once stems from the hypothesis that an infant who often hears music (songs and instrumental music) feels more stimulated to produce various sounds. On the other hand, the difference between various sounds or the same sound repeated several times sprang from the desire to verify what Moog had asserted: when an infant often repeats the same sound, he is exploring his own phonatory apparatus for the function of speaking, whereas when he produces several sounds at different pitches, he is doing so for the function of singing.

When looking at the results, we noted that the average number of infants who produced just one sound is relatively low (12.5%) compared to the average number of infants who produced several different sounds (45%) or the same sound repeated more than once (42.8%).

At this point we wished to check to see if there was a connection between the amount of time dedicated to singing by the mothers and the number of sounds produced by the infants. We therefore separated from the total group (with a system of cut-off points) the mothers who used to sing more and those who sang less. Comparing the results obtained from these two groups with the results from the whole group, we saw that the percentage of infants who only produced one sound is lower for the mothers who sang more often and higher for the mothers who sang less often, with the exception of the age group from six to eight months, a result that was difficult to explain. Our results, therefore, do not give us absolutely clear and certain data, but it is plausible to think that listening to mother singing can often stimulate infants to produce a greater number of sounds.

We now consider the effects of listening to recorded music (CD or audiocassette with songs or instrumental music) on the production of sounds (in the diary we had asked: "While listening to recorded music or when the music has finished, does the child produce any sounds?"). We observed that the average number of infants who produced just one sound is still low (14.9%), even if a little higher than the result when their mothers sang. The average number of infants who produced various sounds was also high (44.5%) as it was for those who repeated the same sound more than once (40.5%).

We applied the same comparison test that we had used in the case of singing (the exposure to listening to music provided by their mothers and the number of sounds produced by the infants). We were curious to see if, after listening to recorded music, the results would go the same way. However, this was not the case. Actually, the results showed us a rather irregular trend between the different age ranges, independently of whether the children had heard less or more music. In fact, it was sometimes quite the contrary. The number of infants who produced just one sound (considered to be a poorer production with respect to others) was often greater in those who had heard more music, and less in those who had listened to less.

Can we assume that listening to recorded music is not so stimulating in encouraging vocal production from small infants? Perhaps so, but the irregular trend makes us think that there are other variables that influenced the babies' behaviour, and these include the mother's behaviour during the listening activity.

However, it is important to be aware that it is not only the mother speaking to the child that prompts vocal reactions, but it is also singing and music, especially if the child is normally surrounded by a stimulating family environment. A comparison with a control group, that is, with infants who did not receive prenatal musical stimulation, would have helped us to better measure the range of this sonorous production, but a comparison of this kind was programmed only with reference to singing dialogues, as we shall see in the next section.

3.5 Communicating Through Singing

As we have said, the study of the sounds produced by infants was not limited to a classification of the responses contained in the diaries. There was also a series of recordings produced at home under controlled conditions for the two to eight month period after birth (Tafuri and Villa, 2002). As guidelines for these recordings, we produced a protocol according to which the mothers had to sing well-known songs to their babies: they were to stop after one or two verses and wait for any vocal interventions, and then do the same thing again a couple of times more. Following this, they were asked to do the same with a new song, and then to sing "cuckoo" (on a descending third minor interval like so-mi) three times, one after the other and to wait for any response. Then they were to speak in rhythm: three short sounds with the same syllable ("pam-pam-pam") followed by a silence of equal length, three times. The total length of each session and its recording could take from ten to 15 minutes. The mothers were asked to do at least four to five recordings in the period of ten successive days after the infants had reached the ages of two, four, six and eight months.

It was rather an undertaking to do these recordings as it was not easy to find a moment that was always best for the child and when the parents were free. However, participation was quite good. Altogether, we received recordings of 39 infants (out of the 70 who were attending the classes). The mothers of only two of the children managed to do the recordings in each of the age bands (two, four, six and eight months). Others made recordings in three, two or even only one of the periods, for various reasons (babies were sick, families moved house or stopped participating in the project, etc.). In short, ten babies were recorded at age two months, 25 at four months, 27 at six months and 16 at eight months.

The recordings we analysed showed an amazing quality of production. The "chatterboxes" joined in several times when their mothers began to sing, whereas others stayed silent for a long while and joined in now and then. The average was quite high, however. The most abundant production came from an infant of four months. Altogether during the four recordings of 20 minutes' duration each, the child joined in 235 times, occasionally with sequences of many seconds. The most limited was from an eight-month old infant who joined in nine times altogether during two recordings of five minutes each.

All the vocal productions of the children (about 4,000) were classified and analysed by two experts separately on the basis of the following categories:

- generic sounds: vocal sounds that are not very definable and syllables;
- glissandi: distinguishing those ascending, descending and mixed;
- intervals: distinguishing those ascending, descending and mixed.

The vocal productions classified as "intervals" (546 altogether) were those formed by two or more sounds in which it was possible to hear and identify a pitch interval that was "in tune", that is, perceivable and reproducible with the voice. These intervals, which we considered to be "musical" because they had the characteristics of our Western musical scale, were also analysed with the computer programme *Cool Edit Pro* to confirm the musical content in terms of pitch relations, and also of duration relations. In fact, the rhythmic aspect was analysed only for the sameness and diversity of the duration of sounds.

Before going on to comment on the results as a whole, let us take a closer look and above all listen to some of the children's productions (in the enclosed CD) with the help of the music stave transcription (the numbers beside the notes indicate the frequency registered by the computer program). These are recordings made at home and the equipment is quite modest. Moreover, these are live recordings and so there are background noises, the microphone is far away, etc. At times the vocalizations are very short, and the children sing with their mouths half open and at very low volume, so one has to listen to it a few times in order to capture the musical aspects. In some of the recordings it is possible to hear the last fragment of what the mother sang, and in others there are short "dialogues".

The transcription of sounds in traditional notation is accompanied by the indication, under the stave, of the frequency of each note. The letter "m" indicates the part sung by the mother, the letter "b" is that sung by the baby.

In this first recording, after the mother sings, a baby of two months sings a descending major third (rec. no. 1):

Now we go to a larger interval, a descending fourth, produced by a baby of four months (rec. no. 2):

In the third recording (rec. no. 3), a baby of two months "replies" to her mother who also "replies" by imitating the sounds the baby made, thus establishing a dialogue (the transcription is omitted because few of the sounds could be considered to be "in tune").

This is followed by an example of what we called mixed intervals: a sequence of sounds, produced by a baby of four months, in which we can make out some ascending and descending intervals (only the central part is transcribed; rec. no. 4):

In the production by this four-month-old baby, there is a particular musical procedure known as "progression": a rhythmic-melodic motif (here of three sounds only) that is repeated (here just once), but at a higher pitch (rec. no 5):

Another child of four months seemed to be about to cry, but the sound went "into tune" and the vocalization concluded with a cadence (a musical formula denoting conclusion) (rec. no. 6):

Another four-month-old child prolonged the sequence: ascending interval (major third), silence, glissando, descending interval (major third) (rec. no. 7):

The same child at six months reproduced two intervals contained in the mother's song, but inverted them. The original song went from a fifth to a fourth, and the child repeated the fourth and then the fifth at almost the same pitch as the mother (rec. no. 8):

This mixed glissando produced by a baby of 6 months lets us hear how shrill their voice can be at that age (rec. no. 9):

In this vocalization there is an interesting occurrence: the mother speaks because the protocol contained the request to follow a speaking rhythm of three short sounds with the syllable "pam", and then this six-month-old child produced "spoken" sounds repeating the syllable "pa". Then the mother repeated the three syllables holding them for longer so that they would seem to be "sung" and the baby also "sang" the two intervals (ascending fourth to descending fifth) imitating the mother (rec. n. 10):

In this vocalization by a baby of seven months, the song the mother was singing is quite recognizable (rec. no. 11):

In recording number 12, the sixth-month-old child is clearly a "chatterbox". The mother's "cuckoo" (descending third major) is the incentive for "improvisations on a theme". A long monologue is evidenced in which, at the start, we can recognize a few times two pitch intervals similar to the mother's "cuckoo" (the transcription is omitted because only some sounds can be considered to be "in tune").

Another six-month-old child is very sparing in his responses, but his vocalizations are already little melodic motifs, and moreover, here his first sound is exactly an octave higher than the last one sung by his mother (rec. n. 13):

The same child at eight months gives us a slightly longer motif (rec. no. 14):

A baby girl of eight months launches into little melodies, here in a low voice (rec. no. 15):

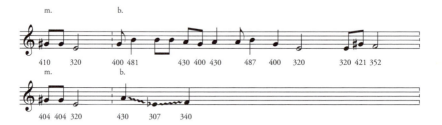

This time the same child sings at full voice, and after the mother sings a descending major third, she concludes with a similar interval (rec. no. 16):

Listening to these examples will surely have contributed to an understanding of what we call "musical vocalizations". Now we look at the results in general. First of all, we emphasize the wealth and variety of the babies' vocalizations that became progressively more varied and longer as they grew older. From a maximum duration of around 45 seconds at two months, they went to about one minute at around four months, and a minute and a half between six and eight months.

In order to better grasp the more musical aspects of these vocalizations in relation to age, we look at Figure 3.1.

In the first group of data relating to the production of glissandi, we immediately notice that the "mixed glissandi" (those in which the sounds went upwards and downwards) were produced by most of the babies after the age of two months. The ascending sounds are the least frequent and, together with the descending sounds, seem to be influenced by age. We should, therefore, affirm that a vocal production of mixed glissandi presents no difficulties and is already possible at two months old.

To produce two or more sounds of "discrete" pitches, that is, to produce intervals, is more demanding than glissandi in which the voice simply "slides" along a continuum of pitches. In fact, on the whole there were fewer babies who produced intervals than those who produced glissandi. However, they were still numerous. Moreover, together with the production of intervals that belong to our musical system and even melodic "phrases" of many sounds, this turned out to be very interesting.

Figure 3.1 also allows us to see the clear difference between the infants who produce ascending intervals constituted by sustained pitches and those (more numerous) who produce descending intervals, intervals that we could consider to be more "physiological" in the sense that they are closer to the exhalation curve.

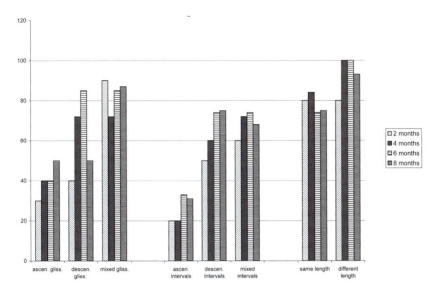

Figure 3.1   Children (in %) who used diverse musical categories between the ages of two and eight months

If we consider the production of mixed intervals (meaning sequences of varying pitch intervals or, in musical terms, short melodic motifs), we would be likely to say that this is influenced by age, in that babies of two months who can produce them are less in number than babies of six to eight months. However, if we compare the results of the category called "mixed intervals" with the other two categories, we notice that the babies of two months who produce these short sequences are more numerous than those noted in the other categories.

Consequently, we cannot state that these short sequences are more difficult than the delivery of one or more intervals that are only descending or ascending. We should conclude that, right from the age of two months, these babies were able to produce short melodic sequences of more and varied pitch intervals with respect to the production of intervals in just one direction.

The reason for this is not easy to identify. If we look for it at a functional level, the hypothesis is that it is easier to stretch the vocal folds a little more and a little less rather than to keep them in the same position of greater or lesser tension for several consecutive stable pitch sounds. If we look for a behavioural reason, the hypothesis is that, on the basis of the same level of ease due to the physiological development attained, the babies show a specific behaviour in response to what is offered by the environment, and that means, in our case, that these children, having heard a lot of music, feel more inclined to use their voices in a more varied way: simply put, they enjoy it more.

A final observation concerns the rhythmic aspect. Contrary to what is commonly accepted, that is, that babies mostly produce sounds of the same length because it is easier, here we see that more of them use varying durations in their sequences (long-short-long, or short-short-long), even if the longest sound is often the last one: the physiological aspect of the end of the breath has come to mean the end of the "sung" phrase.

In order finally to check the significance of these results, we had recourse (as is often done in developmental research) to the so-called "control group", that is, we analysed the vocal productions of babies who had not taken part in this experience.

For this, we asked our colleague the musician Cecilia Pizzorno, who resides in a city where our project was unknown, to contact about forty parents of babies from two to eight months. Of the 39 mothers who accepted the invitation to record their babies' vocalizations, only ten handed in their recordings. The others had given up either because they had no time or because they tried and the babies did not produce any sound at all. Of the ten babies whose recordings we received, the ages were distributed thus: one baby of two months, nine of four months, four of six months and two of eight months.

From the analysis of their audiocassettes, it was found that, in the various recordings made by the parents, seven babies produced no sound but, we were told (verbally or in writing) by their mothers, that they reacted with motor responses (moving their legs and arms, rocking their torsos), which were considered to be expressions of surprise and/or pleasure. Some of them smiled broadly. Only three babies replied sporadically with some vocalization. To be precise:

- One baby of two months from time to time produced some short vocal sounds that could not be classified as having a distinct pitch and being "in tune";
- One baby produced some musical vocalizations which were, at three and a half months, of descending intervals (one second and one sixth) and at four months, some ascending and descending glissandi;
- One baby of four months produced three descending intervals (one fourth and two fifths) and then some ascending and descending glissandi.

In light of what we found, and also by what has been demonstrated by other authors, we feel that we can conclude that the babies who have been exposed to musical experiences during the prenatal and neonatal stages produce vocalizations that we can consider "musical babbling" (see Chapter 1), vocalizations that appear earlier, in greater number and with greater musical value with respect to those of other children who have not had such a rich experience.

3.6 From Musical Babbling to Singing

Monday 8 January 2001, the first Monday after the Christmas holidays, the schools reopened and we recommenced the meetings of the *inCanto* project. The children arrive, one of them running (he is aged one and a half) and some others are still being carried. We greet each other warmly and then we begin. The first song *Benvenuti tutti quanti* [Welcome everyone] is our initial greeting, a verse of welcome after which each child is called by name and their mothers answer for them: "I am here" (*So, So, Mi*). Lorenzo... Irene... Corinne... Martina... and a little voice piped up: "I am here". The little girl was a bit hoarse (the mothers laughed), but the response was perfectly in tune. Great excitement ..., perhaps I had heard wrong, so I call her again. Martina responded again and then again. She was the first baby to sing since the research began two years previously. I looked hopefully at the voice recorder: yes, it was switched on! The long awaited event, the first instance of singing was recorded (rec. no. 17). Martina was 18 months old.

In the previous section, we had left the babies grappling with their musical vocalizations, long or short and varied. Towards the age of one year, the first words appear. The babies want to talk, to express themselves, to be understood. Speech fascinates them. And singing? How did the babies progress from their first vocalizations, their early musical babbling to real singing?

From age one to two is certainly a year of great conquests in the area of verbal and motor language. We were, therefore, curious to discover what would happen with singing (Tafuri, García Rodriguez and Caterina, in preparation). Would it follow a different route? Would it give way to speech and then reappear later?

Some studies on the first signs of singing (see Chapter 1) had already demonstrated that children between the ages of one and two can produce songs; Moog (1976), in particular, in his research with infants, had confirmed that when they learn to reproduce songs, they can first of all imitate the words, then the rhythm and then the pitch intervals.

We had asked the parents to record the children at least three to four times during the first 20 days of each three-month period, for ten to 15 minutes each time. In the protocol that we gave them, we asked, as in the previous phase, to do the following:

- Choose a moment when the child is quiet and well disposed to sing;
- Sing one or two verses of a known song and stop to see if there are any vocal interventions, then do the same again several times with the same song;
- Do this again with a new song;
- Sing "cuckoo" three times (descending minor third); wait and repeat twice more;
- Clap your hands three times and wait in silence, then repeat this twice more;
- Sing the name of the baby and the response "I am here", as we do in our song of welcome during the meetings and wait in silence.

In particular, we suggested that they often sing songs with repeated syllables (such as an action song that we had learnt that finishes with "down, down, down"; or a song about a duckling that finishes with "quack, quack"; or a song with syllables that imitate the sound of instruments, like "pum, pum" or "toc, toc", etc.)

The suggestion arose from the hypothesis that children find it easier to sing repeated syllables before they manage the words of a song.

How did the children progress during this period?

The recordings handed in were unfortunately not very numerous. There were only 19 children recorded several times (out of about 65 doing the course). On the whole, for the age range of 12, 15 and 18 months, 14 children were recorded (even if not always the same children); eight of these at 21 months.

The analysis of the children's recordings was carried out by two independent experts. We had decided to use just "human" evaluation (without a technical application such as computer software) because, except for the precision of intervals, it was sufficient for experts, with their ears and mind, to recognize the musical significance attributed to singing during our meetings. This kind of analysis allowed us to spot the presence of a wide variety of interventions by the children. Immediately after the mother sang (but seldom after the father), and during the song itself, or at times after a ten to 20-second silence, we noticed a great variety of vocal productions from which we derived the following typology:

- generic sounds (ah, eh, boh, mmm, etc.);
- glissandi of various lengths and varieties;
- musical vocalizations: one or more sounds in tune on a vowel, sometimes with mouth closed, mostly short interventions (only one sound on any pitch or on that sung by the mother, or two to three sounds reproducing one to two intervals of our scale, often a descending minor third), or quite long interventions (melodic sequences of six to ten sounds) with recognizable vowels ("a", "o"), or undefined;
- spoken syllables or words that have a contact function ("*tata*", "*mamma*" being the most frequent, or "no", "*nonno*"), or that belong to a song (generally the one that they had just sung with their parents, but not always; for example, "ju, ju, ju"; "qua, qua", "cuckoo", "*dama*", "*piatti*", "*ottolo*"); the words from songs were pronounced with the rhythm used in the song;
- sung syllables that correctly reproduce one to two intervals from the song (sometimes the "cuckoo" is sung with a descending minor third and at times with a different interval, but in tune);
- sung words either from the song ("*tutti*", "*quanti*", "*bimba*", "*rosso*") or free words ("*tonta*", "*oca*", "*dadi*");
- sung phrases or rather a sequence of pitch intervals (from four or five and more) produced with some syllable ("eh-oh" "eh-oh"; "orno-orno", "na-na-ni-na", "ta-ri-ro-to") or fragments of songs, from the shortest "*Sono qui* [I am here]" to "*Bianca sono qui* [Bianca I am here]", "*Canta e balla* [Sing and dance]", "Pum, pum, pum"). These sung phrases also sometimes came from the song they had been listening to, and other times they were free (little improvisations), but always with intervals that belong to our scale.

This material was very rich, but its interpretation was not easy. Was this a variety that came from the freedom and fantasy of the children, or was there a greater or lesser presence of some specific type of vocal production? Did these typologies vary with age? In other words, we wanted to understand if it was possible to glimpse some form of evolution in the fact that some productions might be present in varying quantities, or even might be absent, according to age.

After classifying each vocal production according to the typology listed above, we chose to give particular attention to the study of five types of production:

- musical vocalizations,
- syllables and words spoken with rhythm,
- sung syllables,
- sung words,
- sung phrases.

The analysis of the productions present in the last three categories also established if the intervals being produced (imitated or invented) were in tune or approximate. A fairly constant fact was also the imprecise pronunciation of many words ("onno" for "*giorno*", "ono" for "*sono*", "ca" for "*qua*", etc.). On the basis of the collected data, we were able to assess the number of children in each age range who produced sounds that belonged to each of those five categories, and their frequency.

By generally observing the behaviour of the one-year-old children, we immediately noticed that almost all of them (12–14) had produced vocalizations of the type produced at six to eight months, whilst fewer of them (eight) had produced sung syllables (rec. no. 18).

A good number (12) had produced rhythmic syllables and words, like a child of 11 and a half months who reproduced with the syllable "da" the rhythm of the song *Pippo Kid* (rec. no. 19). Few (four) attempted to sing the words (rec. no. 20 and 21) and very few tried short sung phrases (rec. no. 22 and 23). This early data showed us, on the one hand, an element of continuity in the presence of vocalizations of the type already found months earlier, and on the other hand, a new element, that is, the appearance of spoken language. This had the children both "speaking" – even when the mother was singing, and so they uttered syllables or words from the song or even free words (to the extent of their verbal achievement) – and singing, mostly using few syllables and occasionally a word.

Applying this interpretation to successive phases, we felt that this tendency was being confirmed because progressively fewer children were producing vocalisations and the number they produced were also decreasing (from a total of about a hundred down to about twenty). From the presence of rhythmic syllables and spoken words, it was possible to draw the conclusion that almost all children always use them. We noticed a considerable increase in interventions until 18 months and a clear drop at 21 months (less than half), accompanied by an increase in sung words and phrases.

To sum up, we can say that these children, as they gradually acquired verbal language between 12 and 18 months appeared to considered this to be something autonomous; they tried out the spoken word, while from the musical point of view they continued to produce the usual vocalizations. At around 18 months, they began to discover "the sung word" and to venture into this new experience, something that they obviously learned from observing their parents' behaviour.

Meanwhile, how did their spoken language develop? In the diary, we asked the parents how many words the children uttered in the period between 12 and 18 months. The average number of words we were told about is still very low in this period: 6.08 words for children between 12 and 15 months and 11.83 for children between 15 and 18 months (within the range, there was one who had not yet said anything and one who had uttered 20 words).

For the period between 18 and 24 months, we had given the same question, together with three possible answers as guidelines: "few", "many", "makes phrases". The answers (statistically significant) show how the development of language was predictable: in the period from 18 to 21 months, a group of parents (33.6%) replied "few" and a larger group said "many" (45.4%), but there are still a few who say that the children make phrases (21%). This was a skill that flourished during the next phase (21–24 months) in which there is a drop in the responses on the quantity of words ("few" 19.3%; "many" 32.2%) and there is a noticeable increase in the production of phrases (48.5%).

To come back to singing, we noticed that, up to the age of 18 months, there was an increase in the number of children who produced sung syllables and an increase in the quantity of their interventions. At 21 months, we saw that there was also an increase (if more modest) in sung words and phrases and a decrease in the singing of single syllables. For example, if we listen to the recordings conducted in three successive periods by a mother who often sang the same phrase "*Bianca, sono qui*", we noticed that the child first only sang "*qui*". After a few months she sang "*sono qui*" and finally she sang the whole phrase "*Bianca, sono qui*".

The process from 12 to 22 months that we have described does not yet seem linear because of several factors. In addition to the small number of children studied, we also note the problem of the frequency with which the children intervene during the recordings. Some children are very much in the mood and they sing a lot. For example, a child of 12 months produced 67 interventions in a total period of 40 minutes recorded on different days. Others were more parsimonious, like the child, also a one-year-old, who in four recordings that totalled 60 minutes, only intervened 19 times. Evidently the personality, the willingness and the desire to sing each influences production and the number of interventions influence the probability that determines certain responses.

Moreover, we were surprised to detect that the sung interventions were not always the repetition of words or phrases contained in the songs, but that they were often inventions. We found that this behaviour is something interesting and worth emphasizing, that is, the activation of sung inventions. This activation could happen at a moment in which the child is absorbed in themselves and begins to sing softly, perhaps beginning with syllables or words that then become more elaborate. This is what happened, for example, with a child (22 months) who sang a short word he invented at the same pitch with a rhythm of short-long, then he repeated it at a different pitch forming a melodic phrase (*do-do, mi-sol, re-re, do-do*) which he repeated many times in a more accurate way at first and then progressively deforming the intervals (rec. no. 24). At times, however, the improvisation began during a song, activated by a word, as a girl of 19 months did during one of our meetings. While we sang a song with an echo, she began to repeat the echo whilst moving away from the group (who at that point stopped singing) and she repeated it several times introducing new words (rec. no. 25).

This behaviour allows us to emphasize the pleasure that small children feel when expressing themselves in song, as creators and not only as imitators.

3.7 Finally We Sing!

As the meetings came and went, the babies began to join in the singing of some of the songs. They would repeat the last word of a line, sometimes half a phrase, or maybe the lines with animal sounds, or they would imitate the sound of the instruments (pum, pum, pum; din, din, din; toc, toc, toc). Sometimes we would stop before singing the last line and often it was one of the children who continued.

During the meetings, the children were a bit shy to join in, but their parents told us that they were always singing at home. However, we were in no position to go from family to family and so, as foreseen in the project and already tested in previous phases, the main source for our study had to be the recordings conducted at home by the parents. This continued to be the best choice for the recording of such small children, in spite of the unavoidable background noise and possible distractions (not to mention the exhaustion of the parents!).

As in the previous phases, we prepared a protocol on how to conduct the recordings and gave it to the parents. The mothers had to record the babies for at least ten to 15 minutes twice in every three-month period (minimum). They had to:

- find a moment when the child was well disposed,
- begin to sing a song that they knew the child enjoyed;
- stop after the first verse, or between the first and second line little by little as the children grew, and wait for them to continue.

If the child began to sing immediately, the mother was to stop and let the child continue alone, giving some encouragement to continue in case of some interruption. According to the kind of reaction, each mother had to decide whether to continue with the same song until the end or to change song if the child seemed to want that.

The recordings were to include two types of song: those already learned (at our meetings, in playschool, or at home) and those invented (to be encouraged by asking: "What can we sing to the cat? And to the doll? And to Daddy?"). Parents were also asked to record the children when they sang freely while they played.

The children whose recordings we have for the period when they were two to three and a half years old came to 37 in number out of the 60 who were attending the course (with varying degrees of regularity). Unfortunately we did not receive recordings in every three-month period for all of them (lack of time, colds that dragged out, the birth of a sibling, etc), and so the data was not complete for each child according to our original schedule. Some parents made a video recording.

The recordings were mostly conducted whilst the children were playing, or maybe the children were singing whilst they played alone in their room or in the garden. It was also possible to make some recordings during the meetings, although there were few opportunities because the children often refused to sing when they were asked.

Whilst listening to the cassettes, we noticed that sometimes what had been asked for happened, that is, the mother sang and stopped after one or two phrases. Sometimes, there was some conversation, the mother came and went, or she asked the child what he wanted to sing, leaving him to choose his favourite song. As the months passed, there were more frequent occurrences of the child responding by naming a song or by starting to sing it immediately. Occasionally some of them, in answer to the song suggested by their mother, said that they did not remember it or did not know it. We assume that this was because they did not feel like it, they were tired, or because they preferred to do something else.

In all these situations, it was clear that for the child "singing" meant singing a song and that it was a family activity. From the time that they were born (and I would almost say from before that), the babies were used to considering singing as a normal everyday activity, a pleasant activity and a source of appreciation whenever they themselves sang.

Their performances, which at age two often stopped after a few phrases, gradually became longer as the months passed and there was an increase in the children's ability to remember the words and to hold their focus. As might be expected, the rate of maturity was very different from one child to the next, but some of them at the age of two years and two months could sing songs with three complete verses and sing in tune, although the pronunciation of the words was still imprecise (rec. no. 26).

In the "free" recordings, it could be noticed how the children sometimes became a little distracted. They were playing with something and so they started to sing; then they stopped, they were a bit quiet as they played around with some object, and then they continued their song (rec. no. 27), or they changed song (rec. no. 28). Their expressivity in these situations was more variable, from muttered phrases to shouted phrases, from "rallentandi", or rather, stretched out phrases, to "accelerandi", or hurried phrases. The performances made together with their parents were more homogeneous (example rec. no. 29, no. 30). Nevertheless, there were plenty of children who had fun with the songs (rec. no. 31, no. 32) by introducing variations in resonance (making growling noises or squeaky noises), or of speed, intensity or even variations in the melody, but that stayed in tune (rec. no. 33).

Until about age two, the children were not aware that their parents were recording them, but later it became impossible to hide the recorder and so the recording became an explicit game: "If you sing, then this machine will sing for you" or: "Do you want to hear how nice your voice is?"

The recordings were conducted in a rather heterogeneous way from the point of view of child age and session duration. By this we mean that we have recordings of some children in every age band, because the parents were very regular and faithful to the three-monthly deadlines. For others, we only have some periods covered because their parents were very irregular. As for duration, there was also much irregularity here in the sense that some children were recorded for sufficiently long times (20–30 minutes or more per three-month period). Others, however, lasted only five minutes (after many insistent telephone calls ...). The personality of the parents, the work situation, the family organization and the willingness of the children showed that life, naturally, took the upper hand.

The quality of the recordings is generally not very good. There are background noises and the noise of the children banging something. Sometimes, the children moved away from the microphone, etc. Nevertheless, in all the cases reported here, their singing can generally be heard clearly. The songs produced were analysed by two experts independently because, with this age band too, we preferred to have a "human" evaluation that made an assessment from a musical point of view (which is not possible using voice acoustic software).

For the classification, we drew three types of performance from the *Model of Vocal Pitch-Matching Development* by the English scholar Graham Welch (1997), that are considered as three phases from the point of view of development. These are:

1. *approximately in tune*: when the children reproduce the melodic profile of phrases or songs (the melody rises and descends as in the original), but the intervals are vague (exampled in rec. no. 34, no. 35);
2. *singing almost in tune*: when the children correctly reproduce the melodic profile and several of the intervals (rec. no. 36, no. 37);
3. *singing acceptably in tune:* when the intervals are precise (intervals of a third, fifth ...), even if there are still some small errors or sliding tonality because of occasional intervals that fall or rise (rec. no. 38, no. 39, no. 40).

As we stated earlier, at times the children sang songs from beginning to end and at times they stopped after one or two phrases. In view of the abundance of material in hand, we thought it would be more interesting to study phrases and songs separately.

In order to better understand the progression, we felt it was better to make a further study (Tafuri and Welch, in preparation) on three types of performance according to age band. We wanted to understand if, in practice, the children's singing often passed from one kind of behaviour to another, or if there was a gradual movement towards the third kind of performance. In order to evaluate the production of each child, we therefore built a 7-category scale to combine the various possibilities:

1. absence of imitation;
2. imitation approximately in tune;
3. imitation approximately in tune and at times almost in tune;
4. imitation almost in tune;
5. imitation approximately in tune, at times almost in tune and at times acceptably in tune;
6. imitation at times almost in tune and at times acceptably in tune;
7. imitation always acceptably in tune.

What was the result of the distribution of all the productions according to this scale? Let us call on the help of numbers and attempt to interpret them.

We begin with Figure 3.2 which presents the situation of song production in the age band of 2.9 to three years. It is the period in which a larger number of parents made recordings and so it is possible to analyse the situation of 30 children. Of these, 21 had reached (and some passed) level 5 in the grading scale above. What does this mean? It means that all of the 21 children (70%) were able to sing acceptably in tune at least sometimes, if not always. To be precise, there were two who did this always (scored at level 7), five who at times produced songs almost in tune and at times acceptably in tune (level 6), with 14 whose singing included the three possibilities (level 5).

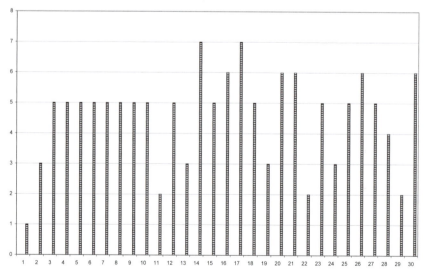

Figure 3.2   Evaluation of song production of each child – age band 2.9 to three years

The results were a pleasant surprise, not least because of the relatively high skill levels being demonstrated by children aged between 2.9 and three years. These were more advanced than expected by looking at previous literature, probably because other studies had participant children who had not followed any particular special musical course. As we saw in Chapter 1 for example, Moog's (1976) study reported that 44% of three-year-old children produce songs that "resembled" the original, whilst an Italian study (Jorquera *et al.*, 2000) carried out in Bologna city and province with two groups of children in their first year of elementary school, showed that only 15% had developed the ability to sing acceptably in tune.

There is also another consideration to be made concerning this data: if a child sings well in many recordings, we have no doubt as to the child's ability, but if they have only been recorded singing two songs, we cannot know what stability they would show if they had sung ten or twenty, even on different days as some other children had done. Therefore, another element that could influence the results is the number of songs sung by each child. In any case, the children for whom we have few examples and that are completely in tune are definitely very few. However, we have compared the number of phrases and songs produced by the children with the evaluations attributed and the result confirms that, when the quantity increased, the quality also increased. In other words, as the children grow and are given the opportunity, they sing more and they sing better.

In order to have an overall view for phrases and for songs in the various age bands, we can look at Figure 3.3 that shows the average of the total ratings obtained by the children.

If we look at the ability to sing complete songs, progress according to age is clear, but if we look at the ability to sing phrases, there seems to be a regression in singing in tune. Actually, this is not the case, but it is in fact an interesting development. As children grow, they are less likely to stop after a few sung phrases;

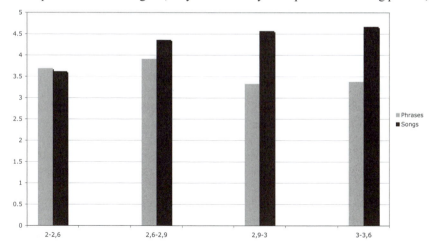

Figure 3.3   Average evaluations of children's ability to sing phrases and songs in tune

therefore, the graph first of all shows a drop in the quantity of single phrases, but not in the entire number of songs. Secondly, those who stop more easily after a few phrases and those who are less secure at singing in tune do not sing an entire song. We say this, however, without forgetting that sometimes children only sing one or two phrases, not because they cannot reach the end, but because they change their minds. After their mother asks, "What do you want to sing?", the child starts a song, then changes their mind and proceeds to sing another. This can happen more than once and at any age.

This difference of quality and quantity between phrases and songs, a difference that favours songs, is nevertheless surprising and initially difficult to explain, because at these ages, as we see from other studies carried out with children who have not had this long exposure to music, the children mostly produce a few phrases at a time. We must, therefore, acknowledge that there is evidence of early singing maturity in this group of children due to the special musical course that these children followed from before they were born, but we can also recognize some causes link to praxis. In fact, both during the course meetings and at home, songs were usually sung from beginning to end; if children at home stopped after a few phrases, they were generally encouraged with "and then?". Studies on infant speech (Cowie, 1989) have shown that children aged two have already developed the sense of the beginning and end of a story ("Once upon a time ... and they lived happily ever after"), even if they have not yet developed the logical connection and coherence between the openings and the outcomes. This ability could also influence the sense they give to a song as something that has a beginning, a duration and a conclusion.

An overall look at the number of children (in percentages) present in the various categories according to the singing profile can be seen in Table 3.1. The data in this table can also be displayed as a figure, see Figure 3.4.

Of the many observations we could make about this Table/Figure, we shall limit ourselves here to pointing out the high percentage of children that come into the fifth, sixth and seventh grades of the scale, particularly as the children get older. The fifth rating level signifies that the children's singing was acceptably in tune, but not always (sometimes they were approximately in tune and occasionally they were almost in tune). The sixth level indicates that their "approximate" imitation was no longer there and that the child had sung almost in tune and at times acceptably in tune. The seventh level means that the child was always acceptably in tune.

The first important finding in this data is the fact that the perceptive-cognitive and phonatory mechanisms are ready, before the age of three, to imitate a melody correctly. The second, and equally important, point is that this ability does not develop at the same time for everyone and, lastly, that it is not yet stable, in the sense that a child who has sung a song perfectly once, could maybe after a few minutes or after a week make errors when singing it again. As Welch (1997, p. 483) affirms, the ability to sing develops along a progressive continuum that may take a year or more, and during this time the children may oscillate between relative successes and less-than-successes. It is rather like learning to walk which involves falling from time to time, or learning to speak which entails making occasional errors.

Table 3.1   Children (in percentages) who sang with different modalities by age group

The seven-grade scale categories	2.0–2.6 13 children		2.6–2.9 11 children		2.9–3.0 30 children		3.0–3.6 24 children	
	phrases	song	phrases	song	phrases	song	phrases	song
1. absence of imitation	23%	15%	9%	0	20%	3%	29%	0
2. imitation approximately in tune	7%	15%	18%	27%	16%	10%	17%	12%
3. imitation approximately in tune and at times almost in tune	7%	23%	9%	0	20%	13%	8%	17%
4. imitation almost in tune	7%	0	18%	0	13%	3%	8%	8%
5. imitation approximately in tune, at times almost in tune and at times acceptably in tune	46%	20%	27%	54%	20%	47%	17%	33%
6. imitation at times almost in tune and at times acceptably in tune	7%	15%	18%	18%	3%	17%	12%	12%
7. imitation always acceptably in tune	0	0	0	0	7%	7%	8%	17%

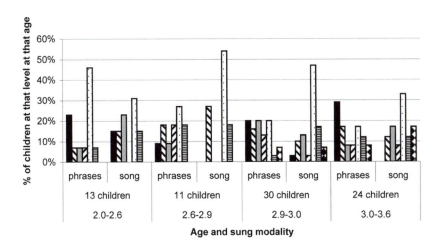

- ■ 1. absence of imitation
- ◩ 2. imitation approximately in tune
- ☐ 3. imitation approximately in tune and at times almost in tune
- ◪ 4. imitation almost in tune
- ☐ 5. imitation approximately in tune, at times almost in tune and at times acceptably in tune
- ▤ 6. imitation at times almost in tune and at times acceptably in tune
- ◪ 7. imitation always acceptably in tune

Figure 3.4   Children (in %) who sang with different modalities by age group

When we look at the numerous factors that influence the development of the ability to sing in tune (Welch, 1994), the data produced in this study convinces us that the most important are a social context in which a musically rich family environment provides encouragement as well as praise, interest and attention for each child.

3.8 Inventing Songs

> Over time, Giulia showed more and more familiarity with singing and music, and there was a sensation that touched my heart when I saw how, while she played alone or was having a bath, she would take a toy or doll and invent a scene, a story, and put it to music, singing a song that she herself composed for the occasion [...]. Now and then Giulia would run into my arms in the evening when I returned home tired from work, and she would ask me if I wanted to hear a song she had composed specially for me. It was such a lovely experience! [Marco]

"Mummy, now I'm going to sing you a hard song. It's called *Love*."

Leonardo, aged two years and seven months, is singing at home with his parents. His mother is interacting with him. His father is video recording and intervenes from time to time. It is a particularly creative moment. His mother had told him that the ice cream was already eaten and he launched into improvising a song with the words "Non è vero" (that's not true) (video no. 3). He repeated it over and over on the same melodic pattern and accompanied this by banging on a bottle. He laughed and continued at this for a while. A little later he announced that he would sing the "hard song".

One day, Claudia, aged two years and 11 months, during one of the meetings asked: "May I sing a song?" "Of course", I answered, but she became shy and would not continue. I asked the others, "Who wants to sing a song?", and Viola, aged three years and five months, a very shy child who was always reluctant to "take the stage", offered to sing: "The whale was looking for her babies in the sea ... ." She was inventing a song. Her mother and I exchanged looks of pleasant surprise.

The attention given to the ability to sing in tune by imitating a melody did not prevent us from studying the same ability through the invention of songs. Above all, we analysed the responses given by the parents in the diaries corresponding to age two to age four, in which they were asked if the children sang freely during the day and if they invented songs. Regarding the first aspect, the parents claimed that they did this very often. Almost all the children sang freely. Some of them sang more often (47%), others several times a week (48%). Most of them sang whatever they had learned from their parents, and also from disks and television, as well as the songs learned at our meetings and at playschool.

As regards the second aspect, that is, the inventing of songs, in the responses it emerges that it was a (statistically significant) frequent activity and quite constant, with oscillations between one three-month period and another. If we look more closely at the results we see that in the period from two to three years, the children who invented songs several times a week were more numerous (40%) than those who did it often (29%). In the period from three to four years, the number who did this often was now greater (40%). Some of them used repeated syllables, seldom sounds of animals, more often single words. Most of them invented as they sang full correct phrases (60%).

The parents also specified the circumstances in which the children invented songs. For most of them it happened as they played (67% of two to three-year-olds; 77% of three to four-year-olds). A small number also invented with other people, especially the two to three-year-olds (24%), and some did so sporadically in other situations: at table, while out walking (rec. no. 41) and especially in the car (rec. no. 42).

The most important study on the invented repertoire was that conducted on the recordings carried out by the parents. There were less of these recordings than there were on the reproduced songs, as we pointed out in the previous section, because it was not easy to record children while they were inventing. They generally stopped singing when they saw the recorder or even when they saw the adult approach.

The examples that the mothers managed to record allowed us to identify and study some tendencies, both of the behavioural and strictly musical type (Tafuri, 2003). Of the 37 children whose productions we had been able to have recorded, we found the invented songs of 21 children. By analysing these inventions, we first identified two categories of song: those with an existing melody to which the children put different words, and those with invented music as well as words.

The songs of the first category we called "imitative songs", and those in the second category we called "original songs", according to the model proposed by Lucchetti (1987).

In the "imitative songs", the more interesting element was the lyrics. They allowed us to see the contents of a normal day that were passed into song. The original song was as follows:

> *C'era una volta un papero, vestito di pelle di bufalo*
> *faceva ballar le papere sull'uscio di dindirindé*
> (Once there was a boy gosling dressed up in a buffalo skin,
> and he made the girl goslings dance out the door of the dindirinday)

In an invention by Clara of two years and nine months (rec. no. 43) it became:

> *C'era una volta mammetta vestita di pipetta*
> *faceva a birichetta ull'uscio 'ndirindé. ...*
> (Once there was a little mummy dressed up as a little pipey,
> and she gave a little winkey out the door of 'ndirinday)

> *C'era una volta papà vestito di torrone*
> *mangiava un bottone ull'uscio 'ndirindé.*
> (Once there was a daddy dressed up as a nougat,
> and he ate a button out the door of 'ndirinday)

The productions considered to be "original songs" were then divided into three sub-categories: *phrases*, when the children invented one or two phrases (for example to call a doll, to tease someone, to ask for water, etc.); *monologues*, when the children were self-absorbed and repeated vowels or syllables using few sounds (rec. no. 44), often while they were doing something else (a child on the swing, or a child with building bricks, etc.); and *songs*, when the children were using song to tell a story or to recount their experiences, such as when their parents encouraged them ("what was that story about the little football?", rec. no. 45), or alone, simply because they felt like it.

The 99 "original songs" that we collected were classified as follows: 26 phrases, 26 monologues and 47 songs. Many (67%) children invented monologues and/or songs. In our analysis of these inventions we noticed that, as in the case of the analysis of the imitative songs, the children were more inclined to invent entire songs (48%) rather than short phrases.

How good were they at singing in tune while they were inventing? Did the children show the same ability as that seen in the imitative songs? In order to answer this question, we analysed and classified the inventions according to the model used previously. On the one hand, we found a clear presence of intervals and rhythmic-melodic patterns pertaining to our musical culture whilst, on the other hand, the level of singing in tune was lower than when singing the imitative songs. According to the 7-point evaluation scale used for the imitative songs (see above), we can see an achievement of level 4 for the intervals produced during the monologues, and levels 4, 5 and 7 during the invention of songs. However, the number of children who achieved these levels is quite low (Tafuri, 2003).

We can, therefore, conclude by saying that there is less control over keeping in tune whilst one is inventing. In fact, if we compare the results of the imitative singing and the invented productions, we notice that in the first case many children (61%) have achieved the median (level 5) and a small group (17%) achieved the maximum (level 7), while in the second case there are very few (10%) who achieved the median (level 5), even if some (10%) – but still less than in the case of the imitative singing – achieved the maximum level (level 7). This can be explained by the fact that imitation refers to an already complete pre-existing model (a song already learned), whereas inventions are improvised and therefore guided by an extemporaneous musical idea that refers to a system that is not yet sufficiently assimilated as such.

Therefore, we agree with Dowling (1984, p. 165) who had the same result with his two daughters. He pointed out that to be able to keep in tune while composing a melody requires much experience and the assimilation of many melodic patterns. At that age, the production of pitch intervals is not yet well controlled by a dominant scale schema, as happens when reproducing known songs.

3.9 Rhythm, Movement and Instruments

Giulia, 11 months old, is sitting on the mat with an instrument in her hands (castanets with a handle) like the other children around her. The parents start to sing a song with piano accompaniment. Immediately Giulia begins to rock back and forth. The rhythm changes for the refrain and Giulia begins to bounce up and down and shake the instrument. When we come back to the verse, Giulia goes back to rocking (video no. 4).

At a different meeting we sing *Pippo Kid*, a song where there is hand clapping on the refrain. The children are just over one-year-old and they are beginning to do this too as they are accustomed to seeing their parents doing this since they were born. In another song there is a part where the parents bounce the babies on their knee, getting faster and then pretending to drop them at the end. The babies enjoy this; they laugh and assimilate it all.

When we give them a percussion instrument, they begin by playing freely and change instrument often, but when we begin to sing or play some music, they play more willingly and are more involved. Rocking, playing, clapping hands, bouncing ... the activities are various, the babies have fun and at the same time they develop their motor coordination, emotional involvement and ability to structure time.

During our meetings, we noticed that from the age of one, as they acquired autonomy of movement in space, the children showed a noticeable increase in their ability to move or play an instrument together with the music. Through the observation we conducted both during the meetings and while watching the video-recordings, we could see how many children frequently gave a motor response when the music started. In particular, it was very evident from the age of six months that they were rocking or bouncing their bodies in their mother's arms or whilst sitting on the mat.

We also noticed how the children were using the instruments and how they progressively became more accurate in their gestures as they played the drum or rhythm sticks together with the music. Their playing was beginning to show an initial attempt to synchronize with the beat of the music. This was the favourite part of our activities. We often got them to bang brightly coloured tubes made of a special plastic material on different parts of their bodies as they listened to a piece of music with a very measured beat.

The parents themselves noticed this at home and often remarked, "Look, he's keeping time". This comment reflects also that this was one of the aspects to which we had drawn their attention by our questions in the diaries.

What did we really want to study through the responses of the parents? Given the importance that psychologists attribute to movement as the main instrument to structure tempo, and given the importance of this ability in musical activity which is basically temporal by nature, we drew the attention of the parents to the frequency and quality of this behaviour, as well as to the interest that the children showed in it.

From the age of one to two, we directed our attention to their motor reactions to music, asking if the children moved spontaneously when their mother sang or when music was played, what movements they made and if they kept time with the music.

On analysing the results, we noticed that a motor response to music was present in most of the children, with a higher percentage at this age phase when it was recorded music (92%), than when it was their mother's singing (86%). This is interesting because it suggests that there is greater incisiveness in the beat (and therefore a greater movement induction effect) when there are instruments playing. This behaviour is constant throughout the four three-month periods.

Which movements are the most prevalent of those that were indicated? Is it rocking, bouncing, moving their arms or clapping their hands? From the age of one and a half we added "dancing" as a global motor behaviour that also has social value, and that children mostly learn from watching television.

As further responses were possible, the results show us quite varied motor behaviour. In practice, the children used all four of the movements indicated, being given full marks for dancing (100%), followed by bouncing (99.6%), moving their arms (99%) and the lowest category went to hand clapping (98.6%). Motor involvement is total.

For the question about keeping time, beside the response "yes/no", we had put "I do not know", thinking that it might not be easy for some of the parents to make this judgement. About one third of them answered that they did not know (31%). Almost all the others, apart from some rare exceptions, answered "yes" (67%). It is interesting to observe that the "no" answers are concentrated in the first three-month period which is when the children were between 12 and 15 months old. This is, therefore, more evidence that motor activity, even though it is a response to music, does not display the synchrony that we classify as "keeping time".

For the two to three-year-old age group we categorized all the motor activity within the category "dancing", and so we asked in the diaries if the children danced when there was music, live or recorded, and if they kept time. At this point we had noted that spontaneous dancing to music begins to diminish in this age group, especially in the period between two and a half and three when there is an increase in the percentage of children who never do it (from 3% to 13%) and a decrease in the number who do it often (down from 52% to 41%). The percentage of parents who claim that their children move in time to the music increases considerably (84%), especially after the age of two and a half. Could this be true? We shall take this question up again later.

With this age group (two to three-year-olds), we also asked about another category and that was if the children displayed a preference for any of a choice of musical activities. In order to find out about any such preferences, we asked the parents to indicate the kinds of behaviour the children adopted most often, choosing between singing, playing instruments, dancing and listening. From the results, it emerged that singing remained the most common activity and the most constant during this period (38%), maybe because it can be done almost anywhere. Dancing came next (32%), far ahead of listening (19%) and playing instruments (12%).

For the three to four age band, we only asked the parents to indicate an order of preference from among the four activities given above. As regards the first preference, singing remained in first place far ahead of the other activities (57%), followed by dancing which was almost at the same level as listening (24% and 21% respectively). Similarly, when asked about a second preference, these two activities as received almost the same scores (30%), well ahead of playing an instrument, classified in last place as only 9% of the children chose this as a first preference. Even though we saw a clear tendency in this period (three to four-year-olds) towards a certain order of preference, they were not stable preferences. We noticed a certain oscillation from one three-month period to the next, perhaps because at that age children's choices are affected by other factors (school, friends, cinema, etc.).

In order not to leave the observation of the development of such an important skill in music as "keeping time" entirely to the parents' impressions, we looked for an instrument of analysis that would be as accurate as possible. We decided to use a protocol designed and tried out very successfully by Silvia Malbrán in her research undertaken in Argentina, and of whom we have already spoken (see Chapter 1).

We procured the necessary instruments for the data collection. These were a digital drum (a round plastic surface with loudspeakers attached that responds to the drumbeats by transforming them electronically into sound), a computer program (Cakewalk) to collect and analyse the children's performances, as well as a MIDI interface to connect the digital drum to the computer so that the performances would be recorded directly onto the computer.

The test consisted of asking the children to play the digital drum with a stick as they listened to a highly rhythmic piece of music that was recorded on the computer and transmitted over the drum's adjacent loudspeakers. The piece of music was March no. 10 from *Music for Children*, Op. 65 by Prokofiev. The first ten bars had been recorded, played with as regular a beat as possible (almost mechanical) at sustained speed (Metronome $\frac{1}{4} = 105$).

The children were simply asked to play the drum "together with the music". They were not given time beforehand to explore it, and they never showed any sign of needing to do so, probably because they were used to banging the drum together with music during our meetings.

The appearance of the digital drum fascinated the children and they ran over to play it, except for the more timid ones who needed a lot of encouragement before they decided to try. While each one played, the others were present, but they were held back by their parents (not always easy) so that their companion would not be disturbed (video no. 5).

The first recordings were made between February and May 2002, but although we allowed this much time, it was not possible to record all the children who attended the project because of their absences and other logistical difficulties. The study was conducted on the performances of 42 children who at that time were between 24 and 35 months.

In order to ascertain if their early familiarity with music had produced any benefits, we had a control group of 21 children who were also between 24 and 35 months old. They attended a playschool in Bologna where there were no particular musical activities besides a few songs and rounds. These children took the test in the same way as the children on the *inCanto* project.

The performances were analysed together with Silvia Malbrán (Malbrán and Tafuri, 2006) and they were assessed by taking into consideration the four variables that she had determined in her previous research, namely:

- *Correspondence* between the number of bangs on the drum and the beats in the piece of music (the music had ten bars in 4/4 time, so it contained 40 beats in total);
- *Sustainability*, the degree to which the children continued performing without interruption (starting from a minimum of four continuous sounds);
- *Adjustment*, the degree of proximity of each of the child's striking gestures to the precise beat of the music (maximum proximity, that is, perfect concurrence = 0; limits of tolerance for a sound slightly anticipated or delayed to be accepted as synchronous: 1/8 of the temporal interval between one sound and the next);
- *Regularity*, the degree of stability of a level of synchrony.

The results obtained are very interesting and can be summarized as follows: First of all, it is important to point out that the children showed great interest in playing this particular drum individually "together with the music", which means that interest in this activity can be seen very early. Already between the ages of two and three, the children do this task with enjoyment and pleasure. What is the level of synchrony achieved in this age range?

If we examine the level of *correspondence* in each child's performance, we notice that the sounds that they make are more than half of the beats contained in the piece of music. To be more explicit, out of the total of 40 beats contained in the March, the experimental group made 55% and the control group 58%. The values reached are statistically significant (meaning that they were unlikely to be by chance) and they tell us that the children's early familiarity with music had no influence over their performance because both groups achieved almost the same results. In fact, the control group was slightly higher. How did that happen? Here we have to look at two factors.

The first is the age factor. Analysis of the data showed that the older children reached a higher level of *correspondence*, and this suggests that this variable depends on their perceptive-motor development, which is connected to age. By observing the two groups of children, we could also see how the control group had more children between the ages of two years and eight months and two years and 11 months (43%) with respect to the experimental group (24.4%) which had a greater number of younger children (75.6%). Therefore we can hypothesize that the slightly better performance of the control group might depend on the larger number of older children.

There is, however, another consideration that I would personally like to put forward as I was present during the performances. Some children from the experimental group sometimes played the rhythm of the melody (semiquaver-dotted quaver, a typical cell found in many marches) instead of the beat, because often in our meetings we marked out the rhythm of some of the songs. Nevertheless, according to the analysis protocol, if a child performed two or more sounds in correspondence to one beat, this intervention was not counted among the valid sounds and so it was discarded. Some children, therefore, obtained a lower score and this influenced the total percentage.

The second variable examined was *sustainability*, that is, the number of sounds in sequence that the children could reproduce without interruption. This variable measures the level of attention paid during the task. This also turned out to be age-related. On the whole, the scores were quite low for both groups, even if the experimental group showed a slightly better result. They performed continuous groups of sounds to a total of 37%, a little higher than the control group (33%). We can, therefore, suppose (even taking into account the fact that the average age of the experimental group was slightly lower) that musical practice had helped them to develop greater attention when playing instruments.

We now go to the third variable, *adjustment*, which is the degree of proximity of the percussion to the beats and, therefore, the level of co-occurrence – which is synchrony in the strict sense. Here the difference between the two groups is clearly greater. Even though the level of synchrony is low, also because of their young age, the experimental group performed 31% of the sounds within the limits of tolerance and the control group reached 23%.

Finally, a look at the results corresponding to the fourth variable, *regularity,* allows us to say that in early childhood there is still much instability at the levels of synchrony, in the sense that it easily passes from one level to another and is therefore highly variable. Nevertheless, the extent of the variations is clearly lower in the performances of the children of the *inCanto* project. The statistical processing of the data showed that all the differences between the two groups are significant.

We can, therefore, conclude by saying that the children on the *inCanto* project had reached a level of synchrony that, although still modest because of their young age, was nevertheless greater than that of the control group, and that this edge is likely to be due to their early musical exposure.

We then asked the children to repeat the same test a year later and again two years later in order to study their progress (Tafuri and Malbrán, submitted). They did it with great enthusiasm, and they were always thrilled when the digital drum arrived. Unfortunately, it was not possible to gather all of the children who did it the first time to come and do it a second or third time. This meant that the comparison of results over the period of three years was only done with the performances of 25 children. The second time, they were all (except one) aged between three and four (35–47 months) and the third time they were aged between four and five (48–58 months).

Comparing the results achieved in the first year of the experience with those achieved in the second and third, we see a clear progression towards synchrony. In particular, most of the improvement was in their ability to make a sound *correspond* with each beat of the music they heard, to play without interrupting for longer periods (*sustainability*) and to make their sounds co-occur better with the beat of the music (*adjustment*). The factor that remained very low and that did not really show any improvement was the *regularity*, in the sense of the stability of the synchrony achieved.

A final interesting observation was noted regarding the differences between the three age bands: the improvement was more marked from age two to three than from age three to four. This would confirm those psychological theories (Piaget *in primis*) that locate a series of transformations (cognitive, motor, sensorial) at around three years of age.

In order to complete the picture of rhythmic skills, we wanted to analyse the precision shown by the children in performing known songs (Tafuri, Privitera and Caterina, in preparation). Actually, playing another piece of music "in tempo" is a different activity from singing in tempo. In the first, we have another musical event with which to synchronize, while in the second we alone keep the beat of the song, a beat which in some way needs to be interiorized so that it can be sustained without outside support. Furthermore, each song has, in addition to its internal beat, its own rhythm that needs to be respected. Is this easier or more difficult?

In order to find an answer, it was necessary to analyse the songs sung by the children aged from two to three and a half. The analysis was carried out by two experts independently and the assessment was attributed according to the degree of accuracy shown in two different aspects: the beat and the rhythm of each song.

Both elements were judged on the basis of a scale of 4 degrees which showed if the beat or the rhythm (considered separately, first one and then the other) were: 1 = absent; 2 = inaccurate; 3 = nearly accurate; 4 = accurate. These tests were done "by ear", that is, without recourse to computer instruments, because we preferred (as in the case of assessing singing in tune from the age of one, to have human assessment of a comprehensive musical meaning in which the beat and the rhythm form an integral part together with other aspects.

This choice gave rise to the first problem because – as we know – a "musical" performance, even of a children's song, cannot be perfectly "in tempo", but must show the necessary flexibility to make it humanly "expressive". Therefore, the assigning of scores by two experts according to the scale indicated above, gave very diverse results precisely because the judgement of this aspect in function of expression can vary notably even between experts, and so it was not easy to come to an agreement.

Regarding the accuracy of the beat in a song, if we compare the average scores obtained from the children in each age band, we observe a tendency towards improvement, but it is not like this with rhythmic precision which sometimes shows progress and sometimes regression. This is because, besides the demands of expressive performance, other factors emerged as a hindrance.

The first is surely breathing because, as children do not know how to measure their breathing well, they sometimes pause to breathe (and so lose time). Another factor is the pronunciation of words which is not yet very accurate and the children sometimes swallow some of the syllables ("dindirinday" becomes "ndirinday"), thus changing the rhythm. Other times, they stumble over words or do not remember them well, and this makes their performance unsteady. From all of this we can deduce that it is not so easy at that age to respect the rhythm of a song.

To these considerations we add that the recordings were sometimes made while the children were playing, and so the performance was likely to slow down or accelerate according to the action being effected at that moment. Besides, the children often played with the songs and had fun spontaneously introducing rhythmic and metrical variations. This is something that their mothers and playschool teachers had done on many occasions from the time that they were infants. For an expert who has to assess the performance, it is not easy to decide if the rhythm is not correct because the child made a mistake or because he or she is having fun distorting a song.

In conclusion, to keep to the beat is more difficult when one is singing a song than when one is synchronizing with a piece of music. The children showed a clear improvement from the age of two to three and a half, even if there still remained some difficulty in not losing time between one phrase and another in the song. Finally, rhythmic accuracy, although it was very good in some performances, is affected by other factors that appear to be connected to breathing, the pronunciation of words and the situation (of playing or of attention) in which the children find themselves at the time of the recording.

Before finishing this section, it is important to give space to the presence of musical instruments (to which we have referred a few times) in the experience of the children. In our project, which was specifically devoted to singing, we also attributed much importance to instruments. We conveyed to the children that music is sound and that sounds are produced by the voice and also by a series of "objects" that we construct as an extension and boost to our abilities. This is not only to immerse ourselves in the pleasure of producing sounds beyond the limits of vocal production, even though it can be varied, but also to enrich ourselves with an almost infinite range of possibilities made possible by the instrument-objects.

As the children grew, they developed their ability to hold things in their hands, and it was with great eagerness that, during the meetings, they seized and shook the little percussion instruments that we offered them: maracas, bells, jingles. Then they started to bang drums with their hands or even with other instruments (maracas, rhythm sticks, etc.). The parents sang and the children played their instruments. Were these the first forms of ... manipulation, expression and accompaniment? The children were certainly fascinated by the sound, and more generally, by a global situation in which the object, with its forms and colours, the action of shaking or banging and the sound that came from it were all part of the one experience.

As the months and years passed, their interest in the instruments was always high during the meetings and their ability to join in the songs in ways that were more varied than simply keeping to the beat was progressively improving: rhythmic ostinati, entering in at the end of phrases, inventing, etc. were activities carried out with obvious pleasure and progressive mastery. As regards their compositions in particular, when they were doing this in a collective situation (all/alone/all), we noticed the progressive passage from improvisation of a tentative kind (two to three sounds) to short sequences organised rhythmically or according to pitch (some children even took three or four instruments so they could use more than one in the same improvisation).

We were unable (for lack of time) to control rigorously this development through recordings and the relative analysis, but we can document some aspects of the children's interest through the data that we received from the parents through the diaries.

We should remember that these diaries in our project were an instrument of research that in research methodology is the structured questionnaire. The reliability of the results obtained with this kind of instrument is usually verified, as we have said earlier, through the statistical treatment of the data, that is, the procedure that allows us to see if the responses are statistically significant or the result of chance. The data we present here were subject to statistical treatment and are significant results. Let us now look at them closely.

The questions on "willingness to play", that is, to produce sounds, either with objects they have in their hands (boxes, cutlery, skittles ...), or with musical instruments (real or toy instruments), are questions that the parents were asked quite early from when the children were six months until they were aged four.

We asked first of all if, when they saw their parents playing instruments, they became alert, they wanted to play too, or they tried to grab the instrument. This question was based on the presumption that the parents had instruments at home, and in fact this was the case. Some dusted down instruments that they had at home (a guitar, a piano, a drum), and others went out to buy one after they saw their children's interest.

From the responses, we could see that from the age of six months almost all of the children (97%) became very alert if an instrument was present and, if they saw their parents playing, they wanted to do the same thing, and they tried to grasp the instruments and play them. In what way? The first thing that they did spontaneously (a spontaneity encouraged by their parents' example) was to bang, whilst others shook the instrument, and a few rubbed it. However, was the children's desire to play instruments always conditioned by the presence of music in the environment (someone singing or playing, music in the room), or did they also play instruments in the absence of music? The responses corresponding to the period from six months to two years were very high in all situations, in the sense that almost all the children (95%) wanted to play an instrument, whether or not there was music. This result showed us how instruments are a source of a global sensory-motor pleasure and that, at least in this age range, they exerted a very strong influence.

Then we wanted to find out if it was the instrument itself that attracted attention (its form, its colours ...), or if it was the production of sound in its auditory-motor sensoriality, so we asked if the children also made sounds with whatever object was in their hands. Again, the percentages were very high, in that almost all of them had also made sounds with objects (94%). Whether they were instruments or objects, the children had actually behaved in the same way, banging (44%), shaking (38%), rubbing (13%), in an almost consistent way until the age of two.

If, on the one hand, the children showed a "hunger" for sound, we must say that on the other hand the parents were happy to satisfy them by building up the family collection of instruments. On the list taken from the responses given in the diary, there is just about everything one might think of: from electronic keyboards which were the most popular, to guitars, from the flute to the accordion, to the saxophone, and then the small percussion instruments (maracas, drums, rhythm sticks, bongos ...).

Between the ages of two and four something changes. The children enter nursery school, their interests widen, and they acquire new skills of various kinds (verbal, motor, cognitive, etc.) and these bring about big transformations during this period. The consequences are many, and among these we find a drop in interest in playing instruments.

When we looked at the responses given by the parents, we saw that in fact the number of children who did not play instruments at all had clearly increased (from 5% at age two to 17% at age three to 33% at age four) and that the increase was progressive from one three-month period to the next.

And the others? What did they say about the children who still wanted to play instruments? The questions we had asked the parents in the diaries concerning the making of sounds with objects had three possible answers: often, sometimes, never. When we looked at the percentages of children who played instruments, we saw a reduction by age in both those who played often (23% from age two to three and 21% from age three to four) and those who played a few times a week (60% from age two to three and 45% from three to four). Nevertheless, the drop-off in the first group is more limited and this would confirm the significance of the results in that the children who played instruments more often were the ones who were most motivated to continue in any event.

For this age band, too, we wondered if the willingness to make sounds with objects (often or sometimes) was facilitated by the presence of music in their surroundings (live or recorded). We gathered from the responses that, although there was not a great difference between the two situations, nevertheless the group of those who played instruments often was slightly more numerous with recorded music (from 9% to 11%) and the increase could be due to the presence of instruments in the piece of music being heard.

When we looked at children's willingness to play instruments in the absence of music, we noticed, unexpectedly, that there were more who played often if there was no music in the background (22%). This fact could be interpreted as a sign of an "autonomous" desire to play an instrument, or at least a desire for music that impelled children to create it when there was none. As it happened precisely with the children who played instruments often, this could confirm the fact that there was greater interest.

The number of instruments that the parents gave their children increased between the ages of two and four, and the little ones could decide which to play. A clear preference was seen for the keyboards (electronic keyboard or piano), followed at some distance by the flute or guitar. Among the small percussion instruments, there was the drum (always well behind the keyboards in frequency preference), followed in turn by maracas and rhythm sticks.

The frequency with which they used the instruments in this period was slightly less than the number of times that they made sounds with objects. A possible interpretation for this difference could come from the fact that the instruments were generally kept in a particular place and so it was necessary to "go and fetch them", whereas it was easy to have objects in hand that could be banged or shaken.

There is one more interesting element. We observed during our meetings as the children were approaching three years of age that, when they ran to the keyboard (something that they had been doing ever since they could walk), they played keys as usual (more or less at random) but they also began to sing, something that they were used to seeing us, the educators, do.

We decided to add an explicit question in the diaries, asking the parents if the children sang as they played, and we discovered with a pleasant surprise, that in fact many did so at home, some of them quite often (26%), others sometimes (43%). We also found that we had some examples of this in the recordings (rec. no. 46).

In conclusion, we can say that the interest in musical instruments was very high, even if it began to decline at around the age of two. The opportunity offered to those children certainly contributed to the widening of their sound horizons. At the same time it enriched their opportunities to express themselves and communicate as well as to develop their metric-rhythmic skills and also to play music together.

In this section we looked at three aspects of the making of music that are different but closely interrelated: rhythm (as temporal organization), movement and activity with instruments. Sound and movement share the temporal dimension and they are the first means with which the newborns express themselves and communicate. Vocal sound is certainly the first to appear (wailing and crying), but it does not involve movement in a substantial way, while instrumental playing does. Shaking and banging are movements that are "felt" by the body. Movement also allows us to interpret sound, to express and verify our perception of it, something which happens to small children especially when the sounds clearly mark out the time structure, inducing them to rock, bounce, etc.

These three aspects are, therefore, inseparable in children's education: the positive and enthusiastic reactions of the children allowed us, on the one hand, to realize its importance, and, on the other hand, it confirmed us in our insistence that this need expressed by the children should be satisfied from the time that they are born.

3.10 Evaluation and Comments

Now that we have presented the progress made by the children on the *inCanto* project, we should sum up, although, as the panorama described here is so rich and varied, it is impossible to conclude with simple final deductions. As in all research worthy of the name, the first step is to go back to the hypotheses and compare them with the results.

In the first hypothesis (see the opening of Chapter 2), which is to an extent the key element of the entire project, we predicted that all the children would be able to learn to sing correctly (that is, to sing in tune) over the period of the six years, under certain conditions: that there was music in the environment from the sixth month of prenatal life, with specific moments dedicated to singing and listening, in a family atmosphere of encouragement and praise.

As the hypothesis refers to the entire period of the research, we cannot give a definite interpretation before completing the study of the skills acquired by the children at the age of six. However, from the results presented in the previous pages (and particularly this chapter), two important facts emerge.

The first concerns the good level of singing in tune reached by most of the children by the age of three and a half (25 out of 35, which is 71%). This is already a high percentage compared to the average documented in other Italian and overseas studies (see Chapter 1).

How did this happen? What are the causes? We certainly cannot settle the question by simply saying that "by chance" the children who took part in the research were all born with the ability to sing in tune at an early age.

The answer is likely to be found in the special context surrounding these children as these conditions are not generally part of common experience. We can confirm this by recalling cases that we sometimes hear about of children who sing correctly at the age of two and a half or three. When we make some enquiries, we learn that these were children who had been "helped" by their parents with models similar to those used in our project. Therefore, we maintain that the high percentage of children able to sing in tune before the age of three and a half is due to the rich musical experience that they were given from before they were born, an experience that was accompanied by the support and encouragement of their parents. This is also an important element in light of the role model provided by the adults' behaviour, especially at home, and the need the child has to be surrounded by adults who sing, play instruments and listen to music.

We said that the ability to sing in tune has been achieved, so far, by 71% of the children. So, why not all of them? Here we see coming into play an aspect that is more difficult to deal with and that is the pace of development of each individual. Why do some children say their first words at the age of ten months and others at 18 months? Why do some manage to stand at ten months and others continue to crawl until they are 15 months old? Why does a child sing her first phrase in tune at 18 months and another does so at the age of three? All parents know that the average that is reported in the books that they read during pregnancy does not necessarily correspond exactly to the rate of development of their children. It will always be unique and different from the average reported in those articles they read. The presence of a wide number of variables makes this phenomenon extremely complex.

On the basis of the song productions we have analysed, we can affirm that the first phrases sung in tune were sung at age 18 months, whereas we have no record of some of the children of three and a half years of age singing in tune yet (although the number of examples provided to us by some parents was sometimes so low that we cannot exclude the possibility that they may have occasionally sung a phrase in tune). We cannot explain this difference except by putting forward hypotheses: extreme shyness, a drop in interest in singing in favour of the instruments or other activities, little power of attention ... . Each of these hypotheses would merit the appropriate research.

The other important factor that was not foreseen and that, therefore, brought a new element into the study, is the fact that the ability to sing in tune that we had perceived was not stable. As we have already pointed out, the same children who had sung a particular song very well, some days later would sing some passages out of tune.

This piece of evidence opens up an important question: At what age does the ability to sing in tune become stable? And more generally: Can this skill reach a definitive level? Or does control of the ear over the voice always require much attention and is there need for ongoing practice? If we take the example of target shooting suggested by Welch (1985), we ask if a shot hits the bullseye once, can the shooter expect to be successful always from then on and therefore have no need to continue practising.

These are basic questions with determinant consequences on teaching that could perhaps definitively remove the prejudice according to which one is born "with" or "without" the ability to learn to sing in tune and could allow for educational courses in singing in tune to be seriously undertaken. In other words, instead of "excluding" the children considered to be "tone deaf" as if this were a permanent *dis*ability rather than a still unstable *a*bility (they are children who occasionally "sing off key"), teachers could have the commitment and awareness to spend time teaching and encouraging those who still have this need.

When we come to analyse the song productions of these children from age three and a half to six, we shall certainly be able to offer new elements for reflection about stability, but we can already anticipate that it is a skill that requires constant control and practice. Let us not forget that even some professional singers have been said to "sing out-of-tune" and that we read about famous "fluff notes".

The research project also contained a second and third hypothesis. In the second, we hypothesized that there was a predisposition for music in all children from the time that they are born and that this is demonstrated by consequent displays of interest and attention towards musical experiences. In the third, we foresaw an anticipated development, with respect to their peers, of the more elementary musical skills like singing, playing instruments and keeping tempo.

I think that the readers of these pages, through their contents, will have been able to verify both of these hypotheses. It is useful, however, to briefly take another look at the most important aspects.

We shall start with the term "predisposition" that is so abused in the practice of musical education. It is used in order to establish, almost *a priori* or, in any case, on the basis of one feeble performance, who possesses musical ability and who does not. In our hypothesis, however, we did not use the term in the sense of "innate ability", which only some people have, but rather in the sense of being well disposed, an inclination, an openness to music generally. We affirm, on the basis of the results obtained, that all the children on the project showed that they possessed and had been born with this predisposition. The interest and attention that they demonstrated towards music, their willingness to "feel" its effects, their eagerness to make sounds with objects and their production of musical vocalizations and of songs were common and constant in all the children during the first two years. This behaviour diversified over time, according to changes at home, personal enrichment through different kinds of experience (not only musical) and the development of the temperament-character of each child.

Regarding this last factor, we had in fact seen different ways in approach, exploration and assimilation of the experiences themselves. Some children were more courageous, more exuberant, even more aggressive, and others were more timid, more placid and more diffident. There were children who showed plenty of interest in new experiences (musical, motor, graphical/pictorial, etc.), and children who preferred just one, perhaps excessively. We have observed, and our data documented here supports it, that some children got tired and moved away, while others did not, that some followed a more linear path and others had more ups and downs and even regressions. Progress for some was constant while for others it was not. However, it is difficult to identify the causes of this slowing down and changes in attitude.

Of course, a reduction of stimuli would have an influence and this occurred, for example, when the children missed many of the meetings, or when their parents had less time to dedicate to them for various reasons (bereavement, illness in the family, change of employment, etc.), but this was not the only reason. Another cause has to be seen in the number of other interests the children had, a complex situation difficult to restrain and control. At first, every child had a great interest in music and singing. It was an interest that arose immediately from the time of their first experiences, to an almost preponderant extent, and it was seen in different ways. There were children who asked for or refused particular songs or pieces of music, who were fascinated by singing and instruments, who wanted to hear the same song over and over or to play for hours on end the instruments that their parents had given them. However, these interests, for each child, continued to grow or to recede with the passing of the years without any evident explanation. The demonstration of interest and the changes in the children would certainly require a study apart.

Passing finally to the third hypothesis that predicted the early development of some skills, the reported data speak for themselves. We studied various aspects of the melodic and rhythmic skills:

- the rich and varied production of the first vocal sounds;
- the rich and varied production of musical babbling;
- singing in tune with a few words, with phrases, with entire songs;
- the invention of musical monologues and short songs;
- instrumental performance in tempo with pieces of music;
- reproduction and invention of rhythmic phrases with the voice or musical instruments.

In all of these areas, the results, reported here, were noteworthy. We can, however, add some comments. First of all, we emphasize that some skills (musical vocalizations, singing and synchronization) were controlled in a rigorous and systematic way, and were comparable with data from other studies (Moog, 1976; Welch, 1997; Jorquera, *et al.* 2000), or with control groups formed within this research project. Moreover, most of the responses provided by the parents were subject to statistical treatment and they proved to be significant.

Early development is, therefore, evident here as it was in other studies that began to expose children to music from the prenatal period (Shetler, 1989), but ...

the interpretation of these results is not so automatic and requires answers that are more nuanced.

The first important fact that we learn about early development concerns the existence of certain physio-psychological conditions: if several children carry out certain actions (grab an object, say a word, stand, sing), this means that their physio-psychological conditions are ready. If other children do not show the same ability, does this mean that those conditions have not yet developed? Not necessarily. It might mean simply that these children, although they have attained the same conditions at the physiological and psychological level, they may not have received the stimuli needed to "learn" certain behaviour (even though it is true that something learned reveals, and at the same time facilitates and consolidates, a certain degree of maturity).

Here we have one of the most important scientific contributions of this research: to have possibly identified the age at which the biological clock allows for certain actions. We now know that at six months, at age one, age two ... children are able, from the physiological and psychological point of view, to show certain behaviours. If we compare this with the case of the mother tongue, we all know that children, at the age of one year approximately, are ready from a physio-psychological point of view to speak their first words, but that some children say them at nine to ten months and others at 18–20 months for a series of reasons, but none of them could ever do it at the age of four months, because the development of the vocal tract is not yet complete. If children live in an environment of total deprivation, they may not be able to speak by the age of three, not because they did not receive the "gift" of speech "genetically", but because they did not receive the necessary stimuli to exercise their vocal apparatus at the time when the apparatus was ready to do it. We sometimes read about children held in extreme conditions who at the age of three or four not only had not developed because they did not receive enough nourishment, but they did not speak or walk because they had not been sufficiently surrounded and stimulated by people who spoke, walked and generally "demonstrated" how it is done.

The various musical skills developed by the children in the *inCanto* project are not in fact "precocious", in the sense that nature has jumped ahead, but in the sense that they were developed earlier than would normally happen to children that do not live in a stimulating environment. Therefore, they should be considered as "normal", because they show that nature is ready. These considerations allow us to conclude that if the children in the first year of our elementary schools cannot sing in tune, do not keep in tempo, do not respect the rhythm of a song, etc., this means that they have been kept in a state of "musical deprivation".

How slow and laborious would recuperation be? That depends on the duration of the musical sensitive period, that is, the period (see earlier) during which nature provides a particular aptitude for the various skills (speaking, walking, singing, etc.). Do we know the duration of the sensitive period for elementary musical skills (singing, keeping tempo ...)? Not yet. Until we have completed the study of all the data collected over the six years of research, we are not in a position to say.

However, on the basis of the results obtained so far, we are inclined to think that the first three years, including the last three months of prenatal life, are decisive. Regarding the prenatal stimulation, to be honest, it has not yet been possible to investigate what would have happened if the children had begun at the age of two months. This is a variable that would deserve much attention, but that has not yet been studied for obvious practical reasons. The children that we accepted after birth (four to six months) were in fact children whose mothers had sung to them during pregnancy. We had even decided to recontact children who had left the project as two or three-year-olds when they reached the age of six, but in practice this was not possible.

A second point regarding early development that is closely connected to the first, concerns the role played by the educational process that the researchers and parents facilitated for the children. Of course, it could be revised and improved, but we feel that this has been decisive, and that it is, therefore, possible to derive from this research the real usefulness/need of a musically stimulating environment. It contains educational proposals that can be "models" for learning in a focused way and with a certain amount of systemization. We shall return to this point in Chapter 5.

If it is true that genetic heritage contains the "programme" to acquire certain skills, this first part of the research draws us to conclude that we all possess a basic music, including singing, "programme", and that the various skills are not developed if they are not stimulated during the most favourable period by an environment rich in specific experiences, in an emotionally positive climate.

Chapter 4
The Parents Have Their Say

In the preceding chapter we followed the children's development step by step by observing their progress with the eyes of science. This observation had to be objective and to keep strictly to the data. It had to use precision and methodological rigour and, where necessary, statistical instruments, in order to verify the significance of the results. The reader may have thought that this kind of presentation was rather cold. However, as we wanted to provide a solid basis for the final interpretations, we felt it was necessary to have recourse to a style that would demonstrate the steps taken and the instruments used in the most objective way possible.

This chapter, in contrast, is devoted to the parents' testimonies about the progress of their children and what they thought of the research that was done. They experienced it from the inside, there in the midst of the daily events, and so their contribution gives a more complete picture of the research. They give "warmth" to the scientific data.

We could have gathered all their contributions in an appendix, but that would have reduced their impact. We decided to insert them here, almost as a counterpart to the preceding chapter. In doing this, we felt we should organize them (according to the method of interpretative phenomenological analysis used in qualitative research) around the themes with which we had dealt. This is to ensure a better grasp of the multiple aspects and at the same time to facilitate enjoyment of the testimonies.

We must beg the reader's forgiveness for our detailed presentation that might seem to be rather long, and also apologize to the authors for having had to shorten their invaluable testimonies that should not be missed.

4.1 Parents' Voices

The great surprise in this research, in addition to the remarkable results, was to see the extent of the importance of the role played by the parents. Without them and without a personal relationship with each one of them, the research could not have obtained these results. This is not only because it would not have been possible to collect and review so much material, but especially because the children would not have been able to develop those skills without the patient, dedicated and convinced participation of their parents in the project. Their participation had its moments of elation and its moments of tiredness, but they were always sustained by the conviction that they were working on something important for, and with, their children. As they participated, the mothers and fathers of the children collaborated with each other in many ways, from attendance at the meetings to the musical entertainment at home, activities with videos, audio recordings and photographs.

It is only right, therefore, at this point in the book, to give space to their voices, and allow them to recount their experiences of these past few years with all their hopes, difficulties and joys. When asking them to write a report at the end of the project, we also helped them by suggesting some points for reflection (in practice, a semi-structured questionnaire). These points were indicated (as we said in the letter of request), not to curb their spontaneity and imagination, but in order to help them not to forget some important aspects of their experience. We asked them to tell us whatever came to mind and to their "heart" regarding the experience and to include specific episodes if they liked, but without forgetting the topics that we were following:

1. What had encouraged the mother or both parents to join the Project?
2. What were the greatest difficulties encountered, and what aspects were the most tedious and burdensome?
3. What general attitudes had they observed in the children regarding this experience, and what attitudes did children have to singing and music, comparing those seen during the meetings with those seen at home? What changes did they see over the years?
4. What satisfaction did they feel and what emotions, the positive aspects, the advantages, were evidenced in everyday life and in the musical experiences?
5. What involvement was there within the family? How did participation in the project influence family life and what were the consequences for the parents, both at personal level (especially those who took part in the meetings) and in their relationship with their children?
6. What consequences do they predict for the future?

The quantity and quality of testimonies received (30 reports altogether, of which two were "four-handed") was really surprising. With great variety of styles, many mothers and some fathers told of the many episodes that allowed us a glimpse into their personal and family experience, to see the *inCanto* project through their eyes and hence to be enriched by their points of view.

4.2 Motivations and Expectations

Love for music and the desire to do something for their child were the main reasons that some parents gave for joining the project. Some of them stressed their own previous interest in music:

> I have always loved music and I like to sing, although ever since I had stopped singing with the church choir I really hadn't had much opportunity to sing any more. Another

reason I felt drawn to the *inCanto* project was the desire to "reconnect" with music. Due to work and maybe also due to laziness, I had lost touch in recent years. [Alessandra]

What attracted us to the Project was definitely our passion for music. We felt it was just natural to take part so that we could give Andrea an extra opportunity in life. [Matteo and Anna Rita]

From the beginning of my pregnancy, in the gynaecologist's clinic, I noticed a leaflet ... I had no doubts. I adore music, so when I saw the objectives of this experience, I wanted to join. I was convinced that this course had potential to offer lots of resources. [...] The child wasn't yet born and I was already offering her an alternative with a difference for her first years of life! [Micaela]

Some of the reasons given were quite unusual:

My association with singing and music is connected with the memory of my mother ... Unlike most people, my mother sang when she was angry. My wish was to avoid transmitting to my children the negative emotion that it caused me [...]. Besides, a young woman about to give birth should acquire useful tools for putting a baby to sleep and to soothe and entertain him. The *inCanto* project, as my friend presented it to me, seemed to be a great way to do that. So, I went. [Barbara]

Or sometimes they referred to some previous musical experience:

Participation in this innovative project was decided immediately as soon as I saw some benefit, a possibility of growth, an opportunity for the child I was expecting. It is probably because I had studied piano for many years as an adolescent that I understood the importance of music. [Natalia]

Some other mothers preferred to insist on the effects of music or its usefulness:

I have always felt that music is a language that speaks beyond words, and that it has great power to calm us a little in times of difficulty and to cheer us up even more in the happy moments. [...] I joined the *inCanto* project with great enthusiasm. Even though my child was still unborn, I wanted to start sharing with her one of the beautiful things in life – music. [Armida]

I remember that it emphasized the "usefulness" for mothers-to-be to learn little songs and lullabies to "use in times of need". My repertoire in that department was in short supply, and I must say that this acquisition later proved to be almost "essential". [Valentina]

Or they displayed a confidence that was maybe somewhat excessive:

Music actually helps to channel energy, to give free reign to creativity, to increase curiosity, to acquire logic (after all, it is closely related to mathematics) and so to create a mental frame of mind such that, even if a person does not become a "genius" in the field of music, they will however receive useful help in seeing life from all angles. [Natalia]

Occasionally it was the father who was first to be enthusiastic about the idea:

> The *inCanto* project was presented during the childbirth course. I thought it sounded interesting but certainly not suitable for me (I hardly ever sang). I spoke about it at home with the father-to-be who was immediately taken with the idea and pestered me into joining. According to him it would be interesting, a chance not to be missed (he loves music, especially rock and he plays the guitar, but hardly ever sings). [Giuliana]

> My husband read the article about the *inCanto* project in the newspaper and was interested right away ... It would be a lovely gift for Andrea, a gift for the rest of his life. That's how we started. Our love for singing and for music grew and remained with us. [Gloria]

For an expectant mother, the life growing within her is undoubtedly a mysterious happening. Of course, physiology and biology explain many things, but the gap between the science written in books and the presence of an invisible life still remains. Then along comes music. Sound, like an invisible thread of communication makes the "other" become real though still hidden, a communication that allows the father to be already involved:

> The process and procedures studied by the originators of the project from that moment on became a pretext for us to find a link with which to transmit and communicate love to the life that was growing within us. There was a hidden ear, an invisible channel that brought the sound of our voices inside us, that calmed the anxieties of future mothers who were nervous about what would happen, and that helped the future daddy (separated from the baby growing slowly in the mother's womb that was welcoming and expanding) to feel less left out of the miraculous event.
>
> At first, it was to keep the little one company and to let her hear our voices so that she would recognize us when she was born. It was to cuddle her, to rock her and to sing her a lullaby when she was restless. It was to let her hear music she liked. It was also to ensure that she would not be frightened by the music played by her daddy, a musician of rock, hip-hop, ambient, ethnic, and a guitarist and enthusiast of any kind of sound production, not always easy to listen to ... [Cristiana]

> The meeting venue was difficult to reach, but I was convinced that it would be worth it. Something within me (perhaps my child? It was my seventh month of pregnancy) told me that life was not only about work, about housekeeping, preparing clothes, visits to the doctor to see if the baby was all right, but I also had to "cure" my spirit and heart ... and music seemed to me to be the perfect way to communicate with my child. [Claudia]

> It was in this state of mind that we begin to take part in the *inCanto* project: Noemi was not yet born (I was in the 26th week of pregnancy), but I and my baby were already "building" a dialogue ... [Armida]

> I liked the idea that the baby in my womb could hear my voice, and I felt that in this way we could build a relationship even before we met "in person". [Alessandra]

A daughter. Amazement. Perfection. The newest thing in the world. This encouraged me to discover new marvels with her from the very first day. [Cristina]

First of all I was fascinated by the idea of singing for my child, a new idea for me. I could imagine and feel the little fellow who was not yet seen and present in my arms (I was in my eighth month of pregnancy when I started). It was strange, and I thought perhaps it was rather unusual but certainly intriguing. I said to myself: "How come I never thought of that? Shall I do it? Why not?" I answered, and now after six years I am here to report on my positive experience, and my three children and my husband. [Marina]

For the expectant mothers there were so many things to discover and there was a deep-felt need to talk about this with others in the same condition. They wanted to chat about experiences. The *inCanto* project? Why not? They could meet other young women and share their anxieties and hopes. This was another strong motivation:

I remembered being with a lovely group of mothers during the meetings when I was expecting my first, and I would have loved to find the same kind of group for the second. I heard about the Project, and I realized that I had the chance to take part in the first important experience for my next child. The possibility of taking part in such an unusual activity with such special significance connected to music is something I could never have imagined. [Mary]

The reasons that impelled us to join were varied. The most important was to make the little baby within me feel more "real" to me and that then I would finally get to know him. At the same time I was happy to form part of a new community and perhaps to make friends with people in the same situation as me. And that is exactly how it was. [Giovanna]

From the beginning, I was very happy to have had that opportunity! There was a large group of mothers taking part and, as time passed, our relationship grew with each other and with the teacher. That hour during the week that we spent together listening, singing and doing vocalizations, was very relaxing. It had become a fixed date that could not be missed! [Silvana]

We had to be careful not to neglect the fathers. Singing and music could also help him to communicate with the baby and to reduce (if not quite eliminate) the feeling that the expected baby was a "thing" reserved for mothers.

I found the idea of singing and dancing with my husband and my large soft stomach quite funny, especially as it was not something we usually did. However, it was a way of involving the new fathers in this mysterious affective world. [Marina]

Mummy Federica and Daddy Gabriele have been in the scouts since they were children and have been leaders for the past few years. For this reason, what encouraged them to join this project was the idea that they could transmit all these "values" to their baby as far as possible: the joy of singing, the pleasure of playing with music by dancing, continuing a project because of a commitment made (from before birth until six years of age) and sharing, in the sense that they would be with a group of women who would all try to follow this adventure with their families. It is with this spirit of enthusiasm that Giorgia (still in the womb), Mummy Federica and Daddy Gabriele began to be part of the project and to attend the weekly meetings. [Federica]

The father's participation was also needed after the birth:

I thought of sending Linda there with her father Gianfredo because I worked on Saturdays and they were together all day. As Linda's daddy played in the Imola band and in the parish band, music seemed to be a good thing for them to experience together, a good point of contact that also brings joy and companionship. [Cinzia]

To all the reasons expressed so far, we add another: the *inCanto* project was not simply a "package" of musical meetings, but it was also a research study. This was clearly explained in the letter of invitation to parents, knowing that this could give rise to interest, but also to rejection. For some couples, on the contrary, it was one more reason for joining.

When the *inCanto* Project was presented to us, I was charmed by the idea as it looked like a terrific experience for me and my baby! I was very impressed with what the music teacher said when she presented the project. She said that it is thought that babies from the early months in the womb can hear sounds and therefore music ... So I decided to join! [Flavia]

When, about seven years ago, at the childbirth course they presented the project that was to be absolutely "experimental", I immediately decided to join. [Giovanna]

I must say that the idea that my baby could be helped in her growth by music is something that attracted me, but most of all, the fact that, even though her mummy and daddy were tone deaf, she could learn to sing in tune! [Lucia]

The idea interested me immediately for various reasons. Most of all because I loved the idea of being part of a research project together with my baby, and even from before his birth! [Valentina]

4.3 The Difficulties

At the beginning it wasn't so difficult to take part in the project. Before the birth, I could organize my time freely to go to the meetings with the other mothers-to-be. Afterwards, though, with the baby here things changed, and going regularly to the weekly meetings became a difficult commitment to keep. Something always happened to prevent us from going out, things like illness or work commitments ... [Armida]

That is what a mother tells us now. Indeed there were difficulties in many ways. The venue where the meetings were held was not exactly around the corner:

> The appointment was for one hour a week. That seems little to ask, but in fact that's not how it was. To start with, the bus was always full and I took up more space with my stomach [...] [Claudia]

> The only bothersome aspect was the journey, because I lived on the other side of the city and there was always heavy traffic. [Silvana]

Some of them even lived outside the city:

> I cannot deny that from the beginning participation in the project was materially complicated and tiring. We had decided to live out of town, almost 40 kilometres from where the course was held. However, we worked in the city, and so participation in the *inCanto* project meant that I had to leave work early (and therefore stay for an extra afternoon to make up the working hours), travel 40 kilometres to pick Giulia up from the nursery school, tie her into the car quickly and return those 40 kilometres to take her to the Project, getting stuck in traffic in the city centre, arrive, park ... Then there was the 40 kilometre return journey ... exhausting. But the experience seemed to become beautiful over time, and I felt that I should try to give it to Giulia. [Marco]

And then, the children each had their own timetable ... one had to be organized and learn to manage outings with the babies:

> To take a newborn to an appointment at a specific time far from home was one of the hardest things for me. Something unexpected always happened: he was sleepy, hungry, upset, and all this happened when we were about to go out the door. [Claudia]

In addition to the initial uncertainties, sleepiness was one of the main obstacles:

> As you can imagine, there are many exhausting and tedious aspects that go with small babies: when it was time to leave the house, he could be sleepy. [Annalisa]

> The schedule was a problem for Chiara because she used to be tired and often slept on the bus. [Annarosa]

> I often found it difficult to reconcile the need for him to sleep with the schedule of the meetings. Even when he was bigger he had a morning nap when it was time for the Project. [Marina]

> We had a problem reconciling his afternoon nap with the time of the meeting, and also for us to find time to fill in the weekly diary. [Matteo]

Yes, the diaries. Suffering and delight? Only suffering? Some mothers were happy to remember the activities that had been done and to put down in writing the children's achievements:

> I don't recall any particular difficulties, nor any tiring and tedious aspects. We had the commitment to fill in the diaries and make the recordings, but we felt satisfaction on seeing the work we had done. [Gloria]

But for others:

> One of our difficulties was in finding the time to be faithful and punctual in filling in the diary. [Federica]

> For the first few years, I tried to fill in the diary in a systematic way, a rather tedious task in the long term. [Alessandra]

And the recordings? Even more difficult. It was necessary to find the right moment:

> The difficulties that I really found hardest to overcome, and which still bother me to remember, are those trying to make the recordings at home. It was hard to find the right moment, the appropriate atmosphere, free of things and quiet. [Mary]

> In the early days I had more energy, especially when it was time to do the audio recordings of the baby. She got distracted, said nothing, you couldn't hear her voice through the microphone [...], at times it seemed to be the wrong moment! [Micaela]

Children are not machines! At times, it seemed that they deliberately stopped singing when the recorder was ready:

> It was not always easy to find the moment when the kid was "willing" to be recorded. Meanwhile we were juggling with schedules, work, housework and other commitments ... I remember so many attempts to record some perfectly performed "warbling" before managing to press the "record" button. [Valentina]

> Around the age of two, the sight of the recorder became an obstacle to our attempts at documentary. We had to hide it and be very careful that it wasn't discovered. [Roberta]

And then recording the children was "homework" set by the researchers ... and homework, as we know, "must" be done:

> At times I didn't feel very "spontaneous" in making music with the baby. Making recordings, singing at certain times or monitoring the responses to stimuli made it seem more like a "duty". [Alessandra]

After a year and a half or two or three, little brothers and sisters began to arrive and join the big family, but ... they took up a lot of their parents' time:

> With the arrival of our second child, I had even less time to spend on games and the various activities with Tobia and so I found it more difficult to respect the various commitments and satisfy the request to make recordings. In any case, there was no lack of music at home, especially to listen to it. [Alessandra]

And, even if in some cases they were substituted by the father or grandmother, some mothers found they had to reduce their attendance until they left altogether:

I had no difficulty attending the meetings, nor in filling in the diaries. The real difficulties came later with the second pregnancy, especially as they were twins. I couldn't take part in the meetings except for occasionally. [Silvia]

Some mothers had tried to bring the two siblings with various results, from crises of jealousy:

When she was two and a half, along came a little sister which made it even more difficult to have Bianca alone during the hour dedicated to music. Going with her daddy meant going to have fun, but it also meant leaving mummy at home with "the other one". Going with mummy meant, in general, having to bring along "the other one" who was always in my arms, while Bianca felt that the hour in *inCanto* continued to be a special intimate time between her and me. [Cristiana]

When Miranda was born, the biggest problem was the great jealousy Arianna felt for the baby, and she showed this to an extreme during the *inCanto* project. Arianna had always gone with her mother all by herself. She wanted to be carried instead of the baby, she took part reluctantly, she was tense [...]. Once she shook me with such force that all three of us fell to the ground. It was a difficult time for me too. [Manila]

… to an excess of closeness and complicity between the two:

When his little brother was born, our presence with him was less constant and dedicated. The months passed and Simone grew, and it was nice to bring them both to the meetings although I could not always manage it.
    When the younger one was one and a half, it became more difficult to bring both children to the meetings. So I began to go less often until one awful day when both of them spent the whole time playing together and disturbing everyone. I decided not to go again for a while, and then time passed and it was hard to take it up again. [Flavia]

And the children? Were they always happy? Many reports speak of their enthusiastic participation that was quiet, enjoyable, but not always … Sometimes they preferred to stay at home:

Seasonal colds, tiredness after a day spent at the playschool and later at the kindergarten and the exhaustion felt in spending all those hours out of the house in an activity that was pleasant but that took from our family time, all made our attendance less than constant. But music continued, nonetheless, to accompany the growth of our children. [Cristiana]

They may not have wanted to spend all their time with other children:

There were also times when N. didn't feel like being with other kids to sing. After a day spent at nursery school, to be again surrounded by youngsters … Can you blame him if he wasn't in [the] humour for it? [Armida]

… or they wanted to do something different:

As regards my son, a curious child who likes new things, I think he might have preferred more variety in the songs and activities. [Alessandra]

From the age of three to four, several children went through a period of tiredness, either temporarily or ongoing, and their parents used different strategies to deal with it:

Virginia also went through a period of tiredness, but I didn't give in to her. I tried to include an ice-cream, for example, with going to the course, but I never gave in, even though I can understand how that can easily happen. However, she always showed interest and the proof that she liked it is the way she sings in tune and wants to dance when she hears music, even if it is not special children's music. [Rita]

At times there was a bit of laziness about going to the meetings. I never forced her, and for a few months we went very seldom because I gave in to her wishes. [Valentina]

Francesco, look how much you've grown! You're as high as the piano keyboard ... Yes, it's time to go to nursery school, now that you're three years old". "Francesco, today is Saturday, shall we go to our music meeting?". "No, mummy. I don't want to go to the music meeting any more." And that's how it happened. [Silvia]

Some parents managed to do it well from the time of the pregnancy:

Tuesday afternoon was a fixed date to meet the other pregnant mothers and to challenge the natural laziness that occurs during those months. Neither I, nor Clemente ever thought it was tedious to go to those meetings. We did it most of all because we had fun there all together. Yes, we were a bit comical and awkward, especially when we look back on it now, but at the same time we were all so inexperienced! [Giovanna]

… and they kept it up with the children:

> There were no difficulties, either on our part as parents or on the part of Linda who always went to the meetings and participated willingly. [Cinzia]

> Martina is a vivacious and determined child, and she never wanted to miss the Saturday morning meetings over the years, and so it was never difficult to reconcile our needs (mine and my husband's) with hers. [Cristina]

One person concludes with enthusiasm:

> Difficulties or tedium did not enter during my time on the *inCanto* project. On the contrary, it was an important and satisfying appointment for both of us. [Emma]

4.4 Progress

Mothers and fathers are generally attentive to the progress made by their children, especially during the early years of life. The parents in the *inCanto* project were even more so, as they were aware of being part of an experiment and they were being asked by us, the researchers, to pay great attention to any signs of a particular experience. This could also be done by comparing their own with perceptions of other children (usually a spontaneous activity in all parents). Let them now lead us along the trail of some of these aspects.

4.4.1 Initial Perceptions

In the beginning there was listening … Listening to sounds filtered through amniotic liquid, and later floating through the air. There was movement in the "paunches". Then the little heads turned round just after birth:

> When Andrea was born, we made our first recordings in hospital. Andrea turned his head to listen when he heard the songs we had always sung. I think that it was reassuring for him to know that here too, outside the uterus, we still have music. [Gloria]

As the months went by:

> I remember how he reacted when we sang the songs. He opened his eyes wide and stared at me, always turning his head towards the source of sound, rocking his head in time with the music, making sounds. [Natalia]

Listening worked at the meetings too and soon the parents lost their fear of maybe having to hear a concert of … wailing:

> We could immediately see how all the newborns were attracted to the music. They were relaxed during the slower songs and smiling with contentment with the faster ones. We seldom heard the babies cry during those meetings (those incidences were always

linked to hunger or some kind of discomfort). They were all very attentive or so relaxed they fell asleep. [Giuliana]

We were already beginning to see the effects of listening to music:

I remember how we used to calm her crying by playing the music she used to hear before she was born. She immediately calmed down and became alert. [Claudia]

A nursery rhyme like *Occhio bello* or a little song like *Il grillo John* (two of her favourites) could be used as "tranquillisers" when she was restless, or as a game to play with her cousin. [Micaela]

Whenever Andrea hurt himself, I sang a short song and he calmed down. [Gloria]

When she was restless, my singing soothed her and she relaxed. [Manila]

Critical situations also had to be faced outside the home:

At first, when I took her to the paediatrician I was worried. As soon as I started to remove her clothes she cried. But then I found that I only had to sing *Tutte le ochette* (the song I often sang during pregnancy) and she calmed down immediately. [Nago and Cristina]

At times, the songs were a panacea:

The power of song facilitated our difficult task of being new parents. Songs were a great help in making him eat and sleep and take a bath, and generally in communicating with him. [Roberta]

Preferences already began to show:

Her face lit up when I sang her favourite song as I rocked her. It is you who can make her sleep and turn tears into smiles, dispelling fears with just a voice or a simple caress. [Cristina]

The babies never tired of listening to their favourite songs:

Music calmed her when she was restless and at other times it stimulated her to play. Since she started to say her first words, if she liked a certain song she asked me to repeat it umpteen times by saying: "Again." Very soon, she asked for particular songs. [Giuliana]

When she was a year old and we were on our summer holidays, she pestered us in the car asking us to sing an English song that she loved called *Roxen* (pronounced "ocken") and she joined in. What a joy it was for us! She already had definite tastes! When we suggested other songs she used to say: "no like" (I don't like it) when they weren't acceptable! [Manila]

… and the mothers, naturally, tried to make the most of this at difficult moments:

At a later stage, while she was seated in the highchair for meals, I used the song that says "pretty white butterfly flies and flies and never gets tired" because the surprise she got when my hand disappeared behind my back made her open her mouth to take the three spoonfuls of soup, which is all she ever took … After she turned one, the audiocassettes from the meetings became very useful. She listened to them on a toy player that had a microphone and then she played with the buttons trying to record her cooing. [Cristina]

It was usually enough for me to sing in order for her to stop crying. It was the same when trying to get her tied into the car seat. [Lucia]

It certainly seems obvious that babies like listening to children's songs, but these were not the only ones that they liked:

I am very happy that Kady Giunia listens to different kinds of music. In addition to children's songs, she likes to listen to classical music and African music that we have at home, given that I'm Senegalese. [Nago and Cristina]

… and so they were happy to listen to instrumental music and even more:

I came home one day with an old edition of *Rigoletto* on CD. I began to listen to it carefully intending to choose some songs. I wasn't able to do that because Bianca was so fascinated by it that she wanted to hear it all. But not just one day. It was from that time forward until exhaustion ... and then the same thing happened with *Turandot*. [Cristiana]

She was a baby! Of course, she wanted to know the stories about young Gilda in love with a duke and about Liu who dies to save her master. In this way, the emotions she always felt when she listened to music (to the extent of not wanting to hear some songs because they would make her cry) would then become a story. She was able to give meaning to those tears she felt coming when she heard sad music. However, what I really find unusual is the constancy with which she was able to listen to hours and hours of opera. [Cristiana]

4.4.2 The Baby as a Partner

One day, there was a surprise:

One afternoon while I was feeding her and the music playing in the background was one of the children's songs from the Project, Arianna stopped sucking, looked at me and repeated: "oh oh oh oh oh". I didn't think it was possible! She was singing! She was ten months old! This episode was repeated on other occasions under the same conditions. [Manila)]

As he got older, he wanted to sing too. He moved his lips and started to talk very early. He pointed to the player when he wanted music and the cassette had to be turned over to the other side. [Gloria]

This surprise happened in many families:

> I remember her smiles and attempts at imitation during the action songs, and later her
> ability to continue singing alone songs started off with me. [Claudia]

It was an activity through which other skills could be seen:

> Later I could see that when she heard music, she moved in tempo and immediately
> began to sing songs learned at school or at the meetings. [Annarosa]

The children usually sang at home:

> Very early on, Francesco proved to be a great chatterbox, and at 16 months he was
> going around the house singing *Forty-four cats* and banging his drum. [Silvia]

> As she got older, she sang more as she played at home, reproducing, mixing or inventing
> words and music, and she still does that today. We are no longer surprised because this
> has become normal for us. [Manila]

They sometimes tried to "relive" the experience of the meetings:

> Linda loves music, and she often sings alone or with a cassette. She likes to listen and
> to imitate the activities done at the meetings, and then she involves the whole family.
> [Cinzia]

The experience of nursery school also had an influence:

> At 18 months she had begun to speak and then gradually to sing with us. Then when
> she went to playschool (at two and a half), it was she who taught us the songs she had
> learned there. [Federica]

In addition to home, the car seemed to be one of the most conducive places:

> When we are in the car, Martina often asks us to play a cassette. I remember one day in
> summer, I had my car window open, we were stopped at traffic lights in the centre of
> Bologna, and Martina was singing *Little sister do you want to dance*. [Annalisa]

> Bianca loves music. She has a good ear and easily learns the songs she hears. Often,
> in the car, especially when the two of us are together, we sing and have great fun!
> [Flavia]

There were also other stimulating "means of transportation":

> I remember that at times when we were out walking with the pushchair we used to sing
> together and people found that very amusing! [Flavia]

Singing was almost a sign of complicity:

It's nice when we sing to keep each other company in the car, or on the spur of the moment at home, or in the presence of other people. It's as if we recognize each other in a song that only we know. We start to sing and clap hands or play any instrument that comes to hand. [Giovanna]

There were other occasions and situations when the children liked to sing. For example, while they were drawing:

When he was about two years and six months old, while he was drawing a snail he was singing the song "The snail". When he had finished the drawing, he showed it to me and explained it by telling me about the snail who moved slowly and stopped under the tree. I was delighted. [Roberta]

While they played:

So many times after the meetings or after listening to the cassette with the songs we had learned together at the meetings, I heard her singing happily as she played with her dolls. [Armida]

Now and again a bit of vanity showed up:

I see that Fulvio still loves listening to music and singing. Nowadays, he often wants to be recorded while he sings the songs he has learned at school or from the TV. [Valentina]

Now, not only does he ask expressly to be recorded, but he loves listening to himself. [Roberta]

At 18 months, the child was able to sing words and phrases from the songs we used to sing, adapting the rhythm (sometimes in tune, but not always) and inventing words. Sometimes he made up songs while he was playing. [Roberta]

4.4.3 The Child as Musician

Composing songs? At such a young age? His mother must be exaggerating! However, this is precisely what happens. As we have seen in the previous chapter, the first musical vocalizations sung in the early months were inventions. This skill was then developed when they began to speak, as documented in the recordings made over the following years (see section 3.8). At that time, we were looking for traces of this behaviour in the reports from the mothers and fathers. It was great fun to play with the words:

The song about the three Chinese who played the double bass with alternative vowels was the "torment" of that summer. Her musical versions are enriched by notes and expressions that are sometimes invented, other times imitated. She is delighted when she manages to make up a song on a musical base with different words, but that make sense. [Cristina]

... or they could invent words and music:

> Sara often makes up new songs and improvises after starting out on a known theme. [Giovanna]

> At around four to five years of age, Greta often set a phrase to music or she made up the words for a tune she already knew. [Micaela]

The car, as usual, was the best place:

> Viola often made up songs, sometimes with known tunes, and she would put the lines in rhyme starting from a sound, an image or an action. During long car journeys on the way to visit her grandparents, at a certain point she would announce: "Now I'm going to sing a song" and for about twenty minutes she would go from one invention to another searching for words to rhyme and perfecting the verses. [Claudia]

Sometimes, the family were involved in the invention:

> I think it was thanks to this new way of offering them music that helped Noemi to develop a great facility for inventing. It could be new words set to the same tune or a new song and, surprisingly, even her little brother who was listening to his sister attentively, now (at age three) has fun doing the same thing. It has really become a game that the three of us often do together. The results are sometimes so entertaining that the song with the original words is never sung again and she prefers her new version. [Armida]

4.4.4 Starting to Play

Singing is central to the *inCanto* project ["canto" means "singing"] and besides, the voice is a convenient instrument. We carry it along with us, it does not weigh anything or occupy space, and it is easy to use ... That is true, but there were always instruments around for these children. In fact, the production of sound with instruments started very early. From the age of three to four months, the babies could bang or hold in their hands things that they could shake (like bells and maracas). During the meetings, the children were fascinated by the instruments, and when it was time to play them, their attention and enthusiasm returned instantaneously.

This passion for sound and its production was constant and the parents give us interesting insights to this. They played during the meetings:

> They soon began to use the instruments with their hands to beat time to the refrains of the songs. They were sitting on the floor listening to the story in music about the bravery of John the cricket in *Il grillo John* and they accompanied the flapping with rhythm sticks, bells and drums. [Cristiana]

This happened at home, too, given that many parents, in view of the interest shown, had gone out to buy percussion instruments, or electronic keyboards and little guitars:

> For a period when he was about four, he had a great passion for the guitar and he often tried to strum it as he listened to music from a CD. [Alessandra]

> It was wonderful to see his interest, when he was a little bit older, in trying to play instruments (drums, tambourine, castanets, little guitar) and to sing songs to himself while inventing the words. [Matteo and Anna Rita]

The grandparents often collaborated:

> My father always took an interest in my participation in this project, and he always tried to help Adriano's musical development by guiding his fingers and giving him little instruments. Naturally, I too, over the years, gave him a drum, xylophone and keyboard. [Natalia]

They liked to manipulate them with different "techniques":

> He always showed an interest in the piano from the time he was small. At first, he banged all the keys of the keyboard with his hands, and then at about 12 months he pressed single keys with a finger and later (at about 18 months) he paused to listen to the sound produced by pressing down on each key, and he repeated this over and over. [Roberta]

There is a game that evolved as the children grew that is really great. Martina plays it often. It is the game of using varying intensity with instruments or voice, "softly-loud-very loud". [Cristina]

They made music with more than one instrument:

They are interested and curious about the musical instruments at home too (many are toys, others are real). They play the drum, maracas, piano, trumpet, rhythm sticks ... and they pretend to be a band. [Marina]

There were objects that could easily become instruments:

Whenever he found jars or bins, he turned them over, maybe four or five at a time, and then he got sticks or bits of wood (and if he couldn't find any, he used his hands) and he began to beat them and sing songs that had no meaning. When he was a bit older he said he was singing "in English". [Silvana]

I noticed that he was quite confident about "creating" instruments with everyday objects or with toys and using them as "accompaniment" to his songs. [Valentina]

4.4.5 Development

Il grillo John è un furbacchion, canta e balla pum pum pum pum pum.
Sale su un muro, suona il tamburo ...

[John the cricket is very smart, he sings and dances, pum pum pum pum pum. Sitting on a wall, he plays a drum ...]

This is what the mothers-to-be sang, the children sang it over and over, and in effect the singing and playing went together with "dancing". This activity began during pregnancy and later continued with the children. The point of view of the researchers on the reasons for this behaviour has already been discussed in Chapter 3 (see section 3.9). Now we shall look for clues in the parents' points of view.

From simple movements:

Then they stood up too. Dancing in the arms of daddies and mummies then became dancing on their own. [Cristiana]

At the age of three, when she heard songs on the television, she beat the tempo with her hands, or she started to dance, or she sang. [Micaela]

To creative aspects:

When they reached the age of three, they began to improvise dances that were more ambitious. [Manila]

To involving their little sister (dancing in pairs is better!):

> Now that her little sister is almost three, when they play together they dress up as ballerinas with some old scarves and they sing and dance freely. The only argument is over the choice of music to play. [Manila]

To situations where singing, dancing and playing instruments become one complete event:

> He has always been very interested in listening to music, and in sound, dancing and singing. While listening to songs, he removes his shoes, climbs onto the bed and begins to dance, sing and clap his hands, play improvised instruments or the guitar, and you dare not interrupt him. [Silvana]

4.4.6 The Wider Benefits

Memory, reading ability, learning skills, artistic sensitivity, character: the reports also make reference to collateral aspects of music. Their relationship to the *inCanto* project was not studied, mainly because, as it was not in our programme, specific behaviour was not observed in a controlled way. However, the parents touched on various aspects. One example is memory:

> Andrea learned the songs very quickly and he had a good memory. We wrote the words on sheets of paper and put them around the house. This could also explain why he started to read early. [Gloria]

> Even now, when she hears a song on the radio, she learns it in no time. After hearing it a couple of times, she can sing some parts of it right away. [Federica]

Memory that could also be helpful for mother:

> Sometimes, when I can't remember exactly how a tune goes, when it's one we have heard together some time before, I would ask Fulvio, because he would remember it better than me. Perhaps that's an individual trait, or perhaps it's thanks to early training. [Valentina]

They talk of facility in learning:

> Riccardo has developed an incredible sense of music. As soon as he had acquired a linguistic base, he sang one of the recurring songs of the meetings (*L'anatroccolo* [The duckling]) from beginning to end with amazing ease. [Giovanna]

… and of creative skills of various kinds:

> He was always very attracted to manipulating objects, inventing stories, singing well-known songs, and also exchanging the words for others that he invented. When he came out of his own little world, he would read and use the computer. [Natalia]

One of Giulia's characteristics is a particular attitude that we could call an "artistic sense" of life. She draws a lot and makes lovely pictures. She is also very creative in working with her hands in all kinds of things available for children of her age. [Marco]

One mother in particular points out many aspects that could have been stimulated by the *inCanto* project:

The musical experience did not only influence their verbal language. It also had an impact on several social-psychological-motor aspects of the children. In addition, it was very much connected with the development of their social skills and, therefore, with personal and interpersonal relations, in addition to normal psychological development. The motor aspect was also advanced and interesting developments could be seen in their free corporal expression. [Emma]

Another mother speaks in laudatory terms about her child, allowing it to be understood that one of the causes was participation in the *inCanto* project:

It is not easy to sum up these six years because there were so many changes. However, if I look at Adriano today, I see a child who is curious about life, who wants to learn, to try out new situations, who is smiling, serene, affectionate, sensitive, has a sense of humour and is always ready with a joke, autonomous, very observant, empathetic (I have often seen him approach smaller or timid kids who were not in a group and he would play with them and make them laugh), determined and naturally I would say ... he can sing in tune! [Natalia]

4.4.7 Beginning School

Most of the children went to nursery school and all of them went to kindergarten. The teachers noticed that these children reacted in a particular way to music and they always said this to the parents who eagerly told us about it. Some of them remembered this in their reports.

They noticed their interest and attention to others during musical activities:

The teacher told me that Tobia seemed very interested and to be accustomed to listening to others while they played music or sang. [Alessandra]

... or their musical gifts in general were praised:

Sara shows no embarrassment when singing in front of others. In fact, she shows pride and confidence. She recognizes pieces of music heard some time ago and she easily remembers all the songs learned at the meetings and at school, and it is here that she has received the most compliments for her gifts. [Giovanna)]

... or their musical skills were seen together with other skills:

Giulia is particularly attracted to creative activity and this has been pointed out by her teachers over the years. They also say that when they listen to music at school, Giulia is particularly concentrated and taken up by the melody and she keeps time with the music. The teachers emphasized all of this to show how Giulia lived this experience more intensely than the other children. [Marco]

Even now, as they start in elementary school, the teachers' praise continues:

> Noemi has certainly developed greater musical sensitivity with respect to her companions. Even the English teacher in the elementary school one day asked me if the child had already learned at kindergarten the songs she was teaching them. Noemi could sing them more easily than her companions, even if she didn't know the exact words in English. [Armida]

> When we went to speak to the teacher of grade one in elementary school, she told us that she is a very free child who is always singing. [Nago and Cristina]

> At the first parent-teacher meeting for grade one in elementary school, one of Adriano's two teachers, as soon as she knew that we were his parents, immediately said: "But what did you do to have such a musical child?" [Natalia]

4.5 Satisfying Moments

We have been following the parents' accounts of their children's progress. What more do parents want than to rejoice in their children's improvement?

Now we would like them to speak about themselves, their emotions, surprise, satisfaction, and also of the changes in themselves. Some project their own "expectations" on their children, while others observe with more "detachment", almost afraid to influence their choices or to condition their future. However, they tend not to think much about themselves. This is why we wanted to draw their attention to this point. Even though we saw in the reports that it was not easy to draw them away from talking about the child, a few of them revealed something a little more personal.

We shall begin with "their" progress. One mother said that she was happy to have learned so many children's songs:

> I am grateful to the *inCanto* project for teaching me a repertoire of songs that I did not have before and that I would have had to search for myself. I have derived much benefit from what I learned. [Nago and Cristina]

Another mother said that she had acquired a greater interest in music:

> Personally, my love for music has increased (I had it within me, but it had not been cultivated). I learned rhythms and different melodies, and our family have more melodious, resonant, fun-filled moments together. [Marina]

Others acquired more confidence in singing:

As far as I am concerned, I now have a different relationship with music. I like to sing, not in front of anyone at all, but certainly without any problems when I am with my children. [Giovanna]

Participation in the *inCanto* project gave us a lot. It allowed me, as a mother, to sing without apprehension and to learn lots of songs that come in useful in times of stress, to spend some time having fun with the children, and as inspiration for new lyrics and new melodies all yet to be composed. [Claudia]

Personally, I have acquired agility and confidence in singing and now I do it with more facility and pleasure, without fear. Her father was obliged to learn many (too many) children's songs, but he sings them too! [Manila]

More satisfaction with their own singing ability (with perhaps an underlying sense of redemption):

As regards myself, having always accompanied Virginia on this adventure, I must say that I sing far better in tune and now feel quite pleased with myself. [Rita]

Perseverance revealed that even my voice, which is terribly low and most unfeminine, with practice could approach something like a reasonable timbre. [Cristiana]

Better communication:

Singing was a special link between me (the mother) and my daughter. It was a way of communicating, of establishing contact. When we returned home in the evening (we live outside Bologna), because of the dark my daughter couldn't see me any more and so she started to cry. All I had to do was sing and immediately contact was established. The crying stopped. [Nago and Cristina]

Singing and listening to music very soon became a regular means of relating to Sara, something I could never have imagined happening. I sang to put her to sleep, while I was changing her, in the car, while I was feeding her ... I sang around the house and always turned on the stereo to have different kinds of background music.

It was lovely to see her completing the songs and refrains as soon as she had learned to speak, and to see her dancing and moving whenever she heard music.

I believe that this project taught me a new way to communicate with Sara (and also with others in general): I sing for me, I sing for you, I sing with you, we sing together, we sing because we are sad, because we are happy, so that we don't have to think, so that we can think, for love, because of dislike, through desperation, for joy and ... just for the pleasure of singing. [Giuliana]

Other channels of communication were also discovered:

I, whom am a bit of a hermit, found that participation in the project allowed me to be close to my daughter during little dances or rhythmic activities, and it gave me an experience of verbal communication that I don't usually permit myself. I don't think I have ever taken my wife to a dance ... . [Marco]

Some improvements were remembered as moments of deep satisfaction:

> The deepest satisfaction came immediately when, after the birth, we played the music or song to Riccardo (and later also to Virginia) in a different context, at home or at the grandparents home, and we saw that they recognized them. [Giovanna]

> With the passing of time, when she was still very small, our greatest pleasure was to hear her sing the melodies of the songs we used to sing at the meetings. We were thrilled that she loved the song we chose for the videocassette and she still asks me to sing it with her from time to time. [Lucia]

They remembered some emotions, some simple and commonplace, others powerful and now indelible:

> I remember the astonishment at seeing how accomplished our children were, even though they were so young. [Cinzia]

> The emotion of singing together with my son, to see his efforts at singing songs that were increasingly more complex, all of this filled me with joy. Even to hear him singing to himself during other activities always touched me. [Valentina]

> I was thrilled to discover that my daughter was able to repeat rhythms or remember tunes at a very young age. [Mary]

> I remember my first emotions: Adriano moved and kicked when he recognized the voice of his father, during that long hot summer, as he sang the prenatal songs close to me. I remember that we listened to countless types of music (except heavy metal) at home, in the car, everywhere, and I remember the dances I did alone (I who am shy!). Most of all I remember that day when we recorded Adriano as we let him hear his song (*Per te* by Jovanotti that we had sung and played every day of the month) and the music that he had never heard before (metal, in fact!). When I think of it now, tears come to my eyes. The little bundle in my arms looked rueful as we listened to the metal music, but as soon as we played "his" song, he turned his head towards the source of music. It was as if we had already transmitted "values" to Adriano. [Natalia]

> The loveliest emotion that I associate with the *inCanto* project goes back undoubtedly to when Tobia was two days old. It was his second sleepless night in hospital. As he was born by Caesarian section, during the first night I was assisted at first by my husband and later by my mother because I could not get up and was not able to attend to the baby. Tobia spent the second night wailing desperately all the time and I remember well that my mother, exhausted from walking back and forth along the hospital corridors at three in the morning, at a certain point she brought Tobia to me and told me to hold him for a while because she didn't know what else to do. I took him in my arms and started to whisper one of the lullabies learned in the prenatal course: "Fai la nanna bambin, fai la nanna bel bambin, fra le braccia della mamma, fai la ninna fai la nanna" [Sleep my little baby in your mummy's arms]. When Tobia heard the music he turned his head and fixed his misty newborn eyes on me, just as if he had recognized my voice and the song that I had sung so often during pregnancy. This is a precious memory that still continues to move me. [Alessandra]

4.6 Family Involvement

Such a demanding course could not but involve the family. What were the consequences? Was everybody happy about it? Was there resistance? We shall begin with the father's involvement:

> On my husband's part, there was a certain amount of participation in the work done at home, and this increased over time with the satisfaction of seeing progress. [Valentina]

> The child's daddy happily took part in the meetings taking my place. [Mary]

> The project also included fathers and grandparents, and so my husband also sang children's songs. He too listened to lullabies and ditties, sometimes grumbling a bit, but he then confessed gloomily that they were going around his head even when he was at work. Now he is even taking our second child to a similar course to the one followed by his sister ... [Claudia]

For some of them, involvement was total, from participation in the meetings always (or almost) as a couple to activities at home:

> For us too, the parents, involvement was global. We always sang together with him, and both of us tried to be present as far as possible. This is how we then developed friendly relations, in some cases very close, with other participants in the group. We continue to get together, after those six long years, and we often go back over the songs or music of the last few years. [Giovanna]

> We have always been involved as a family because we were convinced from the beginning that this was an interesting project. We did everything together with great commitment. [Annalisa]

In some cases, the roles were distributed. Singing was with mother and playing instruments was with father:

> A closer relationship grew between them and me (the mother) when singing songs. We invented pieces and this amused them very much. With me (the father) they played instruments. The three of us played together and exchanged instruments. [Matteo and Anna Rita]

Music bonded the family together:

> Together with the daddy we used to sing, play instruments, and dance together and we had lots of fun. Our passion for music united us very much. [Gloria]

> It is something that makes us feel united. When singing with them I feel a sense of participation and involvement with them that I don't notice at other times. I hope it is the same for them. [Giovanna]

Naturally, there were some reluctant fathers, but only at the beginning:

> The first time I talked about this with my husband, I saw a flash of uncertainty in his eyes! However, that uncertainty didn't last long. [Natalia]

> My husband likes listening to music, but he has never studied it. Even as a child he never had much opportunity to make music. Consequently he was a bit reluctant to sing and even less enthusiastic than I was about musical activities with the children. Nevertheless, on several occasions, even if I had to persuade him, he accompanied Tobia to the meetings and tried to take part as well as he could. In spite of himself, some of the songs in the *inCanto* project entered his ear and I caught him humming them to himself. The songs and music helped to kill time during Tobia's long convalescence, for he was often sick during his early years. Several afternoons we found ourselves listening to music, playing both "serious" and "homemade" instruments and improvising a family concert. [Alessandra]

Not everyone could be moved:

> Francesco, my husband, supported me in this initiative, but he found it hard to remain involved. If I could not go to the meetings or I didn't feel like singing with Bianca, he never took over for me! Perhaps it was because I did not manage to involve him or maybe it was something that didn't interest him much, even if he never complained when we had to go to lessons on Saturday mornings, even if we had been able to organize ourselves differently. [Flavia]

What about the grandfathers and grandmothers? They are precious and sometimes irreplaceable members of the family who often collaborated in different ways, after some initial scepticism:

> The experience was constructive and unforgettable. I remember particularly a car journey with my mother who was sceptical listening to her daughter who was about to give birth singing *Il grillo John*, and she was shaking her head. [Rita]

The grandparents participated very much in the project. They often accompanied the children to the meetings:

> Thanks to the help of the grandmothers who substituted my husband and me when we were at work, both in caring for Giorgia during the day and in going with her to the weekly meetings of the *inCanto* project, Giorgia's attendance was mostly constant. [Federica]

> I tried over time to interest my husband and parents. On most occasions during those six years, I was the one who accompanied the children, followed by my mother and then my husband, but perhaps not with the same conviction and determination as I had. Maybe it was more to satisfy the children's request. [Giovanna]

They sang with them:

> The most involved grandparent was my mother. She was able to use her lovely voice by launching into *Il grillo John, L'anatroccolo*, and lullabies. [Silvia]

And why not involve the great-grandparents?

> I remember the songs, *L'occhio bello* [the pretty eye], *La pantera* [the panther], *Il grillo John* [John the cricket], *L'anatroccolo* [the duckling], *Fratelli d'Italia* [brothers of Italy] … that we (Alessandro my husband, my mother and I) sang all the time: while we played, while we changes nappies, when it was bath time. My grandmother Clementina was there too reciting the nursery rhymes of her childhood. [Natalia]

There was no lack of musical grandparents:

> Her father hopes that all this will serve to encourage her to take up an instrument. His grandfather plays the saxophone and his father used to play the clarinet. They love jazz in their family. [Cristina]

> Giorgia was born into a musical family. Her maternal grandmother sings in a choir, her paternal grandfather and her father both play instruments at amateur level, so it's not surprising if she loves music. [Federica]

Some were invited to collaborate specifically in some way during meetings:

> We all loved the experience of *Peter and the Wolf*. For several months, we listened a few times a day to the recording we had been given. We could all recite long parts of it by heart and we could hum the music. Fulvio always imitated the characters. Fulvio's grandfather, a clarinetist, was involved during some of the meetings devoted to *Peter and the Wolf*, playing the part of Peter's "cat". He fondly remembers that episode. [Valentina]

There is also a role for little brothers and sisters, wide-eyed pupils whom a little teacher decides to teach the songs that she has learned:

> The habit of singing at home increased when her little brother, Stefano, arrived. Now I hear her singing a lot because she wants to teach the baby the songs. Stefano is very happy with this "new game" and tries as hard as he can to repeat the sounds and words his sister is teaching him. [Armida]

… or companions in musical games:

> The children sing together and they might spontaneously play at dividing a song where each one sings a bit and they wait for their turn. At times we all sing together or we say things in a singing voice (for example, 'Dinner's ready!'). [Marina]

New friendships were made that grew from similar motivations and experiences:

It was really lovely and you could feel involved. The people we met on those occasions are still our companions as we go forward. A shared sensibility led us like a magic pipe to the rooms of the project. Our experience of sharing and working together created special links that would continue in the future. [Cristiana]

I feel that the presence of other children and other parents encouraged us to continue in the project. For the children, particularly in the last two years, it was an occasion to play with their companions and for the mothers it was a chance to exchange news and share experiences. [Federica]

Friendship grew among the mothers. I used to see some of them on other occasions and we exchanged opinions on how the project was proceeding, and gave suggestions on how to improve some things at home. We all felt involved in a beautiful experience!

I still get together with some of the mothers. With the others, when we see each other around we stop to talk. It's lovely to see the children growing and their little brothers and sisters that have arrived since. [Flavia]

Music was not a private affair. It was collective, contagious, and involved people.

From the time she was small, and as the months and years passed (six years, I can't believe it!) music and song accompanied us on the way: Sara and me, Sara, me and her father, Sara and her grandparents, Sara and the world. [Giuliana]

Whenever he could, his father also took part in the course, or sometimes he sang at home. Then Marco dragged along his grandparents and wanted them to join in his musical game. Every evening before going to bed we had to play at "the band". Each one of us took a musical instrument, castanets, maracas, tambourine, or anything that would do for an instrument. He was the conductor and we were the musicians, and we had to play our instruments as we marched around the table, and we had to follow his directions or he got very angry. Sometimes he was the soloist who sang and played those instruments while we had to dance. [Silvana]

4.7 Looking to the Future

What will my daughter be when she grows up? This is a frequent question asked by parents, especially when they provide their children with special experiences. No parents, when they are teaching their children to speak, expect them to become orators or writers, or when they give them a little doctor's set or a little carpenter's set, they do not think of directing the children towards that profession. However, when we are dealing with music or any artistic sector, even today we often hear a hint of expectations of genius, of great mysterious gifts that create great artists. Today, this myth has been refuted to an extent, but it still remains in musical circles (one mother said "I let my child study music because I would not like to hinder the growth of a budding Mozart").

During the project, starting with the letter of invitation, our position has always been to invite parents to help the development of their children's musicality independently of future professional choices. There has always been an atmosphere of maximum freedom, on the one hand to ensure a positive experience for the children and, on the other, to allow for different kinds of experience, so that each one could acquire an array of skills from which to choose.

This climate of freedom and serenity also came through in the reports when speaking of future prospects. One mother emphasizes the difference with respect to other children:

> I am convinced that the constant stimulation she has received during these first six years has somehow brought her further, with respect to children who have not had this kind of approach. [Micaela]

Several children manifested the desire to learn to play an instrument and some mothers told us about the fateful encounter:

> Bianca started first grade in elementary school. She told us she didn't want to learn any instrument. I didn't argue. The days were full with eight hours full time out of the house and dancing, which she wanted to keep up. However, we went to a demonstration lesson. She unexpectedly fell in love with the violin ("listen, Mummy, how nice it sounds ...").
>
> Now, two months later, she practises every day with surprising regularity. She has asked Santa Claus for a violin (she's using a borrowed one at the moment) and you can feel her pleasure when she produces notes from the instrument. [Cristiana]

> Giorgia was four years of age when, during a meeting of the *inCanto* project, she was present during a demonstration of students from the school of music playing the harp. I wasn't there, but I experienced the meeting through Giorgia's enthusiasm when she told me about it. From that time forward, she has had the desire to play the harp. We went to a few concerts in our city where children were playing the harp. Giorgia, who is now six and a half, is enthusiastically attending harp lessons. [Federica]

For some, it was a logical way to proceed:

> Adriano still lives this experience as part of his life, just like school and his friends. When the project concluded, he wanted to continue with music, and the instrument he chose was the piano. [Natalia]

Some children expressed this desire some time ago and they were allowed to do so before the age of six:

> Now that he is five and a half, we are letting him study the piano as he has always liked it from the time he was very small. [Roberta]

> This experience encouraged further development in music. In fact, Riccardo began to study piano at the age of five and he is determined to carry this project to completion. Who knows ... [Giovanna]

Some parents took care to insert the study of an instrument into a wider context of development:

> We realized that this first approach to music could serve Andrea in the future. Beyond the possibility of his learning an instrument well, we already had the clear perception that this "gentle" preparation that came early in life, could serve to provide a more balanced development of his mental abilities. This experience had already led him to study piano at his own request and to willingly accept the extra study and application. [Matteo and Anna Rita]

The ability to play an instrument could have interesting consequences on their self-esteem:

> The child herself decided to continue the path initiated with the *inCanto* project by going once a week to piano lessons together with other children. She goes willingly to these classes because she continues to have fun while she is learning fingering on the keyboard and how to play some short pieces. All of this has increased her confidence in her own abilities. Now she can do things that were unthinkable a few months ago, like for example to play a song on the piano. [Armida]

Some children explicitly declared that they did not want to learn an instrument yet, while others simply have not asked and were not encouraged in that direction. Some parents are thinking about it for later, especially when there has been a passing rejection:

> We hope to send the children to the school of music in the new year, as long as my work does not prevent it as it did this year. [Mary]

> I shall certainly enrol her on a course of music next year to see what her interests and abilities are. [Flavia]

> I think that Margherita can attend a course of music in the near future and then at some stage she can take up the instrument of her choice. [Emma]

There were children who had other ideas in mind which their parents respected thinking that they were just temporary:

> Giulia expressed the desire to take up dancing and now she is doing it twice a week. We feel that this commitment is enough to add to her schooling. However, I think that this is only an interruption to her music studies and that she will surely go back to it. [Marco]

> As we approached the end of the *inCanto* project, I asked her to choose between singing and playing an instrument. She always said she wanted to sing. Even though she has recently taken up other activities (tennis and ballet), I am certain that it will be no problem for her to join a choir or take a music course. [Micaela]

However, there is a general desire not to force the children but to give them freedom in their choice in the conviction that the experience they have undergone has been positive:

> I don't know what will happen in the future. Our hope is that what has been sown will emerge when she decides. We have only directed and encouraged her. In the future she will have to feel the urge to continue. [Annarosa]

One mother wanted to keep a record of everything:

> The rhymes, nursery rhymes and little songs learned over these few years have been collected in a diary with lots of photographs of the music meetings and other important episodes (newborns at the massage course, mothers at "water and pregnancy") and they are a legacy that Martina can keep. [Cristina]

Many parents concluded their report by expressing satisfaction, enthusiasm, gratitude, and some regret that it is over. It was not an "aseptic" research study, but rather an intense adventure with full participation on all sides, and we are deeply grateful to all the parents for their collaboration and commitment.

In that letter written way back in 1999–2000, we said: "One day you will feel proud of having contributed to scientific progress by offering your child this gift. It is a story you will tell your child later." We say this again today to every mother and father.

However, the loveliest gratitude will come tomorrow, your children's "tomorrow".

PART II
From Research to Teaching Practice

Chapter 5
Promoting Musical Development

5.1 Musical Intelligence

In the previous chapters we presented the main stages in the development of some musical skills in children from birth until age three, taking into account the data received from the *inCanto* project. We did not simply document events and the corresponding analysis. We preferred to enter into the heart of the progression that was occurring within a specific educational context. We concluded Chapter 3 by saying that this particular context had functioned because, as pointed out earlier in another publication (Tafuri, 1988), the acquisition of any skill must wait for the maturing of the biological and psychological processes required, but that it is also true that learning does not mature if the individuals do not receive the relevant stimuli, encouragement and example that allow them to try to do certain things.

In the second part of the book we shall deal with the role of education and some learning mechanisms, and we shall look in particular at a series of activities that proved to be effective in the *inCanto* project.

We begin by considering the relationship between education and genetic endowment, a relationship on which this book with the results of our research study would like to cast further light. Taking our cue from the famous book that was published in the United States in 1981, "Intelligence: the battle for the mind", written by two researchers H.J. Eysenck and L. Kamin, we too ask: Are we born musical or do we become musical? This question immediately gives rise to another: what does it mean "to be musical"?

On raising this issue, we come to realize the complexity of the adjective "musical" when it is attributed to people. The term "intelligent" has been and continues to be very much debated, especially in the wake of the theory presented by the American psychologist Howard Gardner (1985) on the different kinds of intelligence – one of which he believes to be musical intelligence – a theory that has disarranged the apparent clarity and univocality of the terms "intelligent" and "intelligence", terms that have also been discussed by some Italian authors (Mugny and Carugati, 1988).

We could say the same about the terms "musical" and "musicality". Ever since the earliest studies on the psychology of music that emerged towards the end of the nineteenth century, these terms were the object of numerous research studies and they remain so until now (Hallam and Shaw, 2003; Addessi *et al.*, 2006). This is precisely the reason why our research was not intended for the study of "the development of musicality", but rather some "musical skills" that are clearly outlined. These have a specific role in a person's "being musical" which is an attribute that does not simply indicate the sum of various skills. For a behaviour to be considered entirely musical, it is more important that different musical skills mature and interact with each other.

In order to enter into the educational perspective with more understanding of the question, it is helpful to ask ourselves what we possess that is due to education and what comes from genetic endowment. Every child born awakens amazement in parents: "How can this little thing become an adult person?" The child is already complete, but not fully mature. He/she has a series of tendencies or bents, a "programme", but at the same time is in tremendous need of help. "What about his/her physical looks, health, temperament? What will he/she turn out like?"

Recent studies in genetics confirm that many characteristics present in each individual are multifactorial, that is, they are controlled by more than one gene. As these include most of our somatic traits, it is all the more likely that other more complex characteristics will be multifactorial, like a "musical ear", resistence to effort or stress, quick reflexes or intelligence (Boncinelli, 1998, pp. 119–120). The presence of joint action by several genes means first of all that none of these has direct control over the result and it also indicates that there is notable interference by the environment. Therefore, in the case of any characteristic (including those just mentioned), to be determined by more than one gene automatically means to be forged to a large extent by the environment (Boncinelli 1998, p. 128).

Studies in genome mapping are making huge advances nowadays, and they may possibly be able to offer more precise information on how many genes control intelligence, or as Gardner says, multiple intelligences, including the musical. For now, there are no scientific reasons that allow us to believe that nature is particularly parsimonious with most people and generous with the chosen few. In fact, there are good reasons to think that we all receive sufficient genetic endowment for "good" musical development and that the differences actually found are due to the influence of numerous other factors. As Howe (1990) says, "all individuals are forged by their experience [...]. The way in which a particular person experiences a particular situation depends on the way in which he/she perceives and interprets the information that reaches his/her brain. That, in its turn, depends on many factors [...], for example, his/her acquaintances, interests, attitudes, personality, self-confidence, temperament, prejudices, state of mind and expectations" (translated from Italian edition, pp. 63–64).

The hypothesis (or conviction on the part of many) is that everyone, or perhaps we should say, most people, start off musically "gifted", that is to say, they possess "normal" genetic endowment for music. However, only those people who have been facilitated with a very positive and stimulating interaction with the environment, with education, and with many other factors including above all interest, are the ones who fully develop their potential skills. This is maintained by the Canadian expert, Sandra Trehub (previously cited) who carried out many studies on newborns and who believes that children are "inherently" musical (2003, p. 402).

If we look, for example, at the results attained by Japanese children who studied the violin according to the Suzuki method (and used all over the world today), by Hungarian children who learned to sing following the Kodály method (again, universally recognized) and the children of the Anang people in Nigeria in their ability to sing and play instruments (Gardner, 1985), we have to admit that nature's generosity with those people is definitely inexplicable. To play an instrument, sing a song, talk about a piece of music, compose a ditty or instrumental piece – there are so many possibilities for our "musical intelligence"! This expression could substitute the term "musicality" in order to indicate, as with Gardner (1985), a specific ability to carry out particular "musical" tasks. To be more precise, given that the requirements he identified are "the ability *to solve problems*" and "the ability to *create products* valued by a culture", we can say that "musical intelligence" is the ability to solve problems of performance, composition and analytical-interpretation or to create performances, compositions and interpretations. Put this way, we immediately think of advanced abilities. However, even a child of six to eight months creates his/her little song, as we heard in some of the recordings, and at the age of two to three he or she can beat out the pulse synchronizing with a melody. Naturally, we are speaking here of "normal" or maybe "basic" musical giftedness, that everybody should possess at birth. I shall not enter into the merits of "exceptional" giftedness, which we might think of in the case of "genius" composers and performers, except to say that we know very little about this as yet. However, I repeat my conviction that in order to know how to make music, to express oneself musically, it is certainly not necessary to be a genius.

To summarize, musical intelligence is the ability to *understand or produce music*, where "produce" includes both the ability to perform and to compose/ improvise. Each skill starts out from an initial stage and goes towards a final adult stage; along this journey (as we are told by Gardner) there is need for the combination of different intelligences. In our case, it is not hard to presume that for musical tasks we need, for example, bodily-kinaesthetic intelligence and also spatial intelligence. What interests us here is to understand the role of education and environment in the various phases that musical intelligence passes through on its way to the state of adulthood.

5.2 Education and Learning

The question is often asked concerning who the "subject" of education actually is: Is it the one who educates or is it the one who is being educated? If we transfer the emphasis from the subject to the educational relationship, the perspective changes, and we discover that there are two equally important "subjects". In practice, there are two protagonists.

It is a delicate and complex relationship in which the educators certainly have the task of facilitating learning in the sense that they must ensure that the necessary situations are provided. One cause of failure to learn (perhaps the primary cause) is precisely the lack of effective learning situations. It is also true, however, that the other protagonist has to be taken into account, the learner, in his/her concrete situation (level of maturity, limits, interests, rejection, etc.). This is the one who must put the process of learning into action by interacting with all that is offered. How can we put this into concrete form in early infancy? What sense do we give to the word "education"?

Aware of the great number of possible definitions, here we prefer to restrict ourselves to saying that the term "education" is most frequently used to refer to the transmission of culture and value systems, to the development of individuals as human and social beings. The first educators are in fact the parents and they transmit values through their behaviour and words. This transmission activates responses from the children. It stimulates an interaction that produces changes in them that, with time, determine the way they find their path in the world.

By observing concrete experience, we can derive three modalities with which the educational process is activated: *informal education*, *systematic* or *formalized education* and *self-education* (Tafuri, 2002). In order to deal with this last modality, we need to take a closer look at learning mechanisms. We shall do this in the next section.

A child hits her little brother and her father yells at her. A grandmother sings a nursery rhyme using actions that are good for motor coordination. These are educational interventions that occur intermittently and casually, that is, just when they happen to take place. However, they demonstrate that, for adults, there is an underlying intention to transmit the value of respect for others or the value of motor control. In the same way, singing or listening to music at random, is an informal act of cultural transmission. A type of behaviour (singing, listening, playing an instrument) happens at irregular intervals, and it is regarded as positive, pleasant and appreciable.

This is what we mean by informal education. It is the sum of implicit or explicit interventions that are intermittent and casual, that come from people who are in the company of children, most particularly the parents.

If, on the other hand, every evening before going to bed, the children have to put their toys away or pray together with their parents, this is a systematic educational intervention in tidiness or in religious sense. The same can happen with music, in a systematic way. If they select some time at home to sing or listen to music, for example, on waking up, when it is time for a bath or on going to sleep.

If this happens in a context that is explicitly devoted to education and most particularly to instruction, understood as the learning of specific skills and concepts (we refer to school in general or to nursery school), we speak of formalized education. In the case of nursery school, we know that, even within the limits of time and children's pace of growth, there is certainly an educational "programme" there, in the sense that the people who deal with children explicitly ensure that there are certain activities that are sensorial, motorial, socializing, etc.

The children are not obliged to "do drills", but they themselves often do so by repeating over and over whatever satisfies them most. In the development of any skill, there are basically three factors involved: age, practice and exercise.

When we speak of age we must remember that there is growth taking place that is guided by our biological clock and is, therefore, tied to the biochemical and psychophysical processes. When we speak of practice we are emphasizing the presence in daily life of casual experiences (a radio switched on, a parent who is singing, the music in the supermarket) with greater or lesser abundance and diversity. When we speak of exercise we refer to an activity organized for the purpose of achieving a specific result. It can be simply the repetition of a gesture (to manage to hit a golf ball into a hole), a song (to continuously ask to hear a song again in order to learn it). Exercise can also be done unconsciously, more spontaneous than organized, but it is something that intellectual development cannot do without.

Potentialities, virtualities and propensities do not become actual skills without exercise. However, practice and exercise depend on the environment, above all the cultural, with its language, customs and value systems. What is the role of the environment? This is an important question from the educational perspective to which, however, it is necessary to add others: What does our environment really offer? How is it presented? Where? With what attitudes? At what times? In what kind of affective climate?

Educators and parents have the responsibility to create a rich and stimulating educational context. It should be rich in content, songs and music of various styles and genres, musical games and dances, instruments to explore and with which to establish sonorous dialogues. However, it should also be rich in opportunities in the sense that occasional moments should also be sustained by systematically arranged times. These activities should be appropriately spaced out so that they are not so long that they cause saturation, nor so short that they leave a sense of dissatisfaction. The activities should take place in a positive affective climate so that the children will find them desirable, they should encourage interaction which is socially important, they should allow them to have sensori-motor satisfaction and at the same time the gratification of feeling praised and appreciated.

In some families, there may be little or none of all of this. Music is considered to be a useless pastime or reserved for the chosen few. The prevalent practice in nursery schools is to sing and play musical games, especially with the older children, but in general the children are not systematically encouraged to explore vocal and instrumental sounds. Sometimes small percussion instruments are distributed (tambourines, maracas, bells). This is certainly positive, as they respond to the extraordinary interest children have in sound. However, they play a limited role if the educators do not involve the children in appropriate activities.

A stimulating environment does not only facilitate, but also brings forward the acquisition of certain musical skills. Such early acquisition confirms, as demonstrated by the results presented in this book, that certain psychophysical structures are ready, and if they begin to function later it is only because they were not stimulated, or we could say nourished, at the right time.

I like to remember an expression used by Maria Montessori. In the early years of the twentieth century, she discovered the great interest children showed in experiences that she offered them at an earlier age than usual. She said that children suffered from "mental starvation". Children have a "hunger" to see, do, experiment, and know. During our project, we discovered together with the parents, that the children hungered for music, for sounds to listen to and to produce with any instrument at all, for participative musical experiences.

To sum up, we emphazise with Gardner that learning requires "appropriate motivation, a favourable emotional state, a collection of values that facilitate a particular type of learning and a cultural context that sustains" (Gardner 1985, translated from Italian edition, p. 394).

5.3 Observational Learning

After having looked at the educational relationship mainly from the angle of the person who is educating, we now consider learning mechanisms more closely, with particular attention to the zero to three year age group. Here, we do not have the compulsory requirements of school, there are no teachers who "explain" and there is no homework. However, the children learn very much, and the gap between "nothing" (but is it really nothing?) at the moment of birth and what they are able to do at the age of three is amazing if it is compared with the learning that takes place over the following years.

It happened to us, now adults. It happened to the children on the *inCanto* project, and it generally happens to all children. A greater understanding of these mechanisms could certainly help us to educate better, to allow the children to follow their path in a more beneficial way. In order to find out more, we shall ask for the help of learning theories from which we shall choose two.

A contribution of pivotal importance was made by Piaget, a Swiss psychologist whose theories emerged and were established around the 1950s. He worked out his model of cognitive psychology on the basis of numerous experiments. Ever since, his work has been one particular blueprint for showing us the course of intelligence development, a course divided into phases considered to be genuine "stages". Each stage is characterized by "key" behaviours that must mature before children can pass on to the next stage.

Things that can be easily observed by educators and attentive parents (vocal sounds, words, standing up, searching for lost objects, manipulating different materials) were carefully studied in order to derive concepts of development (assimilation, accommodation) and behavioural models.

Contrary to a once commonly held belief that newborns are impassive beings incapable of reacting, Piaget (1951) developed a theory that gave great importance to imitation. The mother is the newborn's model for imitation and she, in turn, imitates what the child has just done, for example, the reproduction of sounds. In this way, a series of alternate imitations is activated, made possible precisely because small babies are relatively unable to imitate something that they have not experienced spontaneously, at least not until the corresponding schemata for that action have become mature.

This sequence of alternate repetitions from the age of three months onwards marks the beginning of socialization. This has been studied more recently by the psychologist Daniel Stern (1977) and, in the area of its application to musical development, by the music psychologist Michel Imberty (2002). He demonstrated how repetition and variation (the mother never repeats in exactly the same way) that regulate social and affective interaction between the mother and baby are also the basic principle of musical organization, with interesting consequences on musical development.

Returning to imitation in Piaget's theory, we must add that, with the maturing of the mental schemata, the child's imitation becomes more autonomous and can (from 18 months onwards) be deferred in time.

Other theories have been put forward by a number of authors, partly to explain any less convincing aspects of Piaget's theory, and partly to present new aspects of the problem that led to other conclusions.

One theory that introduces interesting elements came from the American psychologist Albert Bandura (1986) whose field of study was learning in general and not only in the zero to three age group. He was interested in the phenomenon of imitation and at the same time in the social aspects of this behaviour. For this purpose, he studied the various components and formulated a more articulated model in order to allow for better understanding of what happens during the first years of life in particular.

Bandura places emphasis not on imitation, but on observation. His theory of "observational learning" was prompted by the statement that even the simple observation of human behaviour allows one to learn the rules and to acquire skills, and this saves time with respect to actually having to carry out the actions in order to learn. How much learning takes place, at home and outside, simply through observation (how to make an omelette, comb your hair ...)! This is observation that generates a change, without which we could not claim to have learned something.

By giving more emphasis to learning rules of behaviour rather than faithful reproduction – to know the rules also means to be able to vary – Bandura decided to use the term "modelling" to better represent the process that he had identified. This term is present in social cognitive science to indicate those psychological processes that happen when observation of certain behaviour is followed by an action that uses the same structure and the same rules. To put it in a circumlocutory way, we could say that modelling is the reproduction of an action that has been learned through observation of a behaviour that assumes the function of model.

We shall just mention in passing that the same term (modelling) is used with a different meaning when we want to define an educational strategy that an adult can put into effect to "motivate from within" children's games. With this meaning, modelling corresponds to an intervention by an adult that is intended to "demonstrate the solution to a task that the child wants to do, but cannot manage to do alone. In this case, the solution provided by the adult through example, besides being able to perceive the intention of the child and to identify in a sonorous context the instruments needed to solve the problem that is presented, must be placed within the scope of the potential development of the child. Therefore, the proposed solution must be sufficiently close to the child's abilities in order to be done by the child him/herself" (Mazzoli, 2003, translated from the Italian, p. 15).

As an introduction to his analysis on observational learning, Bandura identifies four subfunctions by which it is governed. These are four components or groups of constitutive processes: attention, retention, production and motivation.

A baby of eight to ten months hears some sounds, turns his head and sees a person who is playing a drum. He remains still gazing for a long time at that specific behaviour. Unless attention is paid to a particular activity, the relative information cannot be processed. It is a case of selective attention (as always), that is, attention that chooses some elements on which to concentrate and that depends on various factors: first of all, the characteristics of the person observing (level of perceptive-cognitive and motor maturity, foreknowledge, skills already acquired, etc.); in the second place, characteristics of the action being observed (the action that functions as model: easy, difficult, simple/complex, lively/dull); in the third place, the value being attributed to it (the person whom the child is observing is praised or yelled at for playing the instrument); and finally, the attraction it holds over the one observing (the instrument producing the sound wields particular fascination on the child observing).

Returning to the previous example, it is possible that, after observing for a while, the child crawled towards the drum and started banging in a way similar to what he had just seen done. Here the second and third sub-functions have been activated: retention and production. The child has in fact "retained" a certain image of the observed action and immediately produced something similar. It is the beginning, at an elementary level, of those "retention processes" of which Bandura spoke, indicating with this term the processes through which the observed action is transformed into a symbolic representation that serves to remember general rules. These allow for reproduction of a similar action immediately afterwards or after some time.

The processes of symbolic representation are nevertheless formed quite soon and the development of language often helps this very much. Already at the age of one and a half, a child who observes certain actions, for example, on television (like dancing, jumping or even shooting), can produce similar actions even the next day, as parents often notice. This demonstrates that something was learned from the behaviour that was observed.

We wish to point out, though, that here Bandura does not touch on the problems related to the influence of the mass media. He is dealing with psychological rather than educational problems, and only wishes to emphasize that an action can be reproduced later when the memory has matured the capacity for symbolic representation. This opens another window of reflection: what if a child never does what he/she has seen on television or in play school? The fact that a child does not spontaneously produce the observed actions does not signify, according to Bandura (op. cit. p. 88), that he/she has not learned it. In order to verify the presence of certain skills, it is necessary to create situations in which the children feel encouraged to demonstrate what they have learned.

However, I would also like to draw attention to the fact that the opposite can also occur, and that children do things right away after they are told not to do them. On this issue, what some parents in the *inCanto* project said is very interesting: a child of two years and one month refused to sing a song in spite of his father's affectionate and encouraging requests. After asking him several times, the father said severely: "Don't sing it because I don't want to hear it!" The result was that the child immediately sang the song with all three verses.

A mistake often made by educators and parents is to presume that the skills learned through modelling, those matured by the children through observation, are those that the children choose to do, spontaneously or with some incentive. This is in fact, according to Bandura (ibid.), a gross underestimation of their cognitive skills. On the basis of research conducted on this theme by him and by other experts, he observed that smaller children certainly find it hard to integrate several sequences of an observed behaviour, that is, to remember which gestures or actions (for example in daily life like washing, dressing, etc.) should be done first and which later.

Nevertheless, Bandura continued, with age there is a progressive increase in the ability to understand and retain the global structure of a specific behaviour. It can then be observed in the production phase, that is when the children themselves put into practice the behaviour that they have observed, even if some errors remain in their mastery of the details.

A child (aged three and a half) in our project who had watched a representation (of ten minutes approximately) of a section of Stravinsky's *The Soldier's Tale* several times, one day was very enthusiastic about accepting the invitation: "Who wants to be the soldier?" and he played the role respecting the sequence of action with amazing accuracy (apart from some wavering in the dialogues), without having had any "rehearsals". (An aside: How often do we subject children to useless and tiring rehearsals for the little end-of-year shows?)

In practice, there is reciprocal influence between cognitive skills and modelling, in the sense that the immaturity of the former limits the production of the observed actions, but the attempts at production stimulate in their turn the maturing of those skills.

We have spoken of attention, retention and production and now we come to the final subfunction: motivation. According to Bandura (1986, p. 91), this is a theme that is often dealt with too easily by separating internal and external motivations. Included in the former are the need to know and to act, and in the second, external appreciation and the use of prizes and punishments. According to the author, the problem is more complex and requires greater study on why one chooses to produce a certain observed behaviour, why it is reproduced at different times and places and why actions are produced with variations from a model.

The answers, according to Bandura, are to be found first of all in the sensory and social effects of the actions themselves. In the first months of life, interaction with the mother and with adults in general lays the basis for interpersonal relations and is reinforced by affective reward. The first experiences of interchange allow the child to experience the power of social involvement and they generate the desire to frequently initiate similar behaviour. The mother who repeats the vocal sounds of a baby of a few months old is a valued source of stimulation to the child to reproduce other sounds that are more or less similar and to continue for a long time in this game of turn-taking (see Chapter 1).

The production of certain actions also generates the satisfaction of feeling that one is capable of doing something: "Look, Mummy, see how good I am" and this satisfaction becomes a strong motivation. Children feel more and more attracted to *modelling*, that is, observing others in order to learn and to want to demonstrate whatever they have learned. They do this not only in order to be praised, but also from an intimate sense of efficacy (this is the theory of self-efficacy that Bandura would develop later; see Bandura, 1997).

We noticed this satisfaction most particularly during the recordings of the children accompanying a melody with a digital drum (see Chapter 4). Although some children refused to do it, almost all accomplished this task with real enthusiasm and wanted to repeat it over and over. During the first recording (average age two and a half), the children felt that they were the centre of attention and they experienced the sensory-motor gratification of the movement and satisfaction at being capable of doing it.

The children had played the drum many times before, and it was not necessary to provide examples or to "rehearse". A simple invitation was enough: "Play the drum together with the music" allowed them to perform an action that had the same structure and small variants with respect to what they had done so many times before.

We conclude by saying with Bandura (1986, p. 69) that "A model who demonstrates desired activities over and over, who instructs observers to follow the behavior, who prompts them verbally and physically when they fail, and who then rewards them when they succeed, will eventually evoke matching performances". This is what is meant by offering an educational context.

Perhaps this is what took place in the *inCanto* project.

Chapter 6
Suggestions for Musical Activities

6.1 Areas of Musical Experience

The learning activities suggested in this section were among those used in the *inCanto* project. These activities were formulated after careful study of the theoretical propositions required for the design of a programme of musical activities suitable for children aged zero to three.

Our research has tested these models and, as earlier and greater development of musical skills could be observed in the children who took part in the project with respect to their peers, we feel that the activities provided can be considered to be valid (even if there is always room for improvement).

Our first general recommendation is that the planning of activities should concentrate on three fundamental experiences: singing, playing instruments and dancing (or simply moving with the music). In preparing the programme for the children, the educators should focus on the pleasure that children can derive from musical experience and on how this gratification can bring about assimilation of musical models from their own culture. By immersing them in an enjoyable sonorous atmosphere as varied as possible, they are being helped to become more familiar with diverse musical structures.

In choosing a repertoire of songs, we suggest that preference should be given to songs with a tonal system (major and minor) that is clear and stable (according to the criteria given in Chapter 2, section 2.5). Their rhythmic-metrical structure should be predominantly regular and their form should mostly consist of phrases organized in verses and refrain or simply in verses. However, preference does not mean "exclusive use", and so it is also advisable to include some songs of a different type (such as a pentatonic or modal melody, freer rhythms and forms). A repertoire of this kind is found primarily in popular traditions that include songs for children with certain functions (to promote motor coordination, to teach counting, to teach the names of the days, months, etc.) and the words and the musical structure generally suggest how they should be done.

All of this should be complemented by the use of music in other activities that belongs to different genres and styles so that the children are immersed in a varied and stimulating musical experience.

We have spoken about singing, but we also include playing instruments. "At that age?", someone might say. Indeed, it might seem incredible that such small children can play instruments, but in fact the bases are built during this phase. We should actually give them opportunities to play instruments as soon as they are capable of holding something in their hands. There are no reasons to "wait", so why are we reluctant? Is it because they will "make a din"? The first phase of exploring an instrument and the sound it produces is a fundamental stage.

Obviously, this is not a problem of choosing a repertoire in the sense of performance. We cannot customarily expect children to perform pieces of music repertoire (even if there have been cases of classical instruments being taken up by children of two and three years of age). We have to think, rather, of what pieces to choose so that the children's instrumental accompaniment can go along with vocal or instrumental music of different genres and styles. Instruments are also very useful for free improvisation.

What instruments? We can certainly give children small percussion instruments, the kinds that are used in orchestras and in ethnic music. Small dimensions and immediacy of use is what is required. There are some "take and play" instruments that do not require any special skill but that are satisfying because of their immediate sonorous production: maracas, rattles, tambourines, bells, rhythm sticks, triangles, etc. The children can be given real instruments or objects that can be adapted to the same use; two strainers stuck together with a few pebbles inside could substitute maracas, a detergent container could be used as a drum, etc. These are the so-called "poor instruments".

When we give this opportunity to the children, the only limits to put in place are those that prevent the risk of them hurting themselves or where there are difficulties in extracting sound. Let us take the triangle as an example. As the normal striker could end up in the child's eye, it would be better to give them (at least for the under two's) a wooden striker with rounded points. Besides, children under the age of two cannot hold the triangle firmly in order to beat it with the other hand on one of its sides and they often "misfire" (unless the parents hold it steady). So, in this case, it is not enjoyable.

We now turn to the activity of dancing. We wish to make it clear that this is not to be understood exclusively as dancing in the strict sense of the term, but that it also includes any opportunities given to the children to experience music through their body in movement.

The repertoire of popular dances in our culture and other cultures can be useful, although they often have to be adapted to the basic movements that children up to the age of three are able to perform. When choosing, it should be borne in mind that the main function of dancing is the entertainment provided by movement in itself (walking, running, etc.), secondly that of facilitating motor coordination and the control of time and space, and finally to provide, through the formal aspect, the essential requirements for the future activity of segmentation.

In addition to the dances, we also suggest that the children be allowed to listen to music and to experience it through their body in motion. In other words, invite them to move freely with the music, almost like in free dance. Here the repertoire chosen can be quite varied, even if using short pieces (1'30"–2') or sections of longer pieces. Although we always listen while singing, playing instruments or dancing, in this activity listening assumes greater importance.

One educational dimension to which it is important to give time is improvisation. Children easily invent when they are self absorbed – as we have seen in Chapter 3, section 3.5 – but they can also enjoy themselves in games of collective improvisation. It is good to allow for this activity so that they can feel that their ability to invent and their productions are appreciated and valued by adults.

They can improvise songs, melodies without words, rhythms, sung stories, free movement ..., there are no limits. As we emphasized earlier, it is important that they assimilate the models of their own culture, but it is also good that they feel free to express themselves creatively and to know that this is appreciated. In other words, it is important to balance the assimilation of established cultural models with the development of creative thought.

Musical experience can be individual or collective with differing sensations. Individual children can make music spontaneously, at home or in other places, for example at play school, when they are absorbed in themselves. They sing, play an instrument, move alone with the music, urged on by an inner need.

With collective experience, we would recommend, however, both the musical interaction that a child establishes with one person (a parent, an educator) and making music together with others (children and/or adults). We are, therefore, referring to places like home and playschool, but here I would also like to suggest the possibility of musical sessions for children of zero to three years of age to take place in musical centres with people who are experts in early childhood music education. At these sessions, the children are to be accompanied and participate together with their parents. This means that they *all* have this experience and that the parents are not there just to look after their children, but also to discover and build a new kind of relationship with them. When the activity is continued at home, it will allow them to develop this new means of communication and will encourage familiarity with musical language. The presence of parents during these sessions also allows for activities to be undertaken that at playschool the educator alone could not do and so a greater number of activities can be carried out that are beneficial for the children's growth.

The activities that can be carried out at playschool or at a music centre have been presented as collective activities, but perhaps we could also facilitate an individual dimension within a collective situation. This is the opportunity to give children opportunities to sing or play instruments alone or with others in a group. For example, after all have sung a song together, the educator could ask the children to sing the end of a phrase, or the whole phrase on their own, and then for everyone to sing the refrain together. Perhaps it will not be possible to give the chance to everyone (presuming that all want to), but those who volunteer could go first, and some other day you could call on those who never volunteer.

How much time should be dedicated to music? How should we choose the activities? Each playschool has its schedule in which musical activities are inserted according to different criteria.

Singing can certainly accompany different moments of the day, but we suggest that there should be special times dedicated to it, especially for children over 18 months old. There are songs that they like to sing, but there are also new ones to learn. There are times for singing circle games and for free movement activities together with music. There are times for fairy tales that can also be dedicated to stories that have a part for singing or to musical stories.

In sessions organized at a music centre, the activities would have a fixed time, and in that time children have to be offered different kinds of activity that they are happy to join and that are at their level. A short time could be allowed (30–40 minutes) in which to link some activities well without dispersion, and a longer time (50–60 minutes) that would include initial and final greetings with children and parents, and some free time between one activity and another in which the children can satisfy their curiosity and wishes of that moment, seek out contact with others, etc.

For the preparation of sessions dedicated to music, whether short or long, here are some criteria to guide the sequence of activities:

- choose a song to be used always at the start and one for the conclusion (to serve as a signal to begin and to end and so to "frame" the session);
- alternate singing, dancing and using instruments;
- do not prolong the periods too much when children are sitting, or when they are moving;
- change activity when the children have been well satisfied, or may show signs of getting restless;
- tend to have singing as the first activity because the children get more excited with dancing and with instruments. Remember that the transition from singing to dancing, from dancing to instruments and vice versa relaxes and reanimates.

According to the atmosphere of the group, the age of the children, their demands at that time and the repertoire chosen (longer, shorter, faster, quieter, etc.), the educator will establish how many songs they should sing one after another (old and new) before going on to singing circle games or dancing, and how much time to dedicate to instruments – bearing in mind that a change of activity with such small children requires a certain amount of time.

The essential thing is to watch them attentively so that you can observe signs of enjoyment, attention, tiredness and, naturally, improvement.

The suggestions that follow are intended mainly for playschools and music centres. Those that require the presence of more adults are particularly intended for music centres. However, the parents are always there in the background because their contribution is vital. They need to repeat at home the activities carried out at playschool (ask the educator) or at the music sessions. Being with their children and praising and encouraging their first efforts can facilitate the acquisition of this other means of communication and their musical development.

We are also thinking of the parents who do not send their children to playschool or music sessions. They will find ideas here for activities with their children that are enjoyable, stimulating and attractive.

6.2 So Many Ways to Sing

6.2.1 First Experiences

A mother is holding her two-month-old baby on her lap, a playschool educator is on the carpet surrounded by four to five babies aged four to six months that are in infant seats or on a little rug. "Ask them to sing? That doesn't make much sense. Can you really make music with them? They are so small!!".

Let us sing something and carefully observe the children's behaviour, their expression, posture, arms, legs ... Is anything happening?

After the first verse of the song we stop and continue to observe them with an inviting and smiling expression. A force or wavelength has been created that unites us with each child. Something has happened and the little ones are working on it. We wait for five to ten seconds. We are not worried about remaining silent and we are not in a hurry to recommence. The children are working it out and let us respect that.

After a while we sing our song again and continue like that several times with singing followed by moments of silence. It is a way of coaxing the children and arousing their attention, interest and desire to communicate.

Sooner or later it will happen that, in the pauses, there will be some vocal intervention on the part of the infants. At times, a child might begin to vocalize before the adult stops, and at that point the adult, instead of continuing with the song, stops and listens carefully, and then might repeat the sounds produced by the child and wait. This can continue for four to five minutes altogether and even more if the child's attention and circumstances permit. The experience is repeated on subsequent days (ideally every day). The adult will become aware that the infant's sounds are not produced by chance but that they have the sense of a "reply", a first attempt at dialogue or proto-conversation (as we saw in Chapter 1), that will continue and be enriched over time.

These first vocalizations in response to the adult's singing are more frequent if the mother has sung often during pregnancy and if she continues to sing. They are likely to be less frequent or even absent if this experience of singing is new for the infant. However, this should not cause discouragement. As the children gradually experience singing on a daily basis, they begin to respond and to enjoy exploring their voice, a kind of exploration that is different from the kind they do as they prepare to speak. They begin to experiment with their musical babbling with the characteristics that we pointed out in Chapter 3.

The adult can also sing the song without words, but with syllables like "pam" or "ma". As we have seen (also in Chapter 3), the presence or absence of words in the adult's song does not influence the quality and variety of the child's response.

These moments of invitation to "sung" dialogue are not, however, the only moments of musical communication with the children. There are times during the day, at home or at playschool, in which singing enters as entertainment or a game. We sing while the baby is being fed, is having a bath, while the nappy is being changed, and in this way the child becomes accustomed to this second language as another way of communicating. In fact, as we have already seen, there are often reactions with vocal sounds or syllables repeated at the same pitch if the adults speak, and with sounds of varying pitch if they sing (rec. no. 10). This means that the child soon captures the difference between speaking and singing and reacts in a different way to each.

However, we must specify that singing is not the simple juxtaposition of two different languages, but rather a third event having its own significance that comes from the interaction between music and words.

Singing is, therefore, a unique event (not the sum of two events) that asks for symbolic investment, first of all through the rhythmic-melodic structure and the attitude of whoever interprets it (at least while the children do not yet understand the words and so cannot capture their significance), and later they are drawn to the global event. In any case, the infants soon memorize the melody. They recognize songs and make it clear which ones they prefer. The repetition and variation that the structure of a song generally contains create expectations that are satisfied from time to time (through repetition), or surprises (through the variations) that renew the experience of pleasure (Stern, 1977; Imberty, 2002).

Another way of encouraging the children to join in is to sing whilst holding them in your arms and playing with a song. Movement games can be done by lifting them high and then low, for example, or twirling them round or bouncing, etc. Movements can be suggested by the songs or they can be invented.

For example:

Giro giro rosa gialla la mimosa [Ring a ring o'roses, the mimosa is yellow]
prato verde cielo blu [green grass, blue sky (Lift the child up)]
tutti cascan giù giù giù [We all fall down down down (Bring the child down as if he/she were falling down)]

Ring a ring o'roses,
A pocketful of posies.
ah-tishoo, ah-tishoo. [Lift the child up]
We all fall down. [Bring the child down as if he/she were falling down]

Or:

Il grillo John è un furbacchion [John the cricket is very smart]
canta e balla pum pum pum pum pum [He sings and dances, pum ... (jumping)]
sopra un muro suona il tamburo [Sitting on a wall he plays a drum (lift the child up high)]
pum pum pum pum pum pum pum [(bring the child down again)]

Songs can also be used for games of volume and speed. As regards the first, they can sing two lines quietly whispering and two lines loud and strong. The transfer from quiet to loud (or vice versa) can be sudden, or it can be preceded by crescendos or diminuendos. As regards the speed, variations can be introduced, for example, either by singing a verse slowly as if tired and then singing a verse quickly as if in a hurry (*La lumaca e il topolino* [The snail and the mouse], *Jack and Jill*) or by beginning slowly and progressively getting faster or vice versa (*This little piggie*). These variations are more effective and entertain the children more if they move around the room according to the speed of the song. Another possibility is to stop and look mysterious just before a word or a line, maybe the last one of the verse, and then sing it quickly in a lighthearted way.

The variations suggested here should be done with songs that the children have already heard many times before so that the variations can cause surprise and amusement. Once the educators realize how these variations work, they can compose songs that are suited to the situation of the moment. Another kind of intervention is to change the words of a song that the children already know according to the circumstances. For example, if they want to sing *Il grillo John*, instead of the line about the drum, they can sing "sitting on a wall he sucks his thumb" and then conclude with syllables or nonsense words like *suck suck* or *yum yum*.

Songs can also be chosen to mark some daily events like their favourite lullaby, or their bath time song, their going-out song and so on.

For the songs to be incisive there is need for plenty of expression. The songs themselves suggest marked changes of facial expression and vocal characteristics (tone, intensity, speed, etc.) that make this possible.

Just allow yourself to be guided by the situations you wish to represent and emphasize them: surprise, sadness, tiredness, energy, persuasiveness, fun.

This will require use of a repertoire that contains the musical characteristics already mentioned, and that is also varied, enjoyable and flexible enough to have multiple uses.

6.2.2 Let Us Sing Together

When children reach the age of one, they become active in a different way during a song. They no longer make free sounds that are more or less vaguely connected to what the adult is singing. Now they participate by means of imitation, at first with barely a few syllables and then with interventions that lengthen in duration and precision.

Without anyone explicitly asking them, their spontaneous behaviour is that of imitating the adults by singing together with them, urged on by the need to adopt their means of communication. The free organization of sounds in cells or short melodic motifs is left for other moments.

The typology of songs presented in Chapter 2 can give many ideas to encourage the children in different ways according to their age.

The first possibility and easiest is to use songs with an echo, at times on the same notes as the words that they are echoing, at times with different words. With these songs, the children can easily join in at the echo without having to wait a long time to learn the song because there are no words to remember. They can be enticed to sing by opening up a kind of dialogue, then stopping before the echo and wait for them to continue.

For example:

> L'anatroccolo, occolo ... occolo
> nel viottolo, ottolo ... ottolo [...] [The duckling on the path ...]

Here you can stop after the first "ottolo" and wait so that the children have a chance to sing the repeat.

Here are other examples:

> Giovannino perdi perdigiorno
> ha perso il tram di mezzo mezzogiorno... orno orno.
> Ha perso il turno, ha perso la quota,
> ha perso la testa ma poi era vuota ... ota ota [...]
> [Johnny the idler
> missed the midday tram
> He missed his turn, he missed his share,
> he lost his head, but then it was empty]

If no one joins in, the educator just continues, but does not say anything ("Well, isn't anyone going to sing?"), so that musical language is not interrupted by speech. The song might not have an echo, but it could have syllables that are repeated that children join in on quite early, as in "The horn on the bus goes beep, beep, beep" in the singing circle game *The wheels on the bus*. It is up to the educator to notice if the children begin to join in during the song on some words that attract them most, and so these are good points at which to stop and allow for the dialogue.

Towards the age of 15–18 months, the children's singing interventions can become longer and so you should continue to encourage them by stopping every now and then during the song. This could be before a key word (often at the end of the phrase), then halfway through a phrase, before a phrase, etc. The important thing is that the children are being encouraged to continue by your expression or general attitude. Of course, this game can be done with songs that the children have known for a long time.

For example, you can start singing *Happy birthday to* ... and wait to see if any child (if not all) sings a sound that resembles (at first maybe barely) the "you" of the song.

Other examples:

> *Questo è l'occhio bello, questo è suo ... [wait] fratello.*
> *Questa è la chiesina, questo è il ... campanello [...]*
> [This is a pretty eye, and this is its ... brother.
> This is the little church, and this is the ... steeple]

Or:

> *La bella lavanderina che lava i... fazzoletti*
> *per i poveretti della ... città [...]*
> [The pretty washerwoman who washes the ... handkerchiefs
> for the poor of the ... town]

Or:

> *Teresa Teresina fammi cuocere la ... gallina [...]*
> [Teresa Teresina let me cook the ... hen]

> Jack and Jill went up the ... hill,
> To fetch a pail of ... water.

> Hickory dickory ... dock,
> The mouse ran up the ... clock.

> Little Bo-Peep has lost her ... sheep

We stress the need for all this to take place without speaking, because if something is spoken it could mean that they could lose the thread of the musical discourse in which they are immersed.

Number songs are an interesting repertoire to have. In addition to teaching the numbers, they have the advantage of being adaptable to the number of children present and they can be dramatized, that is, a child does what the song says and as the number changes other children join in. For example, with the song *Tre oche andavano a ber* [Three geese went to drink], three children can move around the room. In the verse "Four geese went to drink ..." a fourth child joins in, and so forth. Another example is *One man went to mow ...*

If there is some kind of change with each number (an action, animal, colour, etc.) the next line probably changes and therefore so does the rhyme. Consequently, this kind of song can be useful for introducing the children to rhyming games.

For example:

> *Uno. La signora veste di bruno perché di bianco non vuol vestir,*
> *mira la dondondella mira la dondondà.*
> *Due. La signora scioglie il bue [...]*
> [One. The lady dresses in brown because she doesn't like to wear white.
> Look at the dondondella look at the dondonda.
> Two. The lady unties the ox ...]

> This old man, he played one,
> He played knick-knack on my thumb ...

> The ants go marching one by one ...

If we observe the category of cumulative songs, we notice that here we have to remember all the elements that are being added on each time round so that we can repeat all of them each time.

Children love these songs because they contain the surprise element of something new that is added on in each verse and there is the security of returning to what has already appeared in the song. Here we think of songs like *Old McDonald had a farm, Little Rooster, I know an old lady*, etc. If the words are few and simple and if the children are at least two and a half years old, the various elements can be assigned to different children and each child sings one (with the help of the educator if necessary).

Other elements can be added on (animals, instruments, parts of the body, etc.) and the children can be asked to make suggestions.

With some songs we can involve the children in the choice of what element could come next. If we are singing, for example, *Old McDonald*, the children can decide what animal comes next without necessarily having to follow the order in the original version.

After the age of two, children are able to sing an entire song alone, at first the short ones with four lines (*Hickory dickory dock, Humpty Dumpty*) then longer ones with two or even three verses like *I'm a little teapot, Mary had a little lamb*, etc.

In general it is the educator who starts things off and begins to sing (a few words or the first phrase) and then stops, but at this age the children are able to start themselves. If the activity is collective, though, the educator should be the one to start so that all begin on the same note. Remember to use the medium high register that children use and to avoid (which happens often) starting a song in a key that is too low for them to reach.

It could happen that, when they stop singing, maybe while the educator is busy with something else, a child might begin to sing alone. This behaviour shows us that at that age, children sing when they feel the need to do so. This can happen at any moment during that day or several days later. On the other hand, it is not common for a child younger than two and a half to three years to sing if asked to, especially if the request does not come from the parents. The child is continuously processing the assimilation of experiences accomplished day by day and the work of reprocessing during which he/she periodically feels the need to spontaneously produce something. This can emerge in conjunction with similar events (someone is singing) or at the most unexpected times. Generally, on those occasions, the child is self-absorbed and what he/she is doing is not for the sake of any adult but to satisfy a need. If the adult intervenes, the child generally stops.

When children sing an entire song alone, it is important that they do not always sing it completely from beginning to end on their own, but that they alternate sometimes with the educator and among themselves: alone/everyone (educator/children) or in two groups. In the latter case, they alternate according to the indications given by the educator (two lines for each group, then one line). After the song has been sung a few times in "alternate choirs", the educator from time to time invites a child to "conduct", pointing to the group whose turn it is to sing. It is only later (four to five years of age) that the alternating can be done with only two children. The use of alternating means that the song is repeated over and over (and so helping them learn it) without the boredom of simple repetition. Most of all it helps them to know how to listen and wait their turn, to capture the sense of the phrase and to acquire the skill of segmentation. Actually, the children who have already developed this skill can indicate the change of group on time while those who have not yet developed it just conduct at random.

Activities to help acquire the ability to sing in tune can be stimulated by an echo activity with melodies without words. It is a form of adult-child alternating, and even though it is not a dialogue in the strict sense (there is no "response", but an imitation), it nevertheless stimulates a personal intervention. In this activity that we can call "the echo game", we need to ask the children to "repeat" in order to direct them towards imitation rather than leave them free to respond in a different way, which is something we shall suggest later in the section on invention.

The educator talks to the children and, after inviting them to repeat "exactly what I sing", sings with the syllable "pam" or "la" a short motif of three to five sounds, that can be tonal (for example: *sol-mi-do*) or pentatonic (for example *sol-la-so-mi*) or modal (for example: *re-mi-fa-mi-re*); then immediately afterwards gives a sign inviting them to repeat. After having suggested three to four phrases, inviting all the children to sing together after her, the educator goes on to individual work telling each child that now she will sing a song only for him, so that he will repeat it, and then suggests a motif for each child. If they are two years old, few will agree to repeat alone, but at around two and a half to three they are more willing to do so.

The game can be played in different ways, according to the educator's creativity. For example, she and one of the children can go to opposite corners of the room as if they were really doing the echo at a distance. They could also use toy telephones and pretend to sing over the telephone.

The imitation might be exact or similar (more or less) and, in this way, the educator gets information about the level of progress reached by the child in singing in tune. Here, as in all activities, the children are always and only praised for their effort in repeating, no matter what level of precision they achieve. It is only later, around the age of four to five, that one should begin to give suggestions: "Good! Now we'll do it again, but we'll sing it higher (or lower)" and do the echo again accompanying the sound with your hands as if you are throwing the sound upwards or downwards.

The periods dedicated to singing and, generally, whenever music is being made in an organized situation (playschool, music centre), can be introduced and closed with two songs that frame the period, like two signature tunes that the children can recognize as the delimiters of a temporal event. These can be invented by the educators, or be adaptations of known tunes.

For the beginning in particular, we suggest a structure that includes a response by the children to the individual call made by the educator. To hear oneself called by name is an aid towards self discovery and it produces a feeling of satisfaction. To begin with, the educator will answer for them until the time, from 18–24 months, when they can answer for themselves.

Here is an example of an entrance song (rec. no. 17):

> *Benvenuti tutti quanti stiamo insieme per cantare,*
> *per suonare per danzare ci vogliamo divertir!*
> *Andrea! Sono qui. Virginia! Sono qui.*
> [Welcome all, we are here to sing,
> to play, to dance, we want to have fun!
> Andrea! I'm here. Virginia! I'm here.]

When all the names are called, the verse is repeated.

For the conclusion, a song can be used that says goodbye to each child individually or a singing circle game could be used that contains a farewell in the words:

> *Tutti vogliamo camminare, camminare, camminare.*
> *Tutti vogliamo camminare da oggi fino a domani.*
> [We all want to walk, walk, walk,
> We all want to walk from today until tomorrow.]

Other actions are added: clap our hands, stamp our feet, jump, twirl around, bounce, etc., and the song concludes with the following verse:

Tutti vogliamo fare un inchino, fare un inchino, fare un inchino.
Tutti vogliamo fare un inchino da oggi fino a domani.
[We all want to bow, bow, bow,
We all want to bow from today until tomorrow.]

To work with interactive songs involves giving the children the opportunity to grow, not only in a musical environment, but also in their creative skills, as well as the opportunity to participate with their own ideas and abilities in building this experience that should be emotionally positive, pleasurable and even exciting.

6.2.3 Inventing

When infants of a few months old are vocalizing, they are already inventing. Of course they are exploring and improvising during a phase when they do not yet have control over their vocal capabilities. Newborns cannot repeat what they have produced, yet there is a deliberateness in their vocalizations, especially when they are encouraged to dialogue. This is why we can confidently affirm that they are "producers" before they are "imitators".

If a parent leaves a recorder turned on close to the child, from the age of two months they will hear repetitions of many vocalizations and they will notice how there will be a distinction between them from the age of six months. Some of them will be mostly made up of repeated syllables (in preparation for speech) and others will include sounds of varying pitch (in preparation for singing; see Chapter 1). It is most likely that there will be vocalization directed towards singing if the mother has been singing or allowing the child to hear music.

In order for the newborns to feel encouraged to join in, it is important that the music not be continuous background music, but that it is present at specific moments: 15–20 minutes several times a day, alternating the times in which the singing is directed specifically towards them and times when music is being played for listening. It is best if those musical moments happen together with specific events (bath time, meal times, changing time, etc.).

You will often come across children from two years of age who are repeating vowels or syllables to themselves, singing with few sounds, very often while they are doing something else (like playing with building bricks or swinging). They sing these inventions sometimes as a long monologue that is very repetitive and sometimes in the form of phrases that accompany or describe the actions they are doing at that moment.

They can be encouraged to invent: "Shall we sing a song about this little pebble?", "A lullaby for the doll?", "The song about the donkey?" Children should be encouraged to invent, in other words, to freely express themselves. This demonstrates, as well as develops, the ability to control their phonatory apparatus on the one hand, and on the other, the sounds of our scale and the basic melodic structures of our musical system.

These inventions can also be activated by means of a collective activity in the form of a dialogue: the educator begins a story by singing an improvised melody, for example "Once there was a donkey that ..." and she beckons a child to continue. After the child sings (possibly a bit muffled or barely audible), the educator adds another line and then invites another child, and so they continue to sing the story for another two to six lines.

There can be dialogues even without words, but that use short melodies invented for the occasion. The educator addresses a child by singing a short motif (from three or four to seven or eight sounds) that can be tonal, pentatonic or modal, and waits for a response with a beckoning expression. Here the main objective is to encourage invention and not imitation. It could happen that the child will sing something different, but he/she might also imitate the motif just heard. If this happens two to three times, rather than ask the child to do something different (as that would be difficult for a child of that age to understand), you could say: "This time, you begin". In this way, after being asked to go first, the child might invent. In fact, even in this case it could happen that the child repeats one of the motifs sung earlier by the educator. In that case, she responds with a different sequence thus showing that there is encouragement to sing something different. The educator can even suggest non tonal melodies that are impossible to repeat and observe if the child still tries to repeat that outline or tries something completely different.

One way to encourage the skill of inventing different melodies could be to associate the melodies to objects or events. For example, take two puppets that represent a dog and a horse and say to the children "Now I'll sing a song that the dog will like" and invent a short motif. Then say, "Now I'll sing you a song that the horse will like" and invent a very different motif. Then you ask, "Who wants to sing a song that the dog will like and one that the horse will like?"

We mention in passing that this activity can be used to work on memorization and recognition. You can invent two different motifs and repeat them two to three times. Then ask the children to recognize them (all of them together first to gain confidence, then one by one): "Now I'll sing a song and you tell me if it's the dog's song or the horse's song. Who wants to recognize it?"

Towards the age of two and a half the children begin to play with words and to have fun changing them in the songs, especially if this game has been played previously by educators and parents. This is mostly about linguistic ability, even more so if they look for rhymes, but it is also about musical ability because it is necessary to respect the rhythmic structure of the phrase.

In songs that present a closed event that can be changed, it is easy to substitute the words. For example:

> *C'era una volta un papero vestito di pelle di bufalo,*
> *faceva ballar le papere sull'uscio di Dindirindé.*
> [Once there was a boy gosling dressed up in a buffalo skin,
> and he made the girl goslings dance out the door of the dindirindin]

The refrain is always the same:

> *Allez vous danser alla moda alla bracé.*

Here is a situation where we can change the character, the clothes and the action to make a rhyme:

> Once we saw Jenny Macgillygag dressed up so nicely in a laundry bag,
> With Tommy Mooney she played tag as they hopped out the door of the dindirindag.
> Once we saw Minnie dressed up in a pretty pinnie
> She went into a spinnie out the door of the dindirindinny.

The repetition and the variations hold the attention of the children, the change of name makes them feel they are main players, and the reworking of the lines helps them enter into the rhyming game.

Here is the invention of a child aged two years and nine months (in the recording, the pronunciation is not distinct, but she sings quite well in tune (rec. no. 43)):

> *C'era una volta mammetta vestita di pipetta,*
> *faceva a birichetta ull'uscio ndirindé. Allez vous danser ...*
> *C'era una volta papà vestito di torrone,*
> *mangiava un bottone ull'uscio ndirindé. Allez vous danser ...*
> [Once there was a little mummy dressed up as a little pipey,
> and she gave a little winkey as she went out the 'ndirinday. Allez vous danser ...
> Once there was a daddy dressed up as a nougat,
> and he ate a button on the way out the 'ndirinday. Allez vous danser ...]

They could have great fun changing the words in this nursery rhyme song:

> There was a crooked man and he walked a crooked mile,
> He found a crooked sixpence upon a crooked stile.
> He bought a crooked cat which caught a crooked mouse,
> And they all lived together in a little crooked house.

A song that is generally used for hand clapping along with the rhythm of the refrain can also be used to invent new verses:

> *C'era un cane tanto buffo si chiamava Pippo Kid.*
> *Pippo Pippo Kid [3 volte], si chiamava Pippo Kid.*
> [There was a funny dog called Pippo Kid.
> Pippo Pippo Kid (3 times), he was called Pippo Kid.]

With this song we could perhaps change only the animal and the name:

> There was a funny cat called Clarabel,
> Clara Clarabel [...]

Alternatively, we could change the refrain by putting in the animal's call:

> There was a funny duck called Daisy May,
> Qua qua qua qua qua [...]

The variation could also be in the presentation of the animal in the first line:

> There was a comical cow called Mooleemoo [...]
> There was a huge crocodile called Toothigums [...]
> There was a naughty goat called Spindlilegs [...]

In this case, you can opt for a refrain with the repetition of the name as in the original song (*Pippo Pippo Kid*), or else with the animal's sounds. In either case, this refrain stimulates the children to join in (rec. no. 19).

6.2.4 Songs and Movements

Singing can be enriched and reinforced by two other kinds of experience: the motor and the instrumental. We shall speak more about the use of instruments in a later section. Here we want to give suggestions on how to use the body in singing, both in action songs and in movement songs (circle games and other kinds of singing games). These are activities that help in the development of motor coordination and rhythmic-metric skills.

There is a long tradition in families and nursery schools of entertaining children with action songs. Although it generally depends on the imagination of the mother, grandmother or educator, it is also true that there are songs with words that suggest actions or that have even been composed specifically to help motor coordination.

We can mention a few songs that point out parts of the body (for example: *Head, shoulders, knees and toes*; *Hokey, Pokey*; *If you're happy and you know it*). At first, it is the parents who sing the song for the babies, but later the children are invited to sing along with their parents and other children.

They can sing stories (for example: *Three blind mice*, *Itsy bitsy spider*) and they can sing them with actions that indicate something about the characters (the mice are blind, the farmer's wife has a knife, fingers can be the spider) and the actions described in the song (running, cutting, climbing, rain falling).

The educator or the parent sings with actions, the child listens, observes and reprocesses. If and when the child wants to, they will do something themselves. They tend to imitate the adult but in their own way. In some cases, as we said, the words themselves suggest the actions to the children. For example:

Appare una manina, si mette a ballare,
si apre, si chiude e poi se ne va.
Adesso l'altra mano ... [ecc.]
[A hand appears and starts to dance.
It opens, it closes, and then goes away.
Now the other hand ... etc.]

It would make no sense to sing this song without moving.

Hands are undoubtedly the first means of expression that children begin to use and that they soon manage to control. This is confirmed by tradition in which there are many songs about hands. Some of these include:

Clap hands clap hands till daddy comes home
Where is thumbkin?
Right hand, left hand

These songs in general foster control over movement and they are often good for the kind of substituting we mentioned before. Instead of hands, they can clap their fingers, elbows, fists, feet, etc.

The song keeps the same melody and the parts of the body change (repetition and variation), thus allowing for assimilation of the musical structures and coordination of movements, in addition to learning about the parts of the body.

As to the question of the position of the children, before the age of six months they are being carried or are held in an infant seat. After the age of six months when they can sit up alone, they can begin to sit on a rug or airbed together with other children and the adults at the nursery school. The most usual position is for all to sit in a circle to allow for greater communication (they can all see each other) and to make it easier for the group to relate. It is an arrangement that helps everyone to feel included.

If on the one hand, we must point out that the attention span of small children is very short, on the other hand, it is fair to acknowledge that their capacity to observe, absorb and assimilate is extraordinary. In our experience described in earlier chapters, while we were singing, some children were able to stare at us for an incredibly long time for their age (six to eight months, a year), even for ten to 15 minutes continuously, being the time to sing two or three songs with variations and a story, often with their mouths open. It was as if a spell had been cast. Some of these children, when they were old enough to walk, as soon as they arrived they would run to the airbed to take their place and there they remained without moving until we went on to a movement activity.

We must also recognize that at that age they are quite slow at reacting. For example, if we sang a song with a line that says "Sun, sun, go round and round me" lifting their hands up, it could happen that in the next song a child would lift her hands up singing "sun, sun".

If we continue to introduce new songs and to revise the songs already learned, they will always expect to have to repeat what has been learned and also look for something new. The extraordinary memory that children possess means that towards the age of two and a half to three years they can sing many songs containing more than one verse. This happened with the children in our research when they had this experience daily and it was always encouraged in playschool and at home.

We conclude this section by mentioning circle games and singing games. These are the most common activities in all playschools and even more so in kindergarten schools where children move with more confidence and adeptness.

A circle game is a collective action through which children learn to hold hands, to control time, for example to walk with varying speed and to try to keep to the tempo, and to dominate space, for example trying to stay in a circle (very difficult at their age), exploring up and down, changing direction (right, left, ahead, backwards), turning themselves around.

There are many circle game songs (*The farmer in the dell, Here we go 'round the mulberry bush, We'll all join in the circle, Hokey Pokey*, etc.) and others that can be used for this kind of game (see Staccioli, Ritscher 1988). For example, they can be alone in the centre of the circle, or walk around within the circle and they act out the speed (slower, faster, stopping), the highs and lows (lift their hands up on expressions like "blue sky" and then lower them for "we all fall down") and the soft/loud (walk on tiptoe and then bang their feet on the ground).

In singing games, they could stand in two rows facing each other and go forwards and backwards, either at the same time or one row at a time.

6.2.5 Stories with Singing

We are familiar with the role played by storytelling in infancy and its contribution in so many areas (symbolic identification, narrative structure, sense of time, vocabulary, grammar and syntax, etc.). Stories are there to be listened to, even though children, when they know the story well, intervene and rob the narrator of a phrase, in particular the most typical of a particular character (the wolf, the grandmother, the giant ...) that they have memorized well.

Can stories also call on their musical skills? Yes. You just have to introduce interventions that are sung or rhythmic and that stimulate the participation of children also at the musical level. We can take the example of *The Travelling Star*:

> *Once upon a time high up in the sky there was a little star that loved to travel.* [point your finger to a spot up high] *One day the little star saw lots of little children playing in a garden, and she decided to go down to meet them. Uuuuuuuuh ...* [sing a long descending glissando while moving your hand from high down to the ground] *Bump! Her landing wasn't very gentle and the little star began to cry: "Waaa! Waaa! I hurt myself. I hurt myself."* [sing it in so-mi, see the musical example in the appendix]
>
> *But the children had already gone home and it was getting dark. The little star was still crying: "Waaa! Waaa! I hurt myself. I hurt myself." After a while along came a squirrel:*

"Who are you?"
"I am the Travelling Star."
"What's the matter with you, little star?"
"I fell from the sky and I hurt myself."
"Come here and I'll make you better."
The squirrel took her in her arms and began to rock her and sing:
"Lullaby, lullaby, little star you sleep a while.
When you wake your leave you'll take, and fly up to the big big sky."
[Repeat the song again; the second time gradually reduce the volume and finish very quietly].
The night passed and morning came. Before the sun rose up, the squirrel lifted up the little star and gave her a little push up towards the sky, ooooooooh. ... [sing a long ascending glissando while lifting your arms up towards the sky] *and the little star went far far away and was gone.*

In this little story – which I invented in order to create association between a particular sound and a particular movement – the children immediately join in spontaneously, both on the descending and ascending glissandos and, in this way, they are adopting the bases of the direction of the pitches used in our culture. After hearing the story a few times, the children soon learn to sing the lament and the lullaby (melodies built only on so and mi) and they join in easily as the story proceeds.

You can also sing phrases of stories the children already know by using either a known tune or an invented one. The activity is easier and they join in more if the same phrase is repeated a few times.

The singing part of a story can be a rhyme, like the one (Cornoldi, 1968, p. 34) that I chose for the story about Merlin the Wizard:

Once upon a time in a faraway land, there lived Merlin the Wizard. Merlin liked to sleep very much. One day while he was sleeping [the most common imitation is to bend their head sideways, put their hands under their cheek and snore for a few seconds] *along came some little sheep and they said "baa, baa, baa". Merlin the Wizard woke up angrily and said:* [they can leave out this phrase and make a gesture of waking up and say "angrily"]
"Who has woken me up?"
"It was us, the little sheep, baa, baa, baa."
"Then I'll cast a magic spell and you'll stop singing."
[Recite the following nursery rhyme while banging a little stick like a magic wand against the floor. It can be a rhythm stick or sonorous tube. Follow the rhythm of the nursery rhyme, not the pulse.]

"An dan tickey tan, [voices low, heavy and dark]
se me comparay,
aleh lakeh pumeh te. [voices high, light, quiet]
Beeeeeeeeees!"

An   dan,   ti - ke   tan,   se   me,   com - pa   rè,

a - le   la - ke,   pu - me   te.   Bis!

*And Merlin the Wizard went back to sleep. After a while along came the little
cockerels:*
Cock-a-doodle-doo, cock-a-doodle-doo
"Who has woken me up?" [...]

After several animals pass by (the children's suggestions can be used) and after
repeating Merlin's magic spell, we go to the conclusion:

At that moment Maga Magoo arrived and said: [in a nasal voice]
*"Merlin, Merlin. You are very naughty. You won't let the animals sing. Now I'm going
to cast another magic spell and they will all be able to sing again."*
[Bang out the rhythm of the following nursery rhyme on the ground]

"Bum bum bing bing [voice low on the first two syllables, high on the other two]
now I want you all to sing [voice normal]
zic zac ticky tac [voice high and quiet]
now let us sing."
[and the children sing the lines of all the animals that had appeared before]

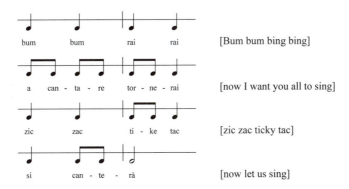

In telling this story, besides needing to vary your voice to depict the characters, it also involves reciting the two rhymes rhythmically and with changes of vocal tone, and instrumental accompaniment so that the rhythmic structure can be better assimilated (voice, movement, instrument). Therefore, the children should also have something in their hands to bang on the floor to beat out the rhythm of the rhyme. On the word "Beeeees" (see Merlin's spell) they can make a wide gesture, lifting their arms upwards to keep the sound long.

A story of this kind – this is one I thought up for the children on the *inCanto* project – allows for different kinds of intervention in that the children can think up the lines said by the animals and respond "it was us, the little sheep" to the question put by Merlin the Wizard instead of the teacher. However, the most important intervention and the one that they all like best is the part where they recite the magic spell accompanying the rhythm with the object-instrument in their hand, an intervention they look forward to and perform with great enthusiasm.

As they get older, they will gradually recite the rhymes with more precision, both with the instrument and with the words. These interventions in stories are not something that is taught and they are not assigned. The children themselves feel the desire to join in and they do it more and more spontaneously as their skills develop.

6.3 ...To Play Instruments

A ten-month-old baby is in the playpen surrounded by toys and objects of various kinds. The mother is apart reading. The baby plays as he takes and leaves different things. Then, all of a sudden, he pulls himself up by holding onto the edge. There is something in his hand and he throws it out. The mother observes with half-closed eyelids. The child takes another toy, shakes it and throws it out. He takes another, shakes it and throws it in the playpen. He does the same with all the objects and toys. Some he throws out and others he throws in. His mother observes curiously trying to understand if the child is doing this at random or if he is making a selection. If it is a choice, what is guiding that choice? The colour? The shape?

All of a sudden she realizes what it is. The child shakes whatever they take up, and some of the toys make a noise and the others do not. The selection is clear. Whatever makes no sound goes out. Whatever makes a noise stays in. The fascination that sound-producing objects have over children in their early months is really extraordinary. The child gazes at it and wants to touch it, especially if it makes sound on its own (like a bell), then shakes it, scratches it, tastes it, bangs it or bangs something else with it (the floor, table, wall).

Parents often notice how easy it is to attract children with a bunch of keys, not only because they contain so many elements but also because they make a sound. In fact, one of the first things a child does with them is to shake them.

An object to explore (not necessarily a musical instrument) is normally shaken, banged, or rubbed. If the children then see the parents or teacher play a tambourine, rhythm sticks or rattles, they memorize this use and, as soon as they see those instruments, they try to grasp them as if they know what to do with them. Then they play them to their heart's content.

As soon as newborns manage to grasp something, they can be given "instruments" (rattles, maracas, etc.) so as to satisfy their desire for sound and at the same time begin to build coordination between ear, eye and hand. If they can manage to sit up, you can put a drum in front of them and watch how they explore it.

At home you can also give them a small electronic keyboard. Infants just bang at it obviously at random, but this instrument has the advantage of producing a long sound if the child's hand remains holding down the keys. When they grow older, children begin to discover the difference between high and low sounds and the possibility of using just one finger instead of their palm, especially if they see their parents do so.

In order to allow children to really experience musical instruments, you can prepare a basket with lots of instruments (we are referring to small percussion instruments) and put it in the middle of the circle and observe the children for a few minutes. They hurry over to the basket (crawling if they cannot yet walk), take the instruments, play them in various ways, they choose them, change them, take one from the child beside them, etc.

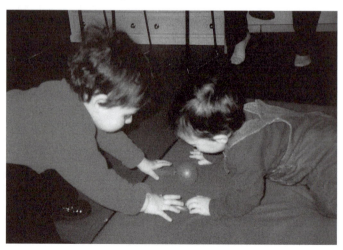

Sometimes they concentrate more on one instrument, other times they continually change; sometimes they bang a drum with the drumstick or with their hands, other times they bang the maracas on the floor or on the tambourine without getting bored. In this way, they are demonstrating a kind of craving for an object that produces sound and the need to satisfy it. Of course there can be timid children that hold back, but later, when the others are already partly satisfied with their choice, the shy child also picks an instrument. Of course, they do not yet distinguish between the gesture that produces and the sound that is emitted. It is still a global experience (seeing, touching, hearing) that fascinates them.

As the children play all together, this produces a sound that we "educated" adults do not consider pleasing: "This is chaotic", "There's too much racket", "What a din". The children themselves are not disturbed because they are "working" and each one is concentrated on what he/she is doing. Some devices can be used to reduce the "density" of sound by eliminating, for example, Basque tambourines (those with the rattles), or tubular bells, that is, instruments with a lot of resonance that are inclined to drown out the others. In this way, the children will be able to hear their own instrument. It is important that these be moments of freedom, of being "bathed in sound" before "organized" time begins.

To have this time of freedom (choosing of instrument and exploring it) and to pass on to organized time (accompanying a song) is fundamental in order to allow them experience two different ways of playing instruments, one individual and the other collective. Children learn this soon and they also learn to accept (at first with difficulty but later on as something normal) leaving the instruments to go on to another activity or to go home.

With children of 18 months and over (although also with newborns if their parents are with them), during exploring time, all of a sudden the teacher gives a signal (claps her hands, plays a trill on the keyboard or with a flute) and begins to sing, beating out the time with the instrument in her hands. Gradually, the children give her their attention and "join in" by accompanying the singing. They really just play what they can and then at around the age of two, they begin to synchronize with the beat, at first in short bursts (they stop now and then) and irregularly (the regularity they achieve for a few sounds is then lost and found again several times), and then it becomes progressively more continuous and regular (see Chapter 3, section 3.9).

In fact, to move and to strike something in time with the music, that is, technically speaking, trying to synchronize with the isochronous beat of the music being listened to, is behaviour that most children do spontaneously before the age of one. You often see them rocking back and forth or banging an object or instrument (even if they obviously cannot yet synchronize). To keep to the beat while singing or listening to music is a practice that allows children to build the bases of this important form of structuring time that constitutes the structure of our western music.

Towards the age of two (but it can be tried earlier), you can begin to invite children to play only at some points in the song. The teacher can invent some expedient means to prevent them from playing instruments all the time. For example, it can be suggested that they lift their instruments up high when they are not playing. The teacher leads the game. With hands held up high they sing the verse, then they accompany the refrain by keeping to the beat or making short interventions of varying kinds. If, for example, they do the songs with an echo or with a verse with animal sounds, they can play only for the echo or for the animal lines. If the phrases of a song in the verse or refrain finish with a long sound on the last syllable, they can give two beats during this long note, that is, at a moment that we might consider to be a bit "empty". This can also be done if there are pauses. For example, the refrain to *Filastrocca a voce bassa* [Whispered nursery rhyme] is formed by four short melodic phrases sung on the vowel "o", that always end with a long sound: Oh oh oh oh ohhhhhhh. On the last long "oh" of each phrase an instrumental intervention would be interesting, for example, two short notes.

Children begin to enter into the game of the two final notes towards the age of two, even if they still find it hard to control it and, instead of two notes, they play three or four. It is as if, once the command to play has been given, it is hard to stop. However, it is all right like that. It is important to remember that development has to come spontaneously.

It is pointless to insist that they do it well, or to say "you should only play two sounds", because it is not the number that is helping them learn (even though the child is capable of understanding it), but the motor control guided by auditory memory. The important thing is to repeat the activity often, until the children gradually develop this specific skill (each according to their own rhythm) and can join in correctly.

As we said in Chapter 5, this is a kind of learning that is done by observation and not by explicit teaching or through drilling. There is no point in drawing the attention of the children to aspects of rationale because their cognitive development is not yet ready. In any case, rhythm requires direct experience of temporal structure, an experience that necessarily passes through the body in movement, not through numbers and calculations. The important thing is that the teachers play the instrument correctly so that the children can feel induced to take part in the activity until they gradually make it theirs.

Classical music can also be used for the children to keep rhythm with instruments. To synchronize with the beat, you can use marches such as Prokofiev's *March Number 10* (from *Music for children*, op. 65) or a *Marche militaire* by Schubert, a mazurka by Chopin and any other rhythmic piece in binary or ternary metre.

With a march, you can play the "band game". On finishing an activity with instruments, the teacher can play Prokofiev's March on a keyboard (or let them listen to it on CD). The beginning of this piece (clear beat with two notes that alternate) can be the introduction. The children are seated on the floor, then they stand up holding their instrument and they begin to move around the room (in a row or a line imitating a band, but freely). They play to the beat with their instrument and walk more or less in time with the music.

This activity could also be chosen as the conclusion of the period dedicated to making music at playschool (or a meeting held in a different place).

A particularly stimulating repertoire for "instrument playing" are the songs about instruments or any other songs where the children can have fun joining in by using their voice to imitate the sounds of instruments or particular syllables. For example, *This old man, Pop! goes the weasel, The ants go marching, Il grillo John*, etc. You can also change the words of known songs to introduce instruments, e.g. *Old McDonald had a band ...*

There can be different strategies used. The instruments can be played when they are named (or when they come to the "knick knack", "pop" etc.) and, in this case, the children keep the beat while they sing the whole line. Alternatively, they just play the rhythm with which their sound is sung (*pum pum pum pum*). They play the rhythm with the named instrument (or sound), but without singing; that is, they substitute their voice with the instrument. Although these alternatives may seem difficult, it is actually what generally happens spontaneously, given that with this repertoire the children hardly sing because they are taken up with the instruments.

When the instrumental interventions are assigned to the children, each one according to their instrument, it is important that the teacher establish a moment in the song when the instruments play together, otherwise the children would only play once in the whole song and this would leave them dissatisfied. The consequence would be that they get distracted and play, even when it's not their turn. This activity gives training in waiting your turn with the music as guide and in memorizing the words of the song.

Towards the age of two, children manage to play not only the beat with the instruments but also some rhythmic patterns assimilated through songs, nursery rhymes and dancing. In the refrain of *Pippo Kid* (see previously), the repetition of the name (or the line with the animal call) can be accompanied by an instrument that plays the rhythm (not the beat!) and later substituted by instrumental playing. This work can be stimulating, even when done with rhymes, provided that rhymes are chosen that have a repetitive rhythmic structure or have small variants like, for example, that used in the story about Merlin the Wizard (see above).

With instruments it is a good idea, from 18–20 months onwards, to have activities of the echo type to help improve their perceptive ability, and the "question/answer" type to foster their inventive ability.

If there are plenty of pairs of rhythm sticks, it is better to make the echo with this instrument as it has a clear sound. Otherwise make the most of the instruments available.

The teacher turns to the children after distributing the instruments, and invites them to play "exactly the same" as she does. Then she plays a rhythmic cell of few sounds:

Immediately after this, she gestures to the children to play. At 18 months maybe few will be able to repeat the same rhythm, but later the children develop this skill. After giving three to four examples, with children of two and over the teacher can go on to ask children individually to play a rhythm. With the instruments, doing it alone is less embarrassing (than singing) and many of them will probably play, even if the results are still approximate.

A slightly more challenging way of doing it for children of about two and a half is to ask them to use their percussion instruments to imitate a given rhythm with rhythmic-melodic phrases played on a keyboard or sung. The teacher plays rhythms on the keyboard with different chords and the children spontaneously select and reproduce only the rhythm. The same activity can be done by singing something: "Now I'll sing some music and you repeat after me but ... we'll pretend that you have lost your voices. What can you do? Do you want to try to play it with an instrument?" The children have no problem following the rhythm, according to the level of development of their ability. The schema for rhythmic invention is similar to that given for melodic invention.

"Let's try to talk with the instruments. Each one can invent their own music." The teacher turns to a child and plays a rhythm, then stops and waits with an air of invitation. In this case too, as we have said in the case of singing, it could happen that the child imitates her. She just has to do a different rhythm a couple of times encouraging them to play their own music. She might even try some irregular rhythms that are impossible to repeat and observe if the response is trying to imitate the structure. Whether the children repeat or change, it is in any case important to let them play the game of "question/answer" with the teacher or with a companion. When this activity is repeated on subsequent days, the children could go first.

With instruments, as with the voice, the inventions can be associated with puppets, atmospheric events, animals, etc. In this case, the children could be asked to invent "the dog's music" and "the horse's music", as suggestions for melodic inventions (see section 6.2.3). You could also distribute different animal puppets to all the children and each one can invent the music for his/her animal.

Instrumental invention can also be done as free expression. A short verse could be used to frame the activity:

> Let's all play music, all together. Loud loud loud, soft soft soft.
> Let's hear yours, please, let's hear yours. Play play play, play play play.

At this point the child who volunteers, or who is indicated by the teacher, invents his/her "music" with his/her instrument. The verse can be repeated between one invention and the next if there are few children, or after every three or four if there are many.

Contrary to what one would expect, the invented music by children in this collective situation is very short, at times perhaps of only two sounds, while in individual situations, like during the free time when they are allowed to choose an instrument, the children often play for a long time, even if in a rather repetitive way.

In this activity that we have just mentioned, we have also introduced the loud/soft element, a fundamental dimension in music that has already been introduced as a fun element in singing and which works very well with instruments too. It is good to turn to this frequently, both in the accompaniments and in the echo and invention activities. In *Filastrocca a voce bassa* [Whispered nursery rhyme]*, for example, when the refrain is sung for the last time, the parts for instruments and voice can get progressively softer using a diminuendo and arriving at pianissimo. Children have great fun with this.

6.4 To Dance and Listen

6.4.1 Dancing

The CD is revolving, lively rhythmic music is coming from the disc-player, and the children run towards the teacher. They have recognized a dance that they have been exploring for the past few days and they are eager to do it again. Perhaps to say "dance" is slightly optimistic. We could really call it "proto-dance", or simply musical activities with dance music. Children between the ages of two and three still want to move freely. Although they experience collective movement through the musical activities, they find it hard to respect the constrictions of a circular structure.

Moving for them is an existential need. From the time that they are very small, their movement is mostly connected to adults, from the swaying during prenatal life when the mother was walking, to being rocked, and the bouncing, being lifted up, twirled around, etc. that parents do with them. As soon as they can move autonomously, they plunge right in, and to do so with music, freely, is a moment of satisfaction from which they derive the incentive to go on to gradually acquire a series of accomplishments (coordination, lateralization, socialization, etc).

We have already said something about musical activities (above). Here we are speaking explicitly about dancing where the children are not asked to sing, but to move together with others guided by the music.

Very often at playschools, there are many two to three-year-old children and only two teachers, and so it is almost impossible to do much more than the classical walking in a circle holding hands like in a circle game. But, if the organization of activities in the playschool permits, it could be done in turn with small groups of six to eight children, as the teachers would be able to manage that. Different kinds of music would allow them to do circle games more slowly or more quickly and, if there are few children, or if they are around three years of age, you can introduce a change of direction into the dance (towards the right and then towards the left) when the music changes.

Wherever it is possible to organize afternoon classes at the playschool with the participation of the parents, or in a musical centre, dancing is an attractive activity. Parents play a fundamental role here, as alternating adult-child in the circle allows for a change in choreography, even if it is always of an elementary kind. The simplest dances for these activities with the parents are mostly those that are done in a circle, either looking towards the centre and moving sideways or facing and moving to the side as in a march in circle games.

In the traditions of one's own and other cultures, it is undoubtedly easy to find dances of this kind. The simplest choreography consists in walking towards the right and towards the left at each change or repetition of musical/sung phrase. With dances made up of two different parts, each of which contains two musical phrases that are repeated, a simplified choreography could be the following: during the first part, for the first phrase you go towards the right, and when it is repeated you go towards the left. In the second part, until the middle of the first phrase you go towards the centre, in the second half you go back to your place moving backwards. The movement is repeated with the repetition of the phrase. They can have arms down and then raise them when going towards the centre and drop them as they return. These elementary schema (right/left, in/out) can be applied to many dances, even if they do not correspond to the original choreography. The purpose here is not to introduce the children to popular tradition with its rituals and specific choreography. It is to help them enter into the organization of time and space with the aid of music so that they can gradually learn to master it.

At the beginning, when they change direction, the children are led by the adults. But, if the activity is done frequently, the children gradually begin to memorize the music and they allow it to lead them along. You have to wait until they are about age four years before you notice that the children prepare their bodies to change direction because they recognize that the phrase of music is coming to an end.

The presence of parents allows for the use of varying types of skips, turns and movements in pairs in which each parent, for example, goes around the circle with his/her child and then returns to the circle with the others, and so on.

If there were continuity between the playschool and kindergarten, and if this activity were done frequently, we would be better able to notice the spontaneous development in motor control that takes place without the need for particular instructions. Children are urged on by a great need to move. They listen to the music, observe what the adults are doing, they try to repeat and ... they learn.

6.4.2 Free Movement

To move freely led by the music is another activity that allows children to be introduced to repertoires of diverse genres. It is a way of listening through the body. Here the teacher can choose short pieces of music (or sections of them) characterized by particular musical structures: fast or slow pace, very loud or very soft volume; in homogeneous mode or with clear changes; alternating between two very different instruments, etc.

To start the activity of listening and movement, the teacher prepares the context. For example, a fast piece could be the *Ballet of the Unhatched Chicks* (from Mussorgsky's *Pictures at an Exhibition* for piano): "There are so many little chicks coming out of their shells. Do we want to dance along with them?". In this piece, there are also some unexpected long notes on which they can stop and then continue to move quickly. For a piece that goes from very soft to very loud and at the same time from slow to fast, you can listen to *The hall of the mountain king* (from Grieg's *Peer Gynt*): "There's a big high mountain where the king has his throne. Let's go there to see what he's doing." If you want to have alternation between two very contrasting kinds of musical sound, try *Samuel Goldenberg and Schmuyle* (from *Pictures at an Exhibition* in the orchestral version by Ravel): "There was once a rich man who was tall and stout who walked stiffly and there was another man who was very poor and very thin who was in a corner lamenting."

Prokofiev's *Cinderella* in the ballet suite version could be used for them to listen, through movement, to the music of a story that the children may already know. This could also be another way of taking part in a story, as we shall see in the next section. In *Cinderella* there are various pieces that are good for this, for example, the *Duet of the Sisters with their Oranges*, a fast and very rhythmic piece, or *Cinderella dreams of the Ball*, a slow piece where the rhythm is not very marked but is quite free, especially in the first part. The structure given to the chosen pieces does not impose specific gestures or movements, but leaves the situation open to free expression.

6.4.3 Musical Tales

There are also stories set to music or compiled for children (e.g. Prokofiev's *Peter and the Wolf*), or adaptable (e.g. Stravinsky's *Soldier's Tale*). Listening to music takes on other connotations when using these pieces.

To listen to *Peter and the Wolf*, we recommend that the teacher (or parents) do the narration and let them hear the musical parts from a CD (this means preparing a CD without narration). This will allow for greater variety in the timing and the styles of narration, as it can be told more slowly if so desired, passages can be skipped and you can go straight to the conclusion or go back, or the children can take part and ask the questions: "Who lives in the white house?", "Who does Peter live with?", "Who were Peter's friends?" In this way, it is not necessary to follow the order, but the musical parts can be played as the children gradually respond. The children themselves can then tell the story. The children can listen to the full narration at home if they like. The story can also be performed by giving the children a role to play, and asking each one to move with the music when their theme is played.

With Stravinsky's *Soldier's Tale* (inspired by a Russian story), we are immersing the children in sounds and rhythms that are more daring and we are giving them the chance to be familiar with the violin. Here is a reworking of the first part in a very reduced and simplified form that generally fascinates children. Two people are required (two teachers or mother and father), one of them is the narrator and later the devil, and the other is the soldier. If reference to the devil creates problems (but children do not ask who this character is), we can also call him a "bandit" or somesuch. A violin is required, either a real one of small dimensions, or one made of cardboard, and a book with drawings left close by.

SCENE I
No. 1 – *The Soldier's March*. Arrange the children in the centre of the room. The soldier carrying a bundle over his shoulder walks around them looking tired. In the bundle, besides a violin in its case, there are several objects, for example a bottle of water, a shawl, a pen ... The narrator begins after a few seconds saying in a rhythmic voice:

A very tired soldier is coming home from war.
He has a bundle on his back and he doesn't let it fall.

The narrator stops for a few seconds and then repeats it again and then a third time until the music finishes.

SCENE II
When this theme is finished the disc is stopped. The soldier sits on the ground and takes the objects one by one from the bundle with a flourish. The last thing he takes out is the violin. He opens the case, pulls out the instrument, stands up and produces a few sounds. At this point the animator turns on the second piece of music *Airs by a Stream*. The soldier walks in time to the music and pretends to play the violin.

SCENE III

After about a minute and a half, the music stops and the dialogue begins between the soldier and the narrator who now plays the part of the devil:

D. *Hello. Who are you?*
S. *I am a soldier.*
D. *And what are you doing?*
S. *I am going home.*
D. *What's that in your hand?*
S. *A violin.*
D. *It's lovely. May I touch it?*
S. *No. It's mine.*
D. *I won't break it. Let me touch it.*
S. *No. It's mine.*
D. *Listen, I have an idea. I have a lovely book.* [He takes the book that is close by] *Why don't we do a swap?*
S. *But I don't know how to read. I'm not interested.*
D. [coming closer and closer] *It's a lovely book, you know. It has pictures. Look!*
S. [looking warily at the book] *Mmmm, we'll see.*
D. *Go on. Take it!* [The soldier takes a closer look at the book and the narrator takes the violin from his hands]

SCENE IV

The soldier continues to look through the book as he sits down. Meanwhile the third piece of music is played – *Pastorale*. After leafing through a few pages, the soldier falls asleep and the narrator with an air of intrigue calls the children to touch the violin.

SCENE V

After a couple of minutes, the soldier begins to wake up, the narrator-devil quickly hides the violin behind his/her back, stops the music, and puts on an air of innocence. The soldier stands up and begins to search for the violin all over the place. He says several times in an agitated voice:

S. *My violin. Where's my violin? Who has seen my violin?*
[Then, turning to the devil, he asks again]
S. *Have you seen my violin?*
D. *I don't know anything about it. I've never even seen it.*
S. *It's you! You took it!*
D. *No, no. I know nothing about it.*
S. *What's that behind your back?*
D. *Nothing.*
S. *Let me see your hands!*
[He shows him one hand]
S. *Show me your two hands!*
At this point, the soldier discovers that the devil has the violin and after a few attempts he finally manages to get it back.

SCENE VI
They listen to theme number 1 again and the soldier invites the children to march with him and he again pretends to play the violin.

After they have had this experience several times, the older children can be invited to tell the story, or to play one of the parts (they all want to be the soldier), with the help of the teacher who puts on the music and is ready to help the story along.

Adaptations can be made of other musical stories, for example, Stravinsky's *Song of the Nightingale* based on a story by Andersen, Humperdinck's *Hansel and Gretel*, Henze's *Pollicino*, Mozart's *Magic Flute*, Prokofiev's *Cinderella* ballet suite version, etc. We recommend that you choose the main events connected to the key characters and the pieces of music that characterize the event. The length could be about 15–20 minutes, narration included. The basic idea is to allow the children to enter into musical worlds of different styles through the magic of storytelling.

Postlude

Johannella Tafuri and Donatella Villa

J. Donatella, our adventure has come to an end. Should we allow the curtain to fall?

D. Certainly not. As far as I am concerned this is not finished and never will be. For me the experience goes on, with other children of course, because this has now become part of my daily work.

J. What do you hope parents will remember after reading about this experience?

D. Perhaps I would like parents to remember how music has helped them to educate their children. And you?

J. I would like them to continue to communicate through music. Do you think that this book could be of help in this?

D. I certainly do. It should help them and many others. I would like it if many other parents, educators, paediatricians and all those involved with children who read these pages, could discover new ways of communicating with the very young. As early as in the first chapter there are plenty of interesting ideas suggested by all the research that is mentioned.

J. Do you remember when I was telling you about the breakthrough made by Tomatis? I was reading his book *The conscious ear* that tells about his intuition, his experiments on prenatal hearing ...

D. Yes, but I already knew this instinctively from my experience as a mother. Right from the beginning, when I sang to my children during the early months, I could see that they recognized the songs I used to sing during pregnancy. For several hours a day I used to accompany myself on the piano, singing the songs that I was teaching children at the music school. After the twins were born, they used to go into "listening mode" as if they were meditating. They seemed to remember the songs that they had heard before coming into the world. It often happened during the night that both were crying and my husband and I were walking around the house rocking them and we would notice that the crying stopped as soon as I began to sing even a line from the songs of the prenatal period. They stopped, opened their hands, opened their eyes wide and looked in my direction. If I then sang a song that they did not know, they either started to cry again or they just lost attention.

J. I heard about the effects of singing during pregnancy while I was doing a course in *psychophonie* in France with Marie Louise Aucher, a wonderful person who not only showed me how to work on my voice and singing, but also opened up that fascinating world to me.

D. Did she work with pregnant mothers?

J.   Yes, and she had been doing so for some time. She said that she had noticed almost by chance some interesting reactions by a baby just born to one of her students to whom she had been giving singing lessons until shortly before the birth. Then she conducted a series of experiments with other newborns in order to verify her hypothesis, until one day she met the famous gynaecologist Leboyer who invited her to work at the Pithiviers Hospital. This is how Marie Louise came to spend many years getting pregnant mothers and the fathers to sing, and there were very interesting results. She speaks about it in her books and she told us about it during her *psychophonie* courses.

D.   I remember that you were enthusiastic about it and that encouraged me and my desire to know. I was so interested in the connection between pregnancy and music that, for lack of specific courses, at a certain point I decided to attend courses and seminars intended for obstetricians and gynaecologists.

J.   Didn't you feel out of place?

D.   Well, it certainly was not my scene, but in that way I could acquire skills I needed. These, together with my studies in musical perception, allowed me to give courses on music in pregnancy at the "Il Nido" Association in Bologna and in that way to come into contact with mothers-to-be.

J.   That was not the first time though.

D.   No, you are right. A few years previously I had already given two workshops on "Music Before" and "Music After" for expectant couples and for parents with their new babies. The objective was to make them more aware of music and sound, to stimulate musicality in the unborn children and to foster the parent-child relationship through music. I remember that well. However, you had another fixed idea in your head.

J.   Indeed yes. For some time I had been fascinated with the question of the ability to sing in tune. Why do some people go off the note and others do not. I had a passion for singing (transmitted from my parents, especially my mother) and it seemed to me that people who could not manage to sing must be very sad. It irritated me considerably to hear over and over again "I'm tone deaf. I've no ear".

D.   I remember when you spoke about it in class. Why did you insist so much?

J.   The topic excited me. Yes, I wanted everyone, beginning with my students, to understand that we can do something about it, that we can open doors that a distorted education and milieu have closed. I was certain that it was not a definite closure.

D.   But not everyone was convinced.

J.   No, unfortunately. I had no instruments, no proof. I found documentation and I studied the question, but it was only when I read about the research undertaken by Graham Welch that I understood what direction I should take. His analysis of the problem was what decided me. I was first of all struck by his idea of the ear/voice coordination in the mechanism activated in singing. At that point I said to myself: Here we need more research. We needed to begin with younger children, in fact, even with children not yet born. Then you came into my mind and I remembered the experiences that you had told me about.

D. How long ago that seems! I remember when you suggested that I should embark on this adventure. I immediately found it fascinating, but I did not foresee that it would change my life (and perhaps not only mine!).

J. Were you worried about it?

D. No, on the contrary. In addition to the basic motivation that I also shared, what urged me to undertake this "voyage" was my curiosity, the desire to discover new situations and to test myself, to be challenged by the mothers, the children, the environment, you ... I wanted to know if I would be able to keep this up for six years, to deal with all I would discover day after day. I was aware that everyday occurrences cannot be programmed, and that the project contained several unknown quantities. But even that attracted me. And you? Weren't you worried?

J. Well, I must confess that the choice of a long six-year research project did rather alarm me. Then there were problems that were not easy to sort out (how to make the project known, how to classify the data, the expenses for required materials, the venue ...). Of course, I had many friends who lent a hand, but ... I wondered: "What if the mothers get fed up soon? What if it doesn't work?" My natural optimism kept me going. I would have to take courage and jump right in. Looking back on the project now, I must admit that I did not really know what lay ahead.

D. I must say that your worries were not apparent. Tell me the truth, you were pretending so that I would not be alarmed!

J. No, it's just that I ... removed them. I was fascinated with the idea of being able to catch a glimpse of the origin of an ability that I consider to be humanly essential. I began to imagine hearing so many children singing, to be able to discover through their voices and their behaviour, the secret of singing. Perhaps this passion is not the appropriate attitude for a researcher. We need objectivity, distance, rigour ... That is all true, but you don't face difficulties and sacrifice without passion. Objectivity and distance would come immediately in the planning of the methodological aspects and in the study of the results.

D. Until that moment the project still did not have a name...

J. How was that story?

D. It was my husband who pointed it out: "You haven't given it a name? If you want to attract expectant mothers you will have to call it something."

J. That's right! I'd forgotten that. Now I remember spending days tossing all kinds of words around in my head ... and then illumination came: We'll call it *inCanto,* the "*inCanto* project" ["*incanto*" means "magical spell"; "*canto*" means "song" or "singing"]. But I must add that our dark moments did not end there.

D. They certainly didn't. There were plenty of critical moments and times of discouragement. It was really bad when the mothers were asked to record their children's vocal productions and to fill in the diary and ... the recordings and diaries didn't arrive. That was hard. Did you find that tough?

J.   Indeed yes! I remember in particular in May or June 2001 (many children were reaching the age of two), I realized that I had recordings of very few children. That was a time of real dejection.

D.   We had clung to the idea that the parents had by then got used to making regular recordings.

J.   That's how it happened. I remember that at that time I began to ask and beg, but by then several months had been lost for some children, and even more as the summer was approaching and it would be difficult to record during the holidays ...

D.   However, some cassettes did arrive.

J.   Few. And so the phase from one to two is the least documented. It is really a pity because it is the least studied and the most delicate. It is precisely the time when children learn to speak and so have the double possibility of expressing themselves by speaking and singing.

D.   It was also a bit sad when people left the project, especially when some mothers just disappeared without a word of explanation, or a thank you ...

J.   I also suffered with each withdrawal. It is easy to foresee on paper that not everyone would continue, but then it's hard to accept those empty places. Faces disappear, and behind each disappearance there is a personal story, sometimes because of lack of time (more work, a second child), the child gets tired of it, and also because of suffering (bereavement, illness). In other cases we never learned the reason ... Now, what can we leave our readers as a conclusion?

D.   I would particularly like to say that there were very many positive aspects and I would like to emphasize the affection I felt for the families, the depth of the relations between the families themselves, the mutual understanding that I had with the children, how we fostered so much learning thanks to the positive atmosphere we built up together. I would like to say that it was very important for us the educators to create a stimulating sonorous-musical environment before and after the birth by offering the mothers and babies the opportunity to make music.

J.   I agree entirely. Affective involvement was the determining factor. I remember the emotions of the first sessions. On paper the project was for "expectant mothers", but there, in flesh and blood there were enthusiastic young women, excited about their babies' forthcoming arrival and about the idea that they could do something for them. They spoke of their experiences, they asked for advice, they sang, they had fun. There were also some fathers there, some of them enthusiastic, others politely sceptical, but they too brought along their share of goodwill. A group was being created, people found themselves to be on the same wavelength, friendships were formed. Even if I only really understood this as time went by, I was beginning to realize how much enthusiasm, conviction, support, but especially mutual affection would be the determining factors.

D.   I was particularly motivated by the fact of "freely offering" an opportunity to be together to have fun and learn new things.

J.   "Learn new things" – you are right. I learned so much over these few years. Being together with so many children and so many families opened up a new world to me. Over that time I tried to learn as much as possible from the children, to let them teach me what was going on in their minds and hearts. I tried to understand how they allow music to enter them, why they feel an attraction towards it, how they make it theirs ...

D.   I also feel more confident now when dealing with children. I feel closer to each one of them. I really think that I have learned to communicate with them in a special way.

J.   I became even more convinced that music is not the monopoly of some but rather the right of all. If we adults, expert educators, and parents too, and let us not forget the policy makers ... give them this opportunity, all of them can take as much of it as they want.

D.   Don't you think that we also learned to work together and discuss things?

J.   That's true. That is another marvellous outcome. But there is one thing that was more demanding for me than for you.

D.   What thing was that?

J.   Well, don't forget that you are a pianist and I am a violinist and so, when we decided to use the piano to accompany the songs during the sessions, I had to brush up my piano-playing skills (which in fact came in useful to play the harmonium in church). In any case, I was happy to do it and I had fun.

D.   If I were to ask you now what struck you most that you still remember, what would you say?

J.   I made a discovery that amazed me and that was the magnetic gaze of small children. I would never have imagined that such small babies could fix their gaze for such a long time without moving. It gives you the impression that there is some inner intense activity going on, a magnetic current that joins them to you. It reminded me of what Maria Montessori said about "absorbent minds".

D.   The most heartening moments for me were whenever I became aware of the progress being made by the children. For example, when the children, accompanied by music, managed to keep the beat with an instrument or with hand clapping.

J.   And the emotion of hearing them sing! First, through the recordings and then live during the sessions. I remember the first "qua qua" in the song about the duckling. You know this is a difficult passage with four different descending intervals in succession that start out from the same note: I hear the second, good, then the third, good, the fourth? Good! The fifth? Incredible! It's also in tune. And the child was only two years and one month old.

D.   I loved it when they asked to sing certain songs or play certain games. I was happy that they had preferences, and that they felt free to intervene during the activities. Hearing them sing at the top of their voices made me smile. You could see that they felt secure. They were expressing pleasure and enjoyment.

J.   So, can we say that it went well?

D.   Yes. It was really wonderful. We have to thank everyone, children and parents.

J.   How shall we conclude?

D.   No, we can't say that it has come to an end. I often think. "I shall continue to work with them!"

J.   That's true. However, the book is finishing and the reader expects a conclusion.

D.   If you really want to, we can say that we have completed one stage and that now we shall take on new energy and resume.

J.   You are right. Let's keep on going ...

Appendix of Melodies

Melody 1   *Giro giro rosa* [Ring a ring o'roses]

Gi-ro gi-ro ro-sa   gial-la la mi-mo-sa   pra-to ver-de cie-lo blu
Gi-ro gi-ro az-zur-ro   man-gio pa-ne e bur-ro   pra-to ver-de cie-lo blu

tut-ti ca-scan giù giù giù
tut-ti ca-scan giù giù giù ecc.

Melody 2   *Il grillo John* [John the cricket]

Il gril-lo John è un fur-bac-chion can-ta e bal-la   pum pum pum pum pum

1. So-pra un mu-ro   suo-na il tam-bu-ro   pum pum pum pum   pum pum pum
2. Sa-le sui tet-ti   suo-na i le-gnet-ti   toc toc toc toc   toc toc toc
3. Tro-va due gat-ti che suo-na-no i piat-ti   ciac ciac ciac ciac   ciac ciac ciac

Melody 3   *La lumaca e il topolino* [The snail and the mouse]

Len-ta len-ta   len-ta va   len-ta-men-te   la lu-ma-ca,   len-to len-to
Len-ta len-ta   len-ta va   len-ta-men-te la   tar-ta-ru-ga,   len-to len-to

len-to va   len-ta men-te il   lu-ma-con.   Svel-to svel-to svel-to va
len-to va   len-ta-men-te il   tar-taru-gon.   Svel-to svel-to svel-to va

cor-re cor-re il to-po-li-no,   svel-to svel-to svel-to va   cor-re cor-re il to-po-lin.
cor-re cor-re il ca-val-li-no,   svel-to svel-to svel-to va   cor-re cor-re il ca-val-lin.

Melody 4   *L'anatroccolo* [The duckling]

L'a - na - troc-co-lo oc - co-lo   oc-co-lo   nel vi - ot-to-lo ot-to-lo
Va nel   la - go a - go   a - go   a nuo - ta - re a - re
Poi ri - tor - na or - na   or - na   pie - no   zep - po ep - po

ot - to - lo   ben con - ten - to   ben con - ten - to   ben con -
a - re   e si   bec - ca   e si   bec - ca   e si
ep - po   e si   sdra - ia   e si   sdra - ia   e si

ten - to se   ne   va,   qua qua qua   qua qua qua qua   qua
bec - ca i pe - scio - lin,   qua qua qua   qua qua qua qua   qua
sdra - ia là   sul   pra',   qua qua qua   qua qua qua qua   qua

Melody 5   *Questo è l'occhio bello* [The pretty eye]

Melody 6   *Tre oche andavano a ber* [Three geese went to drink]

Melody 7   *Uno la signora veste di bruno* [One. The lady dresses in brown]

U - no la si - gno-ra ve - ste di   bru-no che di   bian - co non vuol ve -
Du - e la si - gno-ra sce - glie il   bu - e   al - tra   car - ne non vuol man-

stir.   Mi-ra la   don - don - del - la, mi-ra la   don - don - dà.
giar.   Mi-ra la   don - don - del - la, mi-ra la   don - don - dà.

Melody 8   *Lodoletta* [Alouette]

Lo - do - let - ta   ca - ra lo-do-let - ta,   lo - do - let - ta

ti spen - nac - chie - rò.   Ti spen - nac-chie-rò la te-sta ti spen-nac-chie-rò la te-sta
                                   co-da   co-da

e   la te - sta e la te - sta   lo - do - let - ta lo - do let - ta, Ah!
[e la co - da e la co - da]
[e la te - sta e la te - sta]

Melody 9   *Benvenuti* [Welcome]

Ben - ve - nu - ti   tut - ti   quan - ti   stia-mo in -sie-me per can - ta - re,   per suo-

na - re   per dan-za-re ci vo-glia - mo di-ver-tir   An-drea - a   so-no qui
                                                          Vir - gi - nia
                                                          Bian-ca

Melody 10   *Tutti vogliamo camminare* [We all want to walk]

Tut- ti vo - glia - mo cam - mi - na - re cam - mi - na - re cam - mi-
Tut- ti vo - glia - mo batter le   ma - ni batter le   ma - ni batter le

na - re. Tut-ti vo - glia-mo cam - mi - na - re da og-gi fi -no a do-ma - ni
ma - ni. Tut-ti vo - glia-mo batter le   ma - ni da og-gi fi -no a do-ma - ni.

Melody 11   *C'era una volta un papero* [Once there was a boy gosling]

C'e-ra u-na vol - ta un pa-pe-ro ve - sti-to di pel-le di bu-fa - lo, fa -

ce - va bal - lar   le   pa - pe - re   sul - l'u-scio di Din - di - rin - dè.

Al-lez vous dan - ser al-la   mo-da al -la bra -cè.   mo-da al-la bra-cè.

Melody 12   *Pippo Kid*

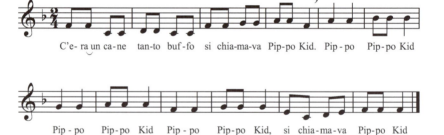

C'e- ra un ca-ne   tan-to buf-fo   si chia-ma-va Pip-po Kid. Pip - po   Pip-po Kid

Pip - po   Pip-po Kid Pip - po   Pip-po Kid, si chia-ma-va Pip-po Kid

Melody 13   *Il codino di un topino* [The little mouse's tail]

Il   co - di - no d'un to - pi - no fuor da un bu - co un dì spun - tò, ven - ne un
Pro - prio in quel - la que - sta è bel - la un gran ca - ne ca - pi - tò, ed il

gat - to quat - to quat - to e coi den - ti l'af - fer - rò, ven - ne un gat - to quat - to quat - to e coi
gat - to quat - to quat - to im - pau - ri - to se ne an - dò, ed il   gat - to quat - to quat - to im - pau -

den - ti l'af - fer - rò.   Il   to - pi - no po - ve - ri - no pian - se   for - te e si la - gnò.
ri - to se ne an - dò.   Il   to - pi - no il suo co - di - no den - tro il bu - co ri - ti - rò.

Melody 14   *Tutti qui si giocherà* [We are all going to play]

1. Tut - ti   qui si gio - che - rà gi - ro - ton - do si fa - rà con la ma - no nel - la ma - no
2. Gior - gia in mez - zo fer - ma sta la ca - te - na gi - re - rà stret - ta a lei si av - vol - ge - rà
3. Un   bu - chin ri - tro - ve - rà sot - to l'ar - co pas - se - rà la   ca - te - na an - cor si fa

gi - ra pia - no pia - no.   Can - ta can - ta can - ta an - cor que - sto can - to è co - me un fior
chiu - sa re - ste - rà
per ri - co - min - ciar

s'a - pre al so - le e di - ce o - gnor   l'al - le - gria dei cuor.

Melody 15   *La stellina viaggiante* [The travelling star]

A. Ahi   ahi   ahi   ahi,   mi so-no fat-ta ma-le,   mi so-no fat-ta ma-le

B. Nin-na   oh,   nin-na   oh,   la   stel - li - na a chi la do,   se la

fac-cio ad-dor-men-ta-re   do-mat-ti-na   si   può   sve-glia-re

Melody 16   *Vogliamo suonare* [We want to play]

Vo - glia-mo suo-na-re   tut-ti in-sie-me   for-te   for-te   pia-no   pia-no.

Se qual-cu-no   vuo-le   suo-na-re   ci   fac-cia   sen-ti-re   co-me suo-ne-rà.

References

Addessi, Anna Rita, Pachet, François, "Experiments with a musical machine: musical style replication in 3 to 5 year old children", *British Journal of Music Education,* 22/1 (2005): 21–46.

Addessi, Anna Rita, Carugati Franco, Santarcangelo, B., Baroni, Mario, *University students, musical teachers and social representations of music*, Presentation to the IX ICMPC, 22-26/8/2006 (Bologna: Proceedings in CD, 2006).

Aucher, Maire Louise, *En corps chanté* (Paris: Hommes & Groupes Editeurs, 1987).

Baldi, Gabriella, Tafuri, Johannella, Caterina, Roberto, "The ability of children aged 7–10 to structure musical improvisations", *Bulletin of the Council for Research in Music Education*, 153/154, (2003): 135–141.

Bandura, Albert, *Social foundations of thought and action* (Englewood Cliffs, N.J.: Prentice-Hall, 1986).

Bandura, Albert, *Self Efficacy: The excercise of control* (New York: W.H. Freeman and Company, 1997).

Baroni, Mario, *Suoni e significati* (Firenze: Guaraldi, 1978, 2nd edn Torino: EDT, 1997).

Baroni, Mario, Dalmonte, Rossana, Jacoboni, Carlo, *Le regole della musica* (Torino: EDT, 1999).

Barrett, Margaret, *Children composing: A View of Aesthetic Decision-Making*, in Bertil Sundin, Gary E. McPherson, Göran Folkestad (eds), *Children Composing*, *Research in Music Education* (Malmö: Lund University, 1998): 57–81.

Björkvold, Jon-Roar, *Den spontane barnesangen – Vårt musikalske morsmål* (Oslo: Cappelens, 1985).

Björkvold, Jon-Roar, "Canto ergo sum", in F.R. Wilson, F.L. Rochmann (eds), *Music and Child development. The biology of music making*, Proceedings of Denver Conference, 1987 (St. Louis: MMB Music, 1990): 117–135.

Blacking, John, *How musical is man?* (London: Faber and Faber, 1976).

Boncinelli, Edoardo, *I nostri geni* (Torino: Einaudi, 1998).

Boysson-Bardies de, Bénédicte, *How Language comes to children* (Cambridge, MA: The MIT Press Cambridge, 1999).

Cornoldi, Antonio, *Ande, bali e cante del Veneto* (Padova: Rebellato, 1968; new edn with CD Rovigo: Minnelliana, 2002).

Cowie, Helen, "Children as writers", in David J. Hargreaves, *Children and the Arts* (Philadelphia: Open University Press, 1989): 87–104.

Davidson, Lyle, "Tonal structures of children's early songs", *Music Perception*, II vol., 3, (1985): 361–374.

Davidson, Lyle, "Songsinging by young and old: A developmental approach to music", in Rita Aiello with John A. Sloboda (eds), *Musical Perceptions* (New York, Oxford: Oxford University Press, 1994): 99–130.

Delalande, François, *Le condotte musicali* (Bologna: CLUEB, 1993).

Delalande, François, "Ricerca sull'esplorazione sonora da 1 a 3 anni. Perché e come", in *Dossier Nido Sonoro* (Lecco: Centro Studi Musicali e Sociali Maurizio Di Benedetto, 2004).

Delalande, François, *Esplorazioni sonore nella prima infanzia: la nascita della musica* (Milano: FrancoAngeli, 2009).

Deliège, Irène, Sloboda, John A., *Musical Beginnings* (Oxford: Oxford University Press, 1996).

Demany, Laurent, McKenzie, Beryl, Vurpillot, Eliane, "Rhythm perception in early infancy", *Nature*, 266 (1977): 718–719.

Dowling, W. Jay, "Melodic information processing and its development", in Diana Deutsch (ed.), *The Psychology of Music* (New York: Academic Press, 1982).

Dowling, W. Jay, "Development of musical schemata in children's spontaneous singing", in W.R. Crozier, A.J. Chapman (eds), *Cognitive Processes in the Perception of Art* (Amsterdam: Elsevier, 1984): 145–163.

Dowling, W. Jay, "Rhythm and the Organization of Time", in Jay W. Dowling, D.L. Harwood, *Music Cognition* (Orlando, Fl., London: Academic Press, 1986).

Dowling, W. Jay, "Tonal structure and children's early learning of music", in John A. Sloboda (ed.), *Generative processes in music* (Oxford: Clarendon Press, 1988): 113–128.

Dowling, W. Jay, "La structuration mélodique: perception et chant", in Arlette Zenatti (ed.) *Psychologie de la musique* (Paris: Presses Universitaires de France, 1994): 145–176.

Dumaurier, Elisabeth, "Le domaine sonore du tout jeune enfant", in François Delalande, *L'enfant du sonore au musical* (Paris: INA GRM/Buchet/Chastel, 1982).

Eimas, Peter D., Siqueland Einar R., Jusczyk, Peter W., Vigorito, James, "Speech perception in infants", *Science*, vol. 171 (1971): 303–306.

Eysenck, Hans J., Kamin Leon, *Intelligence: The Battle for the Mind* (Willemstad: Multimedia Publications Inc., 1981).

Fassbender, Christoph, *Auditory grouping and segregation processes in infancy* (Norderstedt: Kast Verlag, 1993).

Fassbender, Christoph, "La sensibilité auditive du nourrisson aux paramètres acoustiques du langage et de la musique", in Irène Deliège, John A. Sloboda (eds), *Naissance et développement du sens musical* (Paris: Presses Universitaires de France, 1995): 63–99.

Fassbender, Christoph, "Infants' auditory sensitivity towards acoustic parameters of speech and music", in Irène Deliège, John A. Sloboda (eds), *Musical Beginnings* (Oxford: Oxford University Press, 1996): 56–87.

Fernald, Anne, "Intonation and communicative intent in mothers' speech to infants: is the melody the message?", *Child Development*, 60 (1989): 1497–1510.

Fernald, Anne, "Meaningful melodies in mothers' speech to infants", in Hanus Papoušek, U. Jürgens, Mechtild Papoušek, *Nonverbal vocal communication* (Cambridge: Cambridge University Press, 1992): 262–282.

Fraisse, Paul, *La psychologie du rythme* (Paris: Presses Universitaires de France, 1974).

Francès, Robert, *La perception de la musique* (Paris: Vrin, 1972).

Gardner, Howard, *Frames of mind: The theory of multiple intelligences* (New York: Basic Books, 1985).

Gerard, Claire, Auxiette, Cathérine, "The Processing of Musical Prosody by Musical and Nonmusical Children", *Music Perception*, 10 (1992): 93–126.

Gilbert, Janet P., "Motoric music skill development in young children: a longitudinal investigation", *Psychology of Music*, 1 (1981): 21–25.

Goitre, Roberto, Seritti, Ester, *Canti per giocare* (Milano: Suvini Zerboni, 1980).

Gordon, Edwin, *A music learning theory for newborn and young children* (Chicago: GIA, 1990, other edn 1997, 2003).

Hallam, Susan, Shaw, Jackie, "Constructions of musical ability", *Bulletin of the Council for Research in Music Education*, 153/154 (2003): 102–107.

Hargreaves, David J., *The Developmental Psychology of Music* (Cambridge: Cambridge University Press, 1986).

Howe, Michael J.A., *The origins of exceptional abilities* (Oxford: Blackwell, 1990).

Imberty, Michel, *Suoni Emozioni Significati* (Bologna: CLUEB, 1986).

Imberty, Michel, *La musica e il bambino* (Enciclopedia della musica, vol. II, Torino, Einaudi, 2002): 477–495.

Jarjisian, Catherine S., "Pitch pattern instruction and the singing achievement of young children", *Psychology of Music*, 11 (1983): 19–25.

Jorquera Jaramillo, Maria Cecilia, Balboni, Angela, Bella, Chiara, Ferioli, Simone, Minichiello, Alessandro, "Influenza del compito vocale e del genere sulla capacità di intonare in bambini di 6–7 anni", in Johannella Tafuri (ed.), *La ricerca per la didattica musicale*, Proceedings del Convegno SIEM, 2000, *Quaderni della SIEM*, 16 (2000): 165–171.

Jusczyk, Peter W., Krumhansl, Carol L., "Pitch and rhythmic patterns affecting infants' sensitivity to musical phrase structure", *Journal of Experimental Psychology: Human Perception and Performance*, vol. 19/3 (1993): 627–640.

Krumhansl, Carol L., Jusczyk, Peter W., "Infants' perception of phrase structure in music", *Psychological Science*, vol. 1/1 (1990): 70–73.

Lamarque, Vivian, Battaglia, Maria, *L'usignolo dell'imperatore* (Milano: Fabbri Editori, 2004, book with CD, 2004).

Lecanuet, Jean-Pierre, "L'expérience auditive prénatale", in Irène Deliège, John A. Sloboda (eds), *Naissance et développement du sens musical* (Paris: Presses Universitaires de France, 1995): 7–38.

Lecanuet, Jean-Pierre, "Prenatal auditory experience", in Irène Deliège, John A. Sloboda (eds), *Musial Beginnings* (Oxford: Oxford University Press, 1996): 3–36.

Leont'ev, Aleksej, "On the biological and social aspects of human development: the training of auditory ability", in Cole M., Maltzman I. (eds), *A Handbook of Contemporary Soviet Psychology* (New York: Basic Books, 1969).

Leydi, Roberto, *I canti popolari italiani* (Verona: Mondadori, 1973).

Lucchetti, Stefania, "Mi canti una canzone?", *Musicascuola*, 6 (1987): 32–35.

Lucchetti, Stefania, "L'esperienza musicale nel periodo prescolastico", *Quaderni della SIEM*, 2 (1992): 7–73.

Malbrán, Silvia, "The Development of Pulse Syncrony. An Exploratory Study of three-year-old children", *Bulletin of the Council for Research in Music Education*, 147, Special Issue (2000/2001): 109–115.

Malbrán, Silvia, "Tapping in time: A Longitudinal Study at the ages three to five years", *Bulletin of the Council for Research in Music Education,* 153/4, Special Issue (2002).

Malbrán, Silvia, Tafuri, Johannella, "Experiencia musical precoz y sincronía rítmica con el tactus", *Eufonía*, 38 (2006): 14–38.

Malloch, Stephen N., "Mothers and infants and communicative musicality", *Musicae Scientiae*, Special Issue (1999/2000): 29–54.

Mazzoli, Franca, Sedioli, Arianna, Zoccatelli, B., *I giochi musicali dei piccoli* (Bergamo: Edizioni Junior, 2003).

McPherson, Gary E. (ed.), *The Child as Musician* (New York: Oxford University Press, 2006).

Meyer, Leonard B., *Emotion and Meaning in music* (Chicago and London: The University of Chicago Press, 1956).

Mialaret, Jean-Pierre, *Explorations musicales instrumentales chez le jeune enfant* (Paris: Presses Universitaires de France, 1997).

Moog, Helmut, *The Musical Experience of the Pre-school Child* (London: Schott, 1976, or edn 1968).

Moorhead, Gladys E., Pond, Donald, *Music of Young Children: 1. Chant.* "Pillsbury Foundation Studies" (Santa Barbara: Pillsbury Foundation for Advancement of Music Education, 1941, 2nd edn 1978).

Mugny, G., Carugati, Franco, *L'intelligenza al plurale: rappresentazioni sociali dell'intelligenza e del suo sviluppo* (Bologna: CLUEB, 1988).

Nattiez, Jean-Jacques, *Musicologie générale et sémiologie* (Paris: Bourgois, 1987).

Papoušek, Hanus, "Musicalité et petite enfance. Origines biologiques et culturelles de la précocité", in Irène Deliège, John A. Sloboda (eds), *Naissance et développement du sens musical* (Paris: Presses Universitaires de France, 1995): 41–62.

Papoušek, Hanus, "Musicality in infancy research: biological and cultural origins of early musicality", in Irène Deliège, John A. Sloboda (eds), *Musical Beginnings* (Oxford: Oxford University Press, 1996): 37–55.

Papoušek, Mechthild, "Le comportement parental intuitif, source cachée de la stimulation musicale dans la petite enfance", in Irène Deliège, John A.

Sloboda (eds), *Naissance et développement du sens musical* (Paris: Presses Universitaires de France, 1995): 101–130.

Papoušek, Mechthild, "Intuitive parenting: a hidden source of musical stimulation in infancy" in Irène Deliège, John A. Sloboda (eds), *Musical Beginnings* (Oxford: Oxford University Press, 1996): 88–112.

Papoušek, Mechthild, Papoušek, Hanus, "Musical elements in the infant's vocalizations: their significance for communication, cognition, and creativity", in L.P. Lipsitt (ed.), *Advances in Infancy Research*, 1 (Ablex: Norwood, N.J., 1981): 163–224.

Parncutt, Richard, "Pulse Salience and Metrical Accent", *Music Perception*, 11 (4) (1994): 409–464.

Parncutt, Richard, "Prenatal Development" in Gary McPherson (ed.), *The Child As Musician* (New York: Oxford University Press, 2006): 1–31.

Piaget, Jean, *Play, dreams, and imitation in childhood* (New York: Norton, 1951).

Piatti, Mario, *È arrivato un bastimento carico di...* (Assisi: PCC, 1980; edn with audiotape and didactic brochure).

Porzionato, Giuseppe, *Psicobiologia della musica* (Bologna: Patron, 1980).

Pouthas, Viviane, "Développement de la perception du temps et des régulations temporelles de l'action chez le nourrisson et l'enfant", in Irène Deliège, John A. Sloboda (eds), *Naissance et développement du sens musical* (Paris: Presses Universitaires de France, 1995): 133–166.

Rainbow, Edward, "A final report on a three-year investigation of the rhythmùic abilities of preschool aged children", *Bulletin of the Council for Research in Music Education*, 66–67 (1981): 69–73.

Shaffer, L.H., "Rhythm and Timing in Skill", *Psychological Review*, 89/2 (1982): 109–122.

Shetler, Donald, "The inquiry into prenatal musical experience: a report of the Eastman Project 1980–1987", *Pre- and Peri-Natal Psychology*, 3/3 (1989): 171–189.

Shuter-Dyson, Rosamund, Gabriel, Clive, *The psychology of musical ability* (London: Methuen, 1981).

Staccioli, Gianfranco, Ritscher, Penny, *Apriteci le porte* (Teramo: Lisciani & Giunti, 1988).

Stadler Elmer, Stefanie, "Stages in singing development", in Johannella Tafuri (ed.), *La ricerca per la didattica musicale*, Proceedings del Convegno SIEM, 2000, *Quaderni della SIEM*, 16 (2000): 336–343.

Stern, Daniel, *The first relationship* (Cambridge, MS: Harvard University Press, 1977).

Stern, Daniel N., Spieker Susan, Mackain Kristine, "Intonation contours as signals in maternal speech to prelinguistic infants", *Developmental Psychology*, 18 (1982): 727–735.

Street, Alison, *Mothers' attitudes to singing to their infants*, Presentation to the 5th Triennial Conference of ESCOM, Hannover 8–13,/9/2003 (Proceedings in CD, 2003).

Sundin, Bertil, *Barns musikaliska skapande* (Stockholm: Liber, 1963).

Sundin, Bertil, McPherson Gary E., Folkestad Göran, *Children Composing, Research in Music Education* (Malmö: Lund University, 1988).

Swanwick, Keith, Tillman, June, "The Sequence of Musical Development: A Study of Children's Composition", *British Journal of Music Education*, 3 (1986): 305–339.

Tafuri, Johannella (ed.), *Didattica della musica e percezione musicale* (Bologna: Zanichelli, 1988).

Tafuri, Johannella, "Doti musicali e problemi educativi", *Enciclopedia della musica*, vol. II (Torino: Einaudi, 2002): 530–551.

Tafuri, Johannella, "Melodic structures in spontaneous songs of children aged 2–3", Presentation to the 5th Triennial Conference of ESCOM, Hannover 8–13/9/2003 (Proceedings in CD, 2003).

Tafuri, Johannella, Baldi, Gabriella, Caterina, Roberto, "Beginnings and endings in the musical improvisations of children aged 7 to 10 years", *Musicae Scientiae, Special Issue* (2003/2004): 157–171.

Tafuri, Johannella, García Rodriguez, Beatriz, Caterina, Roberto, "Parlare/cantare tra 1 e 2 anni" *(in preparation)*.

Tafuri, Johannella, Malbrán, Silvia, "Sviluppo della capacità di sincronizzazione musicale da 2 a 4 anni" (Lucca: LIM, *submitted*).

Tafuri, Johannella, Privitera, Michele, Caterina, Roberto, "Cantare a tempo. Uno studio con bambini da 2 a 3 anni", *Musica Domani* (*submitted*).

Tafuri, Johannella, Villa, Donatella, "Musical elements in the vocalisations of infants aged 2–8 months", *British Journal of Music Education*, 19/1 (2002): 73–88.

Tafuri, Johannella, Villa, Donatella, Caterina, Roberto 2002, *Mother-Infant Musical Communication in the 1st Year of Life*, Presentation to the XXIV ISME World Conference 2002 Bergen 11–16/8/2002 (Proceedings in CD, 2002).

Teplov, B.M., *Psychologie des aptitudes musicales* (Paris: Presses Universitaires de France, 1966).

Thorpe, Leigh A., Trehub, Sandra E., Morrongiello, Barbara A., Bull, Dale, "Perceptual grouping by infants and preschool children", *Developmental Psychology*, 24 (1988): 484–491.

Thurman, Leon, *Foundations for human self-expression during prenate, infant and early childhood development*, in Leon Thurman, Graham F. Welch (eds), *Bodymind & Voice: Foundations of Voice Education* (Iowa City: National Center for Voice and Speech, 1997): 456–474.

Tomatis, Alfred, *L'oreille et la vie* (Paris: Laffont, 1977).

Trehub, Sandra, "Musical predispositions in infancy", *Annals of the New York Academy of Sciences*, 930 (2001): 1–16.

Trehub, Sandra, "Toward a Developmental Psychology of Music", *Annals of the New York Academy of Sciences*, 999 (2003): 402–413.

Trehub, Sandra E., Bull, Dale, Thorpe, Leigh A., "Infants' perception of melodies: the role of melodic contour", *Child Development*, 55/3 (1984): 821–830.

Trehub, Sandra E., Nakata, Takayuki, "Emotion and music in infancy", *Musicae Scientiae*, Special Issue (2001/2002): 37–59.

Trehub, Sandra E., Schellenberg, E. Glenn, "Music: its relevance to infants", *Annals of Child Development*, 11 (1995): 1–24.

Trehub, Sandra E., Thorpe, Leigh A., "Infants' perception of rhythm. Categorization of auditory sequences by temporal structure", *Canadian Journal of Psychology*, 43 (1989): 217–229.

Trehub, Sandra E., Thorpe, Leigh A., Morrongiello, Barbara A., "Organizational processes in infants' perception of auditory patterns", *Child Development*, 58/3 (1987): 741–749.

Trehub, Sandra E., Trainor, Laurel J., Unyk, Anna M., "Music and speech processing in the first year of life", *Advances in Child Development and Behavior*, 24 (1993): 1–35.

Trevarthen, Colwyn, "Musicality and the intrinsic motive pulse: evidence from human psychobiology and infant communication", *Musicae Scientiae*, Special Issue (1999/2000): 155–211.

Villa, Donatella, Tafuri, Johannella, "Influenza delle esperienze musicali prenatali sulle reazioni del neonato", in Johannella Tafuri (ed.), *La ricerca per la didattica musicale*, Proceedings of SIEM Conference 2000, *Quaderni della SIEM*, 16 (2000): 391–398.

Volman, J.M., Gueze, R., "Temporal stability of rhythmic tapping 'on' and 'off' the beat: a developmental study", *Psychological Research*, 63 (2000): 62–69.

Webster, Peter R., "Refinement of a measure of creative thinking in music", in Cliff I. Madsen, C.A. Prickett (eds), *Applications of research in music behavior* (Tuscaloosa, Al.: University of Alabama Press, 1987): 257–271.

Welch, Graham F. "Poor pitch singing: a review of the literature", *Psychology of Music*, 7 (1979): 50–58.

Welch, Graham F., "A schema theory of how children learn to sing in tune", *Psychology of Music*, 13 (1985): 3–18.

Welch, Graham F., "Onchi and Singing Development: pedagogical implications", in Graham F. Welch, Tadahiro Murao (eds), *Onchi and Singing development* (London: David Fulton/ASME, 1994): 82–95.

Welch, Graham F., "The developing voice", in Leon Thurman, Graham F. Welch (eds), *Bodymind & Voice: Foundations of Voice Education* (Iowa City: National Center for Voice and Speech, 1997): 481–494.

Welch, Graham F., "Singing and Vocal Development" in Gary McPherson (ed.), *The Child As Musician* (New York: Oxford University Press, 2006): 311–329.

Welch, Graham F., White, Peta, "The developing voice: Education and vocal efficiency – a physical perspective", *Bulletin of the Council for Research in Music Education*, 119 (1994): 155–162.

Welch, Graham F., Sergeant, Desmond C., White, Peta, "The singing competencies of five-year-old developing singers", *Bulletin of the Council for Research in Music Education*, 127 (1996): 146–156.

Welch, Graham F., Sergeant, Desmond C., White, Peta, "Age, sex and vocal task as factors in singing "in tune" during the first years of schooling", *Bulletin of the Council for Research in Music Education*, 133 (1997): 153–160.

Welch, Graham F., Sergeant, Desmond C., White, Peta, "The role of linguistic dominance in the acquisition of song", *Research Studies in Music Education*, 10 (1998): 67–74.

Wilkin, Phillys E., "A comparison of fetal and newborn responses to music and sound stimuli, with and without daily exposure to a specific piece of music", *Bulletin of the Council for Research in Music Education*, 1 (1996): 163–169.

Wolff, P.H., "The natural history of crying and other vocalizations in early infancy", in B.M. Foss (ed.), *Determinants of infant behaviour*, vol. 4 (London: Methuen, 1969).

Woodward, Sheila C., *The transmission of music into the human uterus and the response to music of the human fetus and neonate*, PhD Thesis (University of Cape Town, 1992).

Young, Susan, "Young children's spontaneous vocalisations in free-play: Observations of two- to three-year-olds in a day-care setting", *Bulletin of the Council for Research in Music Education*, 152 (2002): 43–53.

Young, Susan, *Music with the Under Fours* (London: Routledge Falmer, 2003).

Zenatti, Arlette, *L'enfant et son environnement musical* (Issy le Moulineaux: ESP, 1981).

List of Audio and Video Recordings

Audio Recordings

Rec. 1: A girl of two months sings a descending major third.

Rec. 2: Here is a wider descending interval, a fourth, by a boy of four months.

Rec. 3: A girl of two months "responds" to her mother, who "responds" in turn by imitating the child's sounds, thus setting up a dialogue (the transcription is omitted because the sounds considered to be "in tune" are few).

Rec. 4: Here is an example of what we called "mixed intervals" – a sequence of sounds produced by a boy of four months in which we can make out some ascending and descending intervals.

Rec. 5: A girl of four months produces a melodic rhythmic motif in an ascending progression.

Rec. 6: Another four-month-old girl sounds as if she is going to cry, but the sound goes into tune and the vocalization concludes with a cadence (a musical formula signifying conclusion).

Rec. 7: A boy of four months prolongs the sequence – ascending interval (major third), silence, glissandos, descending interval (major third).

Rec. 8: The same child at six months reproduces two intervals contained in the mother's song, but inverted – the original song had a fifth to fourth, and the child repeated the fourth and then the fifth, almost at the same pitches as his mother's.

Rec. 9: This mixed glissando, produced by a boy of six months, allows us to hear how high children can sing at this age.

Rec. 10: In this vocalization, something interesting happens. The mother speaks, because the protocol stated that she should perform a spoken rhythm of three short sounds with the syllable "pam", and the girl of six months repeats the syllable "pa" several times; then the mother repeats the three syllables prolonging them to make it sound "sung" and the child also "sings" two intervals (ascending fourth to descending fifth), imitating her mother.

Rec. 11: The mother's voice can be heard singing softly "ed in giro trallallà"; then the child of 11 months makes a short sound with his mouth closed and then two slightly longer sounds, then, after a pause, six sounds that are rhythmic and clear, still with his mouth shut, with the same intervals as those used by his mother.

Rec. 12: This is a six-month-old "chatterbox". Her mother's "cuckoo" sounds (here a descending major third) starts her off "improvising on a theme". A long monologue ensues in which the "cuckoo" interval that had been sung by the mother can be discerned, particularly at the beginning (the notation transcription is not included because only a few sounds could be considered to be "in tune").

Rec. 13: A child of six months who is sparing in his responses, but his vocalizations are already little melodic motifs and, moreover, here his first sound is exactly an octave higher than the last one sung by his mother.

Rec. 14: The same child at eight months gives us a slightly longer motif.

Rec. 15: A girl of eight months launches into little melodies, here in a soft voice.

Rec. 16: This time the same child sings at full voice and after the mother sings a descending major third, she concludes with a similar interval with her mouth closed.

Rec. 17: A girl of 18 months sings the response of "sono qui" [I am here] several times

Rec. 18: A girl of 15 months responds to her mother's song by singing syllables.

Rec. 19: A boy of 11 months, after he heard a verse of *Pippo Kid*, performs the rhythm of the refrain with the syllable "da".

Rec. 20: A girl of 21 months, interacting with her mother, sings some words.

Rec. 21: A girl of 21 months, interacting with her mother, produces words in a way that could almost be called singing ("*tonto*" means "*sono*").

Rec. 22: A boy of 21 months repeats a short phrase a few times between speaking and singing on a descending fourth.

Rec. 23: A girl of 19 months interacts with her mother and sings some words and a short phrase.

Rec. 24: A boy of 22 months sings a short word with a rhythm of short-long at different pitches, forming a melodic phrase that he repeats a few times, more accurately at first and then progressively distorting the intervals.

Rec. 25: A girl of 19 months, during a session when they are singing a song with an echo, begins to repeat the echo a few times whilst moving away from the other children (at which point they stop singing), sometimes introducing other words.

Rec. 26: A boy of two years and two months sings a song with all three verses (*L'anatroccolo*) acceptably in tune, although his pronunciation of the words is still imprecise.

Rec. 27: A girl of three years and four months begins a song, stops after the first phrase and starts again a few times.

Rec. 28: A girl of two years and 11 months begins and stops three songs before going on to sing another one rather freely.

Rec. 29: A girl of two years and eight months begins to sing *Girotondo casca il mondo* and concludes by singing the last line of a lullaby using the same key.

Rec. 30: A girl of two years and seven months sings, with some interruptions, *La barchetta in mezzo al mare*.

Rec. 31: A boy of two years and nine months sings the song of welcome used in the sessions (*Benvenuti*), with flexibility in the rhythm and dynamics.

Rec. 32: A girl of two years and 11 months sings, with the help of her mother, the song *Tutti qui si giocherà*.

Rec. 33: A boy of two years and three months sings the song of welcome used in the sessions (*Bevenuti*) introducing a variation in the melody of the third verse and still keeping in tune.

Rec. 34: A girl of two years and nine months sings *Fra' Martino* approximately in tune.

Rec. 35: A girl of two years and four months interacts with her mother in singing a song approximately in tune.

Rec. 36: A girl of two years and ten months sings *Tanti auguri* almost in tune.

Rec. 37: A boy of two years and three months sings *Fra' Martino* almost in tune.

Rec. 38: A girl of two years and four months sings *Stella stellina* acceptably in tune.

Rec. 39: A boy of two years and nine months sings *Al castello* acceptably in tune.

Rec. 40: A girl of two years and ten months sings a variation of the same song *Al castello* acceptably in tune and then she goes on to invent new words, keeping to the rhythm and melody fairly well at first and then rather more freely.

Rec. 41: A girl of two years and two months, walking through the woods with her mother, sings invented phrases.

Rec. 42: The same child, in the car, sings as she calls her doll *Nunur*.

Rec. 43: A girl of two years and nine months invents words about her parents sung to the tune of *C'era una volta un papero* (text on page 78)

Rec. 44: A two-year-old girl is on the swing in the garden singing a monologue using a few syllables.

Rec. 45: A girl of two years and ten months, encouraged by her mother, invents a story about a blue little ball.

Rec. 46: A two-year-old boy sings a small motif and accompanies himself on the electronic keyboard.

Video recordings

Video 1:   A newborn girl of four days listens to the song that her mother had sung every day in the later stages of pregnancy and then a song that her mother had never heard during that period (see experiment on page 40).

Video 2:   A newborn girl of five days listens to the song that her mother had sung every day in the later stages of pregnancy and then a song that her mother had never heard during that period (see experiment on page 40)

Video 3:   A boy of two years and seven months responds to his mother "singing" (between speaking and singing) and he invents a short sequence (see page 70).

Video 4:   A girl of 11 months rocks and moves up and down as she listens to a song.

Video 5:   A boy of three years and ten months is playing the beat of the music that he is listening to on a digital drum (see page 76).

Video 6:   A girl of two years and ten months sings acceptably in tune, but stumbles a little on the words.

Video 7:   A boy of two years and 11 months sings *Il grillo John*, interacting with his mother and little sister of 18 months.

Index

DATE DUE
